THE BIG TINY
BOOK OF PAINTING

Leslie Stroz

An Artist's Guide to Tiny Painting
Outside in Ink and Watercolour

DAVID & CHARLES
—PUBLISHING—

www.davidandcharles.com

CONTENTS

INTRODUCTION

Hello, I am Leslie Stroz, an American artist living in the United Kingdom.

Painting outside is my favourite thing to do.

Before moving to England in 2014, I taught art at the State University of New York in Geneseo. I am now lucky to live in the English countryside, nestled on a rolling hill between the moors and the sea, where I have an endless array of heather and waves to paint.

I spent most of my life teaching traditional drawing and painting skills, but in 2016 I happened upon a plein air (outside, in the open air) painting festival in Door County, Wisconsin, USA. I was instantly captivated! I had always included plein air painting in the curriculum of my drawing and painting classes and stressed the importance of drawing from life, but HERE was a group of professional artists gathered together for the express purpose of painting the landscape. They even sold their paintings afterwards. I felt that I had finally found my tribe.

For the next few years, I delved into plein air painting in oils, learning as much as I could about painting alla prima (all at once). I enjoyed the challenge of completing a painting in a few hours, chasing light and shadows before they changed. My brushstrokes became quicker and looser, and my ability to mix the colours I saw grew. I'd never enjoyed painting more! The process of being outside, immersed in the environment you are recording is meditative, creatively stimulating, and emotionally uplifting.

It wasn't always easy to cart all my painting gear along, however. The plein air easel, palette, extra paints, water, and wet panels made painting outside an event that required planning and time. Sometimes I wanted to paint on location but didn't feel up to the physical challenges of carrying and setting up my outdoor gear. All of that changed one day when I purchased a tiny, handmade wooden watercolour palette with a tiny sketchbook from a clever artisan.

From the moment I created my first tiny painting, I was hooked! A portable painting studio that I could carry in my pocket and whip out whenever I felt the urge to capture a scene was addictive. I filmed the creation of that first tiny painting, and every one since, and it soon became clear that people all over the world were equally enchanted with the idea of tiny painting. I love sharing my adventures and knowledge about drawing and painting these little gems with others online. The opportunity to record my process in a book that others can use to help achieve their own artistic goals is a dream come true.

In these pages, I'll share with you the secrets of drawing, colour mixing, and painting from life, gleaned not only from my own experiences painting outside, but also from my many years as a university professor. You'll learn exactly how to create your own tiny paintings: which supplies to use, how to build your own, custom art toolkit, the essential skills for drawing and painting, how to avoid common mistakes, and how to plan your own painting adventures outdoors.

I'll also take you along with me on a few of my painting adventures so that you can paint with me, step by step. Soon, you'll be able to create your own delightful tiny paintings.

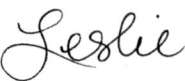

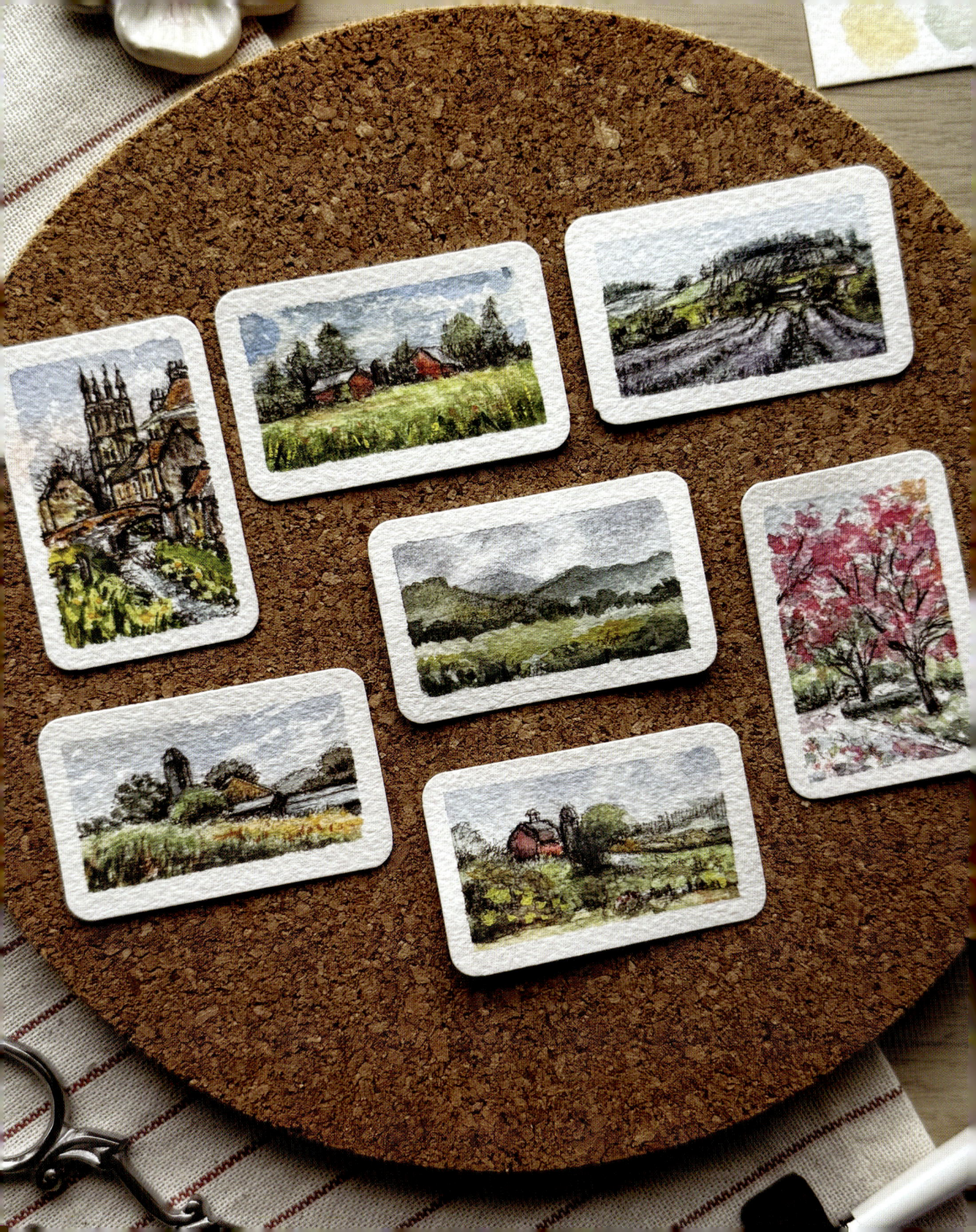

Why Tiny Painting?
(or How Tiny Painting Can Change Your Life)

What if I told you that painting something tiny – just a few inches across – could completely transform your creativity, boost your mood, and even rewire your brain? Sounds dramatic, right? Well, hear me out…

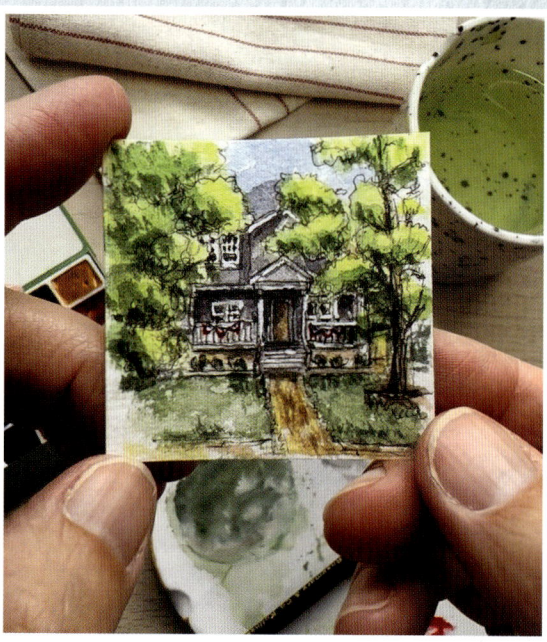

Whether you're an experienced artist or just someone who wants to make more art, tiny painting can transform your creative practice. This simple habit isn't just fun; it's actually really good for you in ways you might not expect.

ENHANCES CREATIVITY

When you sit down to paint – even something tiny – it actually strengthens the creative part of your brain. Studies have shown that making art increases connections in the "default mode network", which is basically the part of your brain that helps you daydream, imagine, and come up with new ideas. Studies on neuroplasticity show that engaging in art helps build new neural pathways, making it easier to generate innovative ideas. So, if you've ever thought, "I wish I was more creative", the secret is just to start creating!

STRESS AND ANXIETY REDUCTION

If you ever feel overwhelmed or anxious, art can seriously help. Even just 45 minutes of making something – no matter if it's good or bad – significantly lowers cortisol, the stress hormone (regardless of prior art experience or ability). Engaging in creative activities, even briefly, can effectively reduce stress, lower anxiety, and promote well-being, regardless of artistic skill or experience. Mindful, repetitive motions, like painting or drawing, activate the parasympathetic nervous system, inducing relaxation. The act of just focusing on the brush, the colours, and the tiny details slows your thoughts down. It's like meditation, but instead of sitting still, you're doing something with your hands.

MOOD BOOSTER

And here's the crazy part – art actually boosts dopamine, the "feel good" chemical in your brain. This is the same chemical that makes you feel happy when you listen to your favourite song or eat chocolate. Expressive arts therapy can significantly reduce symptoms of depression by fostering self-expression and emotional processing. So basically, painting = instant mood boost.

CREATIVE PROBLEM-SOLVING AND MEMORY

Creating art improves memory and problem-solving skills. In fact, a study found that older adults who did creative activities had a lower risk of memory loss and dementia. But it's not just for older people. The reason that most universities in the US require students to take classes in the fine arts is because it's been proven that people in all fields and walks of life benefit from having creative thinking skills, and practising art helps achieve that. Participation in fine arts electives broadens students' perspectives and enhances skills such as creativity, critical thinking, and adaptability. Art strengthens the part of your brain that helps you see different solutions instead of getting stuck in one way of thinking.

SO WHY TINY?

Creating ANY type of art will provide benefits, but there are specific things about tiny painting that make it more conducive to creating. Unlike a small painting, which could be anything larger than 4 inches (10cm), a TINY painting is – well – tiny. It could be 3 inches (7.5cm), 2 inches (5cm), or even 1 inch (2.5cm) – anything smaller than that would qualify as a miniature. My favourite sizes are 2 x 2 inches (5 x 5cm), but I also like to work with 1¼ x 2 inches (3 x 5cm). Here are a few reasons why you might like trying a tiny painting:

1. It's Quick

In our busy world, too many creative people put their art on the back burner because creating art can be time consuming. With tiny painting, you can create an entire painting in an hour. The satisfaction in creating a complete painting in the amount of time it would take to eat a meal or watch half of a feature film is addictive.

2. It's Portable

I love to plein air paint in oil, but I found myself painting less and less as I grew older. The stress of lugging all of my gear, finding a suitable place to set up, and standing for hours was enough to put me off going out at all. When I discovered tiny painting, it reignited my joy in painting outside. You can fit everything you need to create a painting in a small bag that can be popped into your bag or backpack. It can easily be unpacked to create an instant, portable art studio!

3. It's Discreet

Many artists I know would love to paint in public but are too shy or self-conscious. With tiny painting, your set-up is literally small enough to fit in the palm of your hand, so most people don't even realise you're painting. It's a win-win for introverted artists!

4. It's Playful

One of my favourite parts about painting tiny is that I can explore different colour combinations, supplies, and techniques. The tiny format evokes a childlike sense of wonder and curiosity that ignites creativity. And because the surface is small, it's easier to explore different things.

5. It's Fun

Imagine cradling a tiny sketchbook and palette in the palm of one hand. It's a magical feeling to create art in such an unusual way. The uniqueness of this set-up and the immediacy of holding your art studio in one hand connects you directly to your art. This experience creates instant joy.

So, if you've ever felt like you need a fresh perspective in life… maybe painting a tiny painting is the answer. Making a habit of creating – even in small ways – can actually rewire your brain for the better. And you might just fall in love with tiny painting as much as I have!

Chapter One

CREATING YOUR TINY ART TOOLKIT

So, you've decided that you'd like to try tiny painting, but you don't know where to begin. I keep a little tray on my desk that holds all of the items I need to create a tiny painting at home, and a travel art wrap that I can grab and go for painting adventures outside. Once you have created a few tiny paintings, you'll have a better sense of the type of set-up that works best for you. Creating your own custom toolkit for tiny painting is half the fun. You can customise it to suit your needs, and include unusual or unique supplies for experimentation. I'll discuss different travel set-ups in Chapter Five: Plein Air Painting, but here are a few essential items you will need to get started.

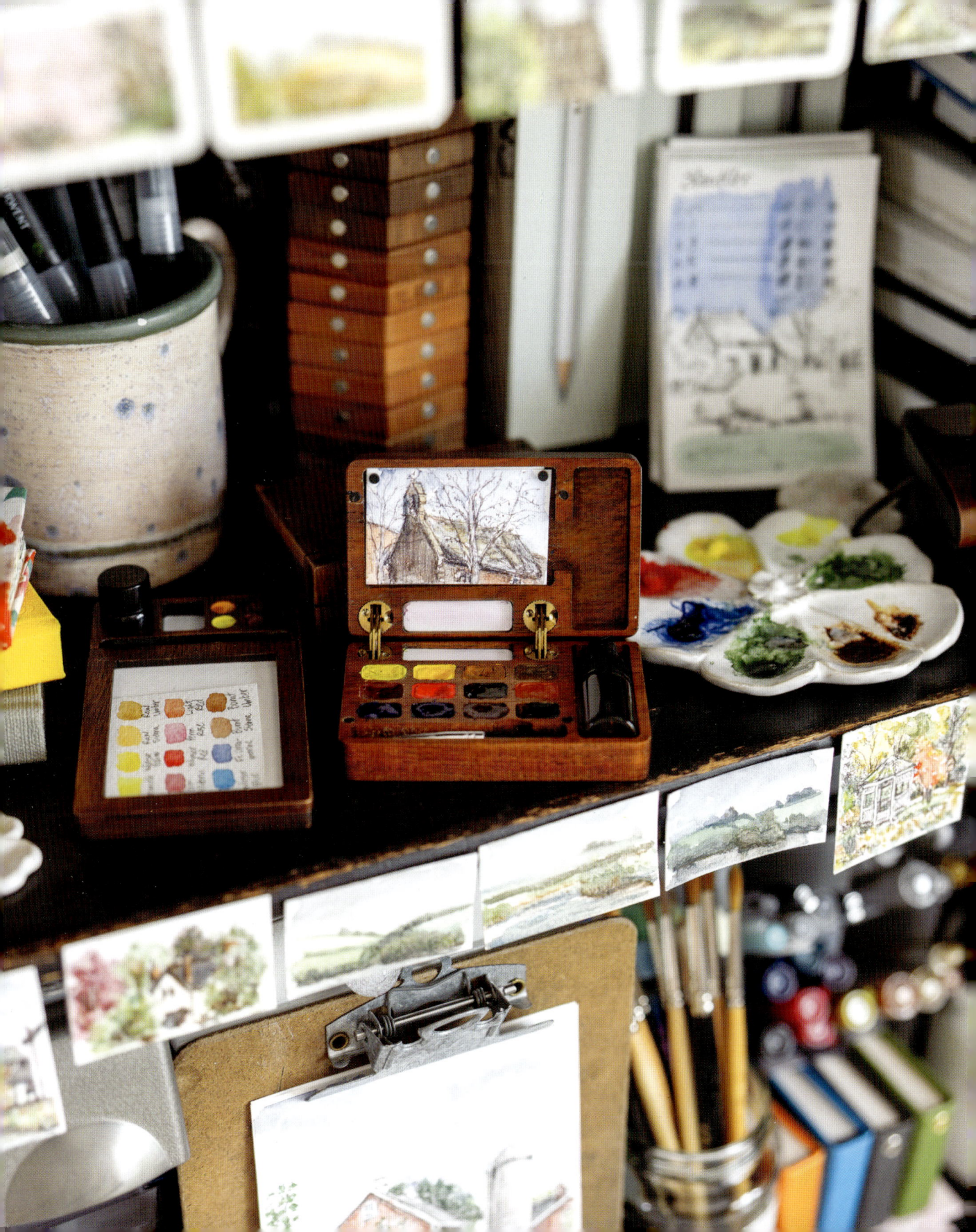

Paints

You don't need many paints to achieve a full spectrum of colours. Many manufacturers sell watercolour sets that contain several colours. It's easy to be tempted by how lovely they look all lined up in a palette like tiny jewels. When you're painting on a tiny surface, however, it's much easier to achieve colour harmony when you have fewer colours and learn to mix with them (don't worry, I'll show you how to do this later).

Student watercolours are more affordable, but to keep the costs down they contain less of the actual pigment (colour) and more of the binder (the agent that holds it all together). This makes them less vibrant than professional watercolours. I recommend purchasing a few of the best paints you can afford from an established and reputable fine art manufacturer. Some of my favourites are Winsor & Newton, Daniel Smith, and M. Graham (see right, for my colour selection).

My Colour Selection

Choose ONE of each:

Cooler Yellows: Lemon Yellow, Bismuth Yellow, Winsor Lemon, Hansa Yellow Light (this one is pretty but less lightfast)

Warmer Yellows: New Gamboge, Indian Yellow

Cooler Reds: Permanent Alizarin Crimson, Quinacridone Rose, Permanent Carmine

Warmer Reds: Pyrrol Scarlet, Winsor Red, Vermillion, Naphthol Red

Cooler Blues: Phthalo Blue (green shade), Winsor Blue (green shade), Prussian Blue, Antwerp Blue

Warmer Blues: Ultramarine Blue, French Ultramarine

Reddish-Orange Earth Colours: Transparent Red Oxide, Burnt Sienna

Yellowish-Orange Earth Colours: Raw Sienna, Raw Umber, Yellow Ochre, Transparent Yellow Oxide

NOTE ABOUT TOXICITY

Some of my favourite colours contain toxic pigments (cadmiums, cobalts, and manganese, among others). For tiny painting, however, it's best to avoid them. In this book, I will only be using non-toxic colours. If you want to know if your paint contains toxic pigments, you can look at the pigments listed on the tube and visit the colour index database online, which categorises all of the pigments used in fine arts paints and inks.

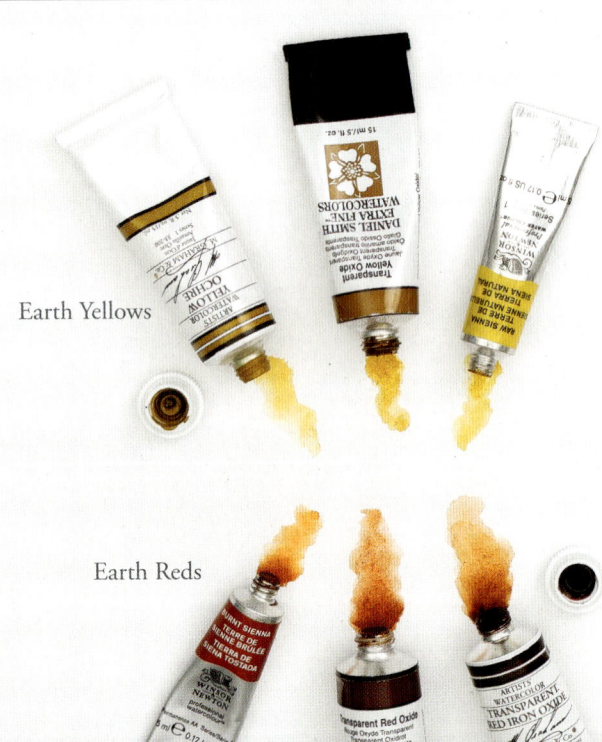

Earth Yellows

Earth Reds

PANS VS TUBES

Watercolours are available in tubes or in small paint pans that contain hardened paint cakes. The latter can be reactivated with water. For tiny painting, I have found that paint pans are easier to control (and more portable). Paint pans generally come in two sizes: half pans and full pans. Half pans are more readily available.

I personally prefer to purchase paint tubes and squeeze the wet paint into empty half pans, or into a custom palette designed for tiny painting that has smaller paint wells. The paint will dry to touch within 24 hours and be dry all the way through within 2–3 days. It is more versatile and cost-effective to purchase tubes and create your own paint pans.

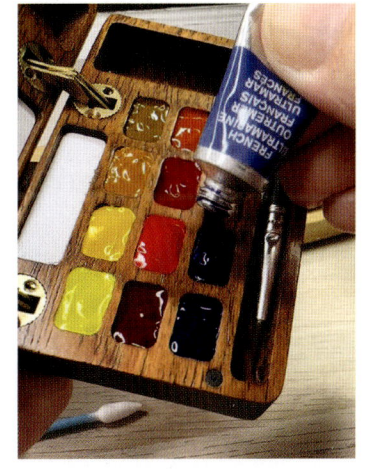

COLOURS

You can paint almost everything you need with just three primary colours: yellow, red, and blue. However, I find that with tiny painting it's easiest to learn if you have something called a split primary palette (a cooler-leaning and warmer-leaning for each of the primary colours). In addition, it's helpful to have a few earth colours. I will explain this further in Chapter Two: The Basics.

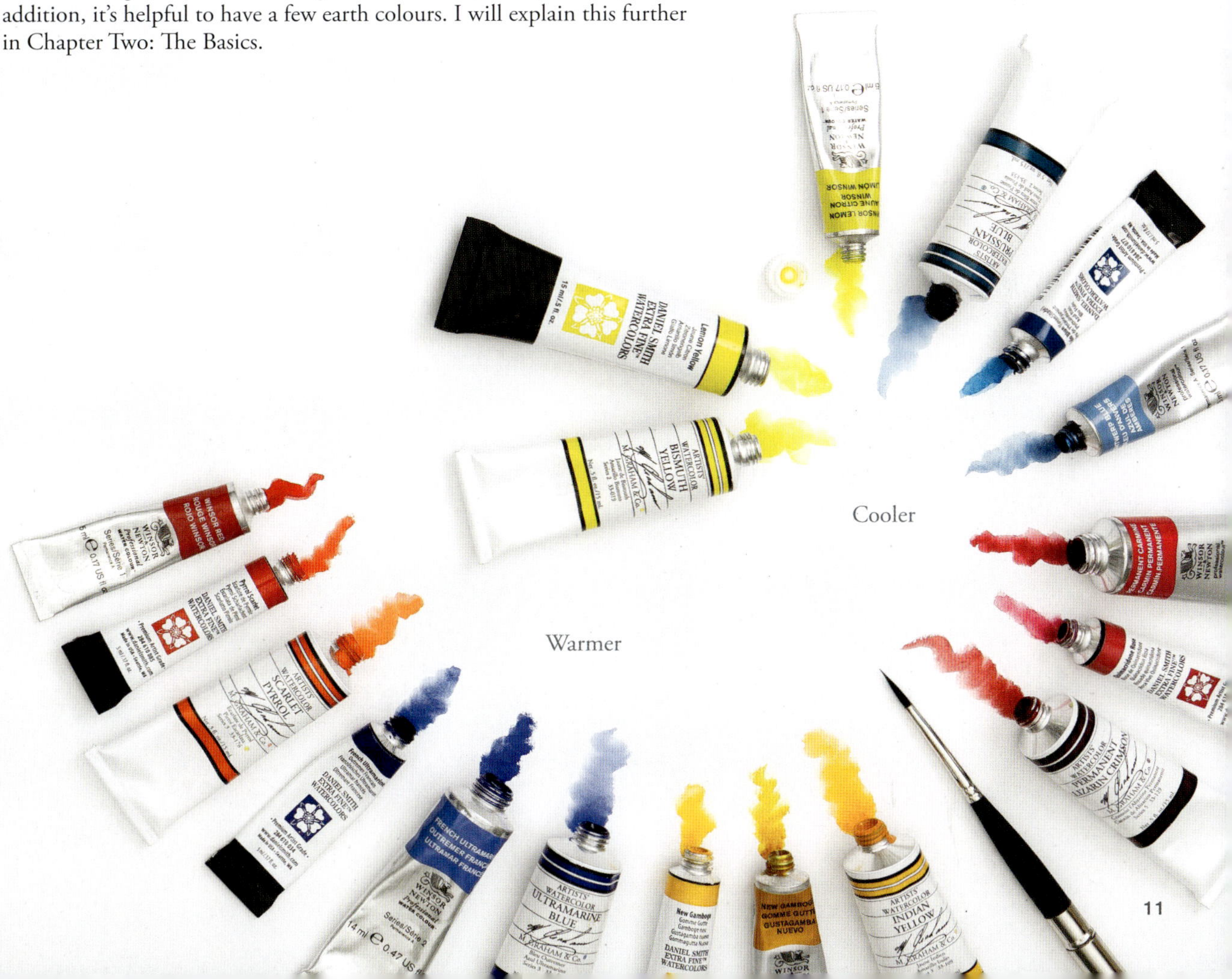

Cooler

Warmer

Palettes and Brushes

PALETTES

You'll need somewhere to mix your paints. If you're painting at home, a white ceramic palette or dish works great, but if you're painting on location, it's helpful to have a tiny palette. This will make things more portable and also enable you to hold both your paper and palette in one hand and paint with the other. You can purchase your own tiny palette from artisans like GoDraw, Blue Star Crafts, or Art Toolkit, or you can make your own by using a small, empty tin and filling it with empty make-up pans or discarded bottle tops that you fill with paint. These can be attached to the tin with sticky tack or magnets. Be creative!

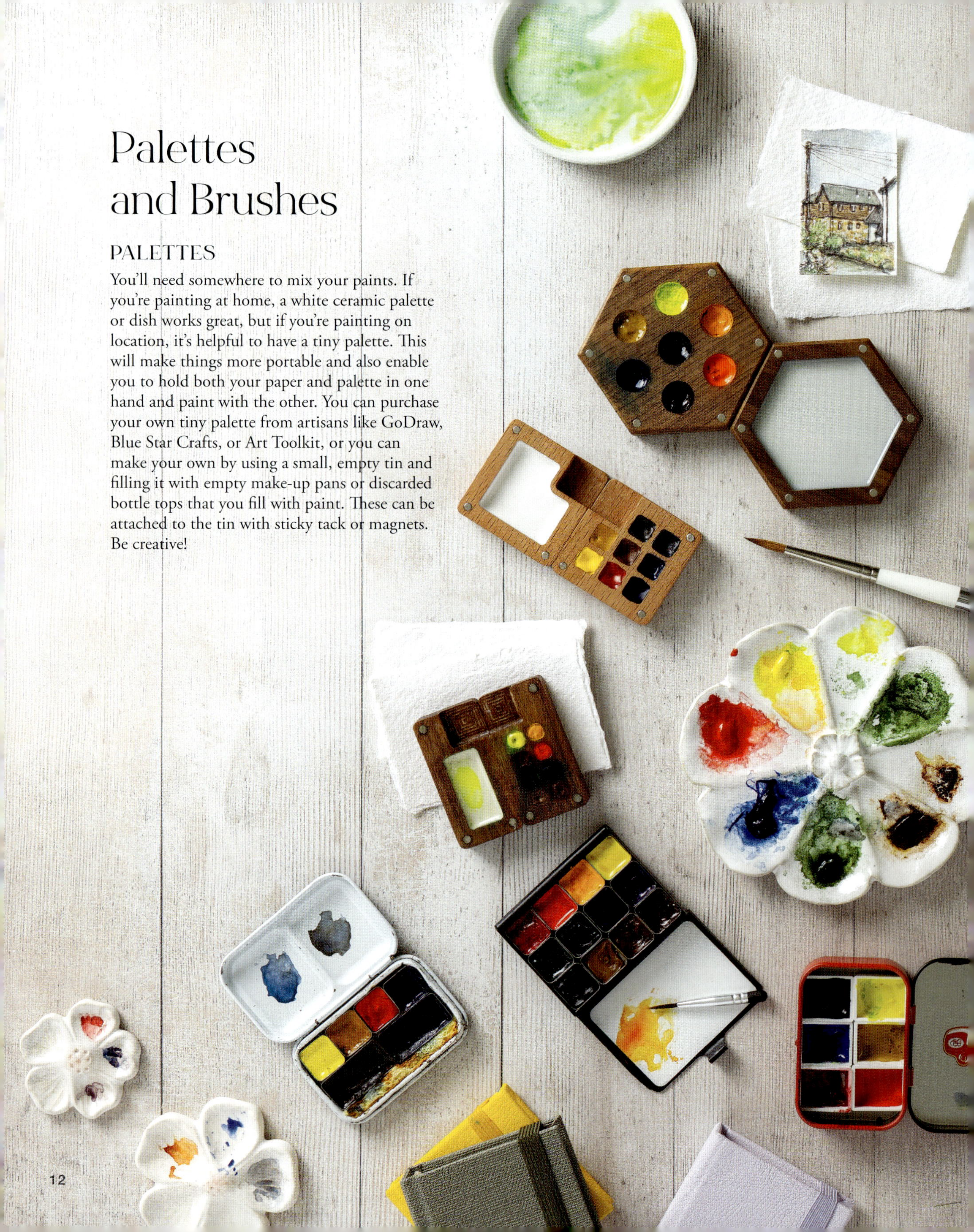

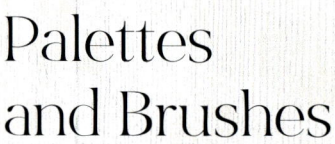

BRUSHES

There are three different types of watercolour brushes: standard, travel, and water brushes.

The standard watercolour brush has a short handle and soft bristles that can hold more water. Sable or sable blends are considered to be the gold standard, but these days many manufacturers make synthetic blends that closely mimic sable and are also more affordable.

The travel watercolour brush is similar to the standard watercolour brush, but the top end of the brush (with the bristles) can be detached from the hollow body, which can then function as a protective cap for the bristles. This both protects the bristles from becoming damaged during transport, and also shortens the length of the brush for portability.

The water brush is an ingenious design that contains water in the plastic barrel of the brush, eliminating the need to use a water pot. The water travels to the bristles with a gentle squeeze of the barrel. It's great for travel painting or painting outside. A few downsides to these are that the synthetic bristles are harder than traditional watercolour brushes, and learning to control the amount of water that comes out can require a bit of patience at first (see Colour in Chapter Two).

I use all three in different situations, but for plein air painting I prefer travel and water brushes.

Sizes and Shapes

You can do just about everything you need with a few brushes. I recommend a pointed round brush in a size 4 or 6. You can create washes with the body of the brush, and lines and details with the tip. A smaller detail brush (size 0 or 1) can also be helpful. A short, flat brush can be used for creating a uniform expanse of colour, or for "rubbing out" accidental colours.

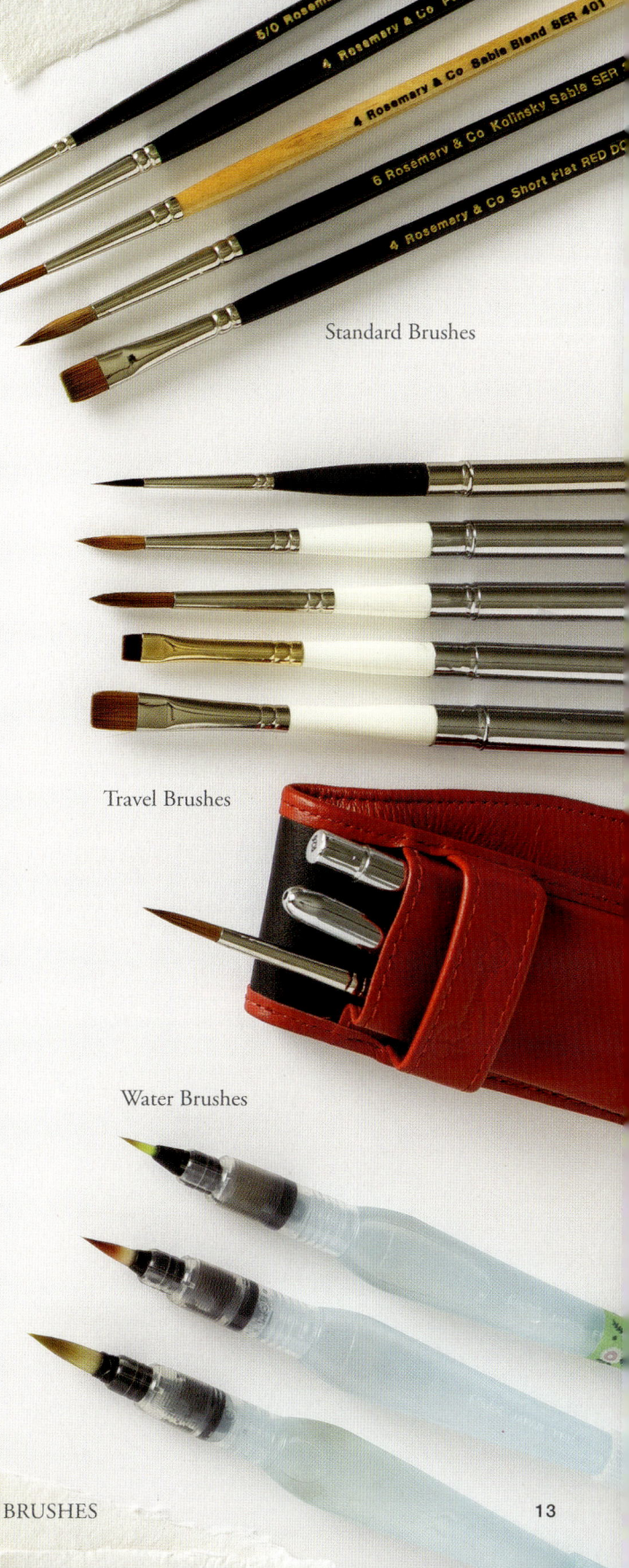

Standard Brushes

Travel Brushes

Water Brushes

Pens and Paper

PAPER

Watercolour paper is made from cellulose (wood pulp), cotton, or a blend of the two (cotton blend). Cellulose paper dries more quickly and isn't as conducive to creating multiple layers or lifting colours. For those reasons, I recommend buying 100 per cent cotton watercolour paper. In fact, if you're going to splurge on one thing, I recommend that you splurge on your paper. You can cut several tiny "canvases" from a single sheet of watercolour paper, so it's cost effective.

Watercolour paper comes in a variety of textures.

• Hot-pressed paper has a smoother surface.

• Cold-pressed paper has a textured surface.

• NOT paper has a lightly textured surface.

• Rough paper has a heavily textured surface.

I prefer using cold-pressed or NOT paper for tiny paintings. The texture allows paint to settle in more interesting ways and creates depth to the painting.

Watercolour paper additionally comes in a variety of thicknesses (weights). I recommend using paper that is 140lb (300gsm) or higher.

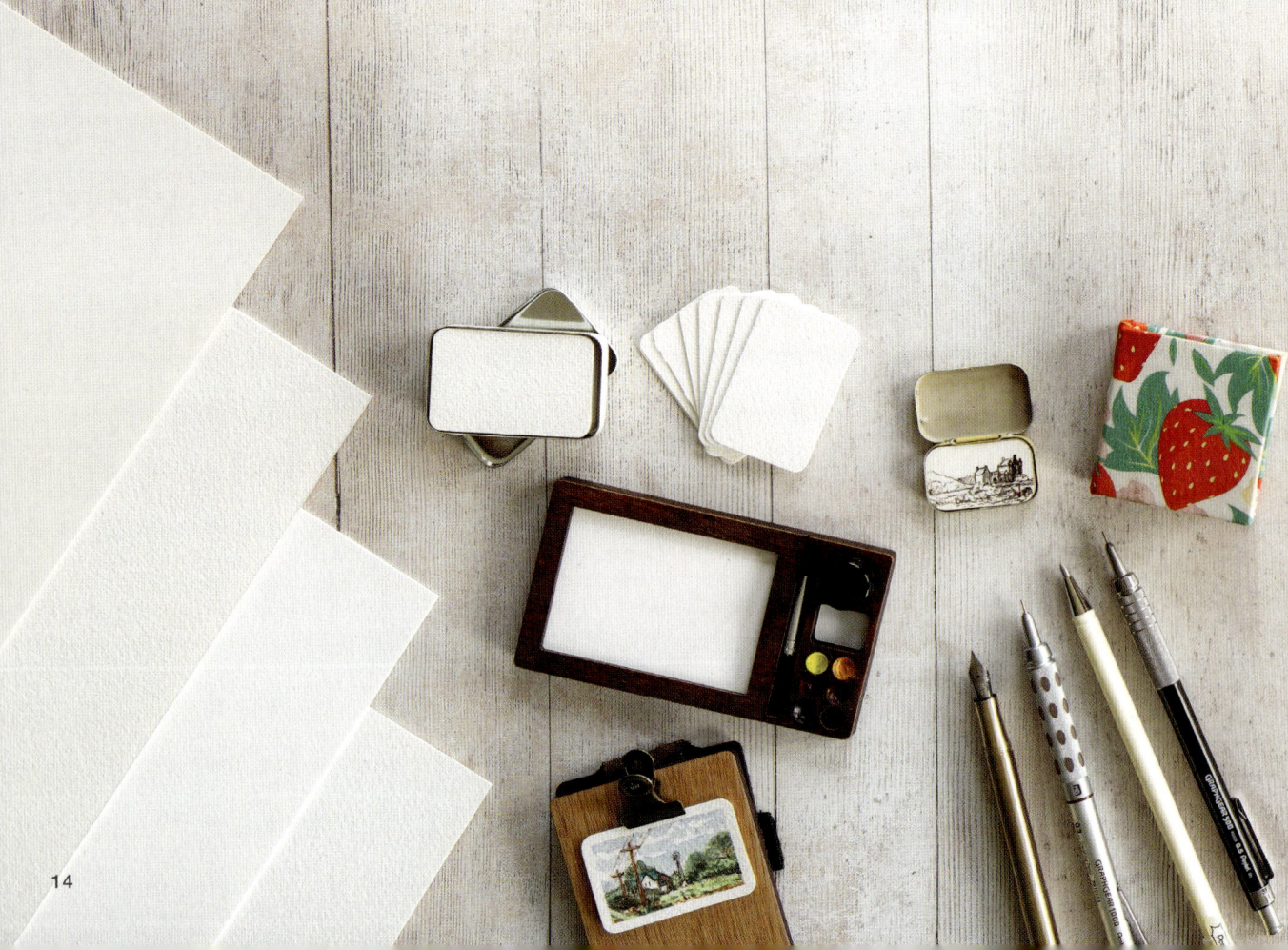

SKETCHBOOKS, CLIPBOARDS, AND POCHADE BOXES

Tiny sketchbooks can be difficult to find, and most of the commercially available ones have cellulose paper. Shop around to find one that contains the best quality paper. Most of these sketchbooks will have a hard cover and closed spine. You can also make your own tiny sketchbooks. There are a number of free tutorials online that will guide you.

Additionally, you might decide to work on loose scraps of paper that you house in a little container or tin. I call these "alternative sketchbooks". These papers can be secured on a tiny clipboard or in a tiny watercolour pochade (paint) box. You can make your own set-up, or purchase one from a company that specialises in making small, portable art products.

PENCILS

Using a pencil to create your initial sketches is helpful. I'd recommend using one with HB lead because the point will be sharper and produce thinner lines. I prefer to use a mechanical pencil with either 0.5mm or 0.3mm lead.

PENS

Line-and-wash is a technique that blends ink drawing and watercolour. It can produce lovely, textured, tiny paintings. You can use fineliners or fountain pens with tiny painting. The finer the point, the more detailed your drawings will be. A finer point also creates softer, less dominant lines. I recommend using fineliners that have a fine point (0.05 or 0.1).

For years my favourite fineliner for tiny paintings was the brown Prismacolor Premier 005 (or 0.05). However, these are becoming increasingly difficult to find. Uni Pin makes a nice brown available in 01 (0.1) that also works well. Staedtler has a beautiful, deep brown, but the smallest available size is 0.3.

If you're using fountain pens, there are a variety of waterproof inks available in different brown and grey hues that are fun to explore. I'd recommend using an extra-fine nib, but make sure to clean it regularly because the waterproof ink can get clogged.

Additionally, I'd suggest using a brown or grey ink and avoiding black, which will dominate in a tiny painting and give your paintings a more cartoon-like look. A white or cream pen also comes in handy for little touch-ups of areas that might have become too dark in a painting. I usually carry a few of these with me at all times.

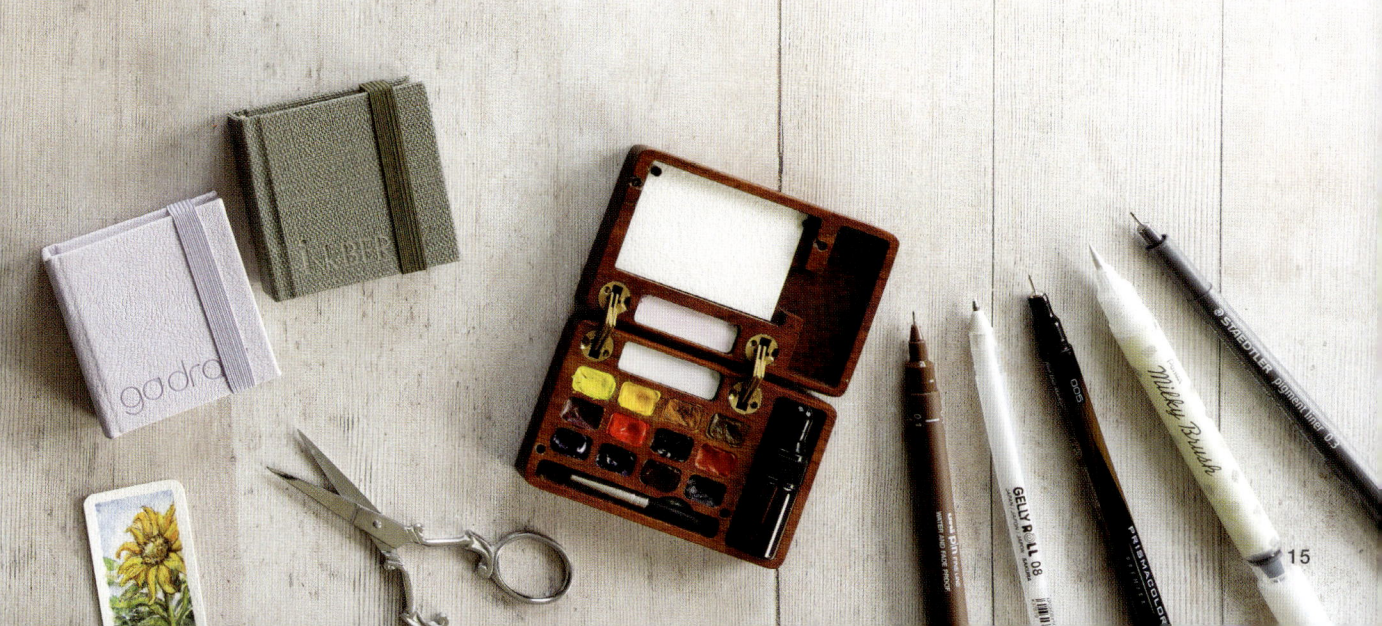

Extra Essentials

ERASERS

A small vinyl eraser can be helpful for removing any fine lines or even for lifting masking fluid. Eraser pens are useful because they have a smaller surface that can enable you to erase detailed areas.

A kneaded eraser is also ideal because it can both lighten and erase pencil lines without leaving any residue on your paper.

WRISTBAND/CLOTH

You'll need somewhere to blot and dry your paintbrushes. A wash cloth or towelling athletic wristband are perfect for this because they are highly absorbent and can be washed and reused.

WATER POTS

A small container or two to hold your water is essential, unless you're using a water brush. You can purchase collapsible ones designed specifically for travel artists, or just bring an empty jam jar or yogurt pot.

CLIPS

It's helpful to have a few additional clips for attaching palettes and paper. I like rubber chip clips, but find what appeals to you. There are bulldog clips, clips with magnets attached, or even woodworking clamps that will all do the job.

TAPE

If you're working on loose sheets of paper, you'll want some type of low residue tape to fix your paper to a board or pochade box. I prefer to use washi tape for tiny paintings, which can easily be removed and won't tear the paper. These are patterned, so it's best to avoid busy designs that will obscure the way you see your paintings. You can also use decorator's masking tape.

CUTTING TOOLS

You can use a paper cutter to cut papers more quickly if you have one. I like to use an inexpensive round corner punch to round the corners on the tiny sheets after I've cut them.

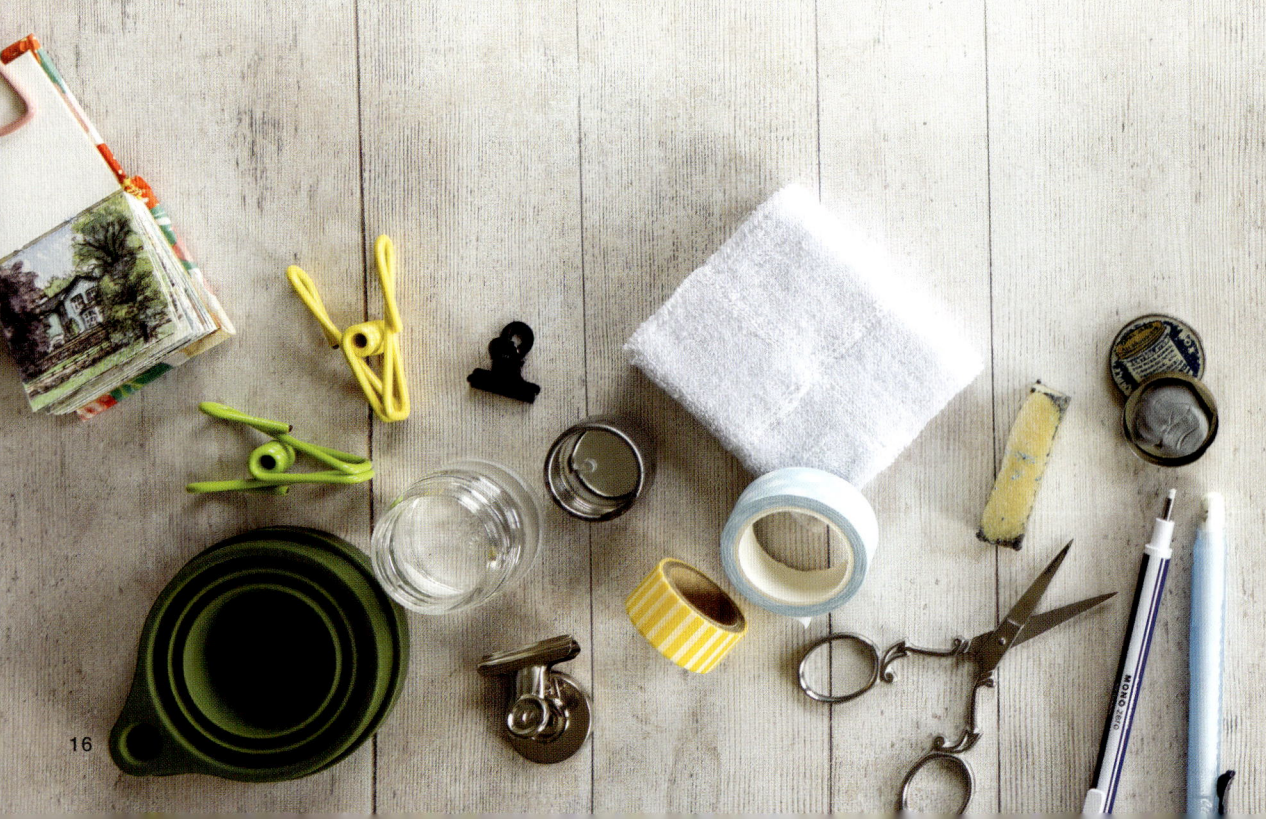

MASKING FLUID

Masking fluid is a rubbery liquid that allows you to block out areas of the paper that you want to remain white. It's incredibly useful for tiny painting to help you preserve certain areas. I like to use masking fluid pens because they are portable. You can also purchase jars or tubes that have a thin, metal applicator, but I find that these take much longer to dry.

NATURAL RUBBER PICK-UP

These little squares are made from a natural crepe rubber and are the BEST way to remove masking fluid without tearing the paper.

BAMBOO SKEWERS/ KNITTING NEEDLES

A bamboo skewer or short, thin knitting needle will help you measure items in a scene and plan your composition. They are more effective than using a pencil or brush because they are thinner and will be more accurate, especially when you're working small. Having a few of these in your art kit is invaluable.

DIVIDERS

Dividers can be tricky to find. They are sometimes called Academic Dividers or Calipers (like the sort doctors use to measure ECG readings). Like the skewers and knitting needles, these will help you measure and perfect your drawings.

VIEWFINDER

When you're painting outside, it can be overwhelming to have an entire 180 degrees of scenery in front of you. A viewfinder will help you isolate interesting scenes. You can purchase one or make your own by cutting a window into cardboard that is the same ratio as your paper.

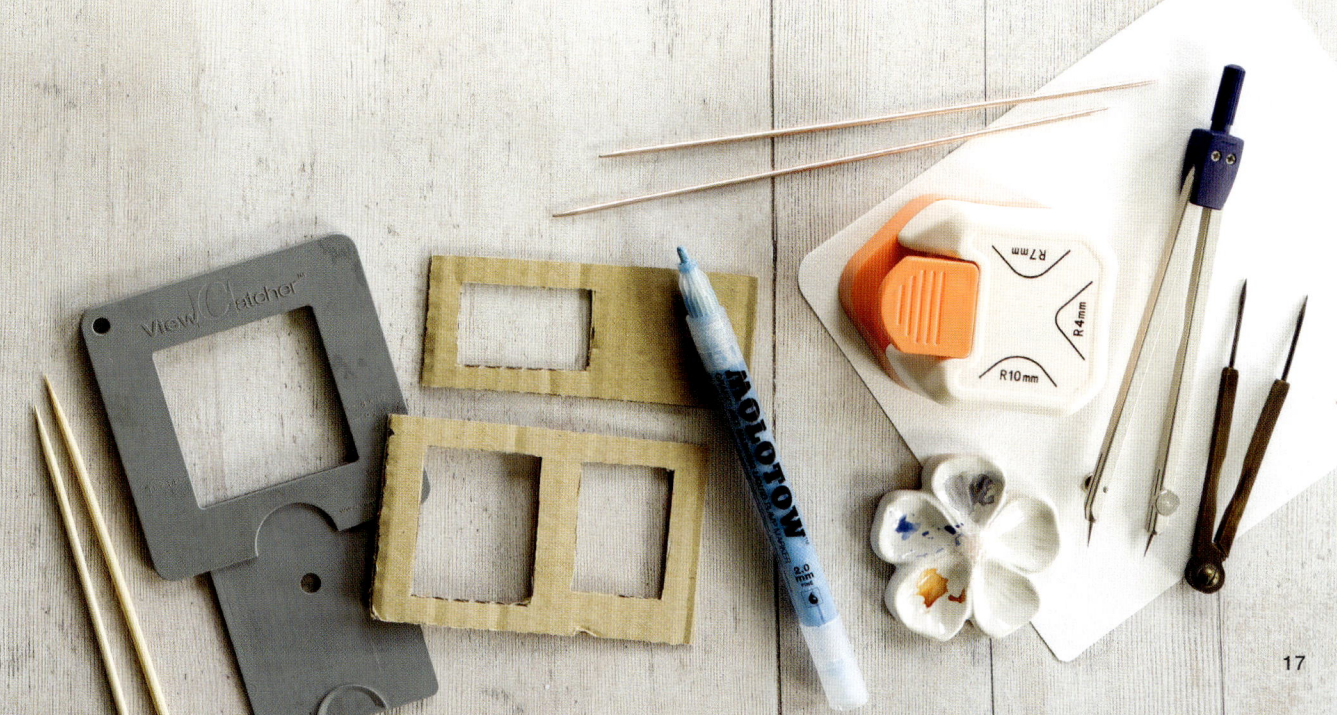

Chapter Two

THE BASICS
(Techniques)

You are going to want to skip this section. Don't.

How do I know you'll want to skip it? After 30 years of teaching drawing and painting to all different age groups, I have observed that if an art student can get away with skipping the basics, they will. After all, it doesn't sound fun to shade basic forms or create value scales. It's far more appealing to rush straight in with colour and play. But consider this: a few weeks or a month spent REALLY focusing on learning and understanding the basic skills and Elements of Art will make you a better artist.

Still not convinced?

When I taught drawing and oil painting at university, students relied on me to give them a grade. If they completed the requirements of the class, they would receive higher marks. Because I required them to fully explore the Elements of Art, they excelled quite quickly. When they left the class, they could draw any scene with confidence and mix colours with precision.

As I transitioned into teaching adults, I observed that many of my adult students were much slower to progress, and some didn't improve much at all, despite painting regularly. This baffled me. Were adult students less able to tackle new skills? Were they less creative than younger students? I didn't think this was the case since I'd had adult students in my university classes and they had performed at the same level as their younger counterparts.

When I delved deeper, I discovered that many of my adult students were cutting corners. They might watch a demonstration of me shading or mixing value scales, but they didn't put in the time to perfect their own understanding of these concepts. If they made a value scale, for instance, and it didn't show a clear indication of varied values, they often didn't devote the time to create another one, and another, and another, until they had perfected it. Instead, many of them moved on to the next assignment before fully understanding the ones before it.

It became increasingly clear to me that the students who not only explored the basics but also spent time perfecting them, produced stronger paintings than those who skipped or skimmed over them. The biggest favour you can do for yourself as an artist – especially if you're interested in painting tiny – is to learn the basics.

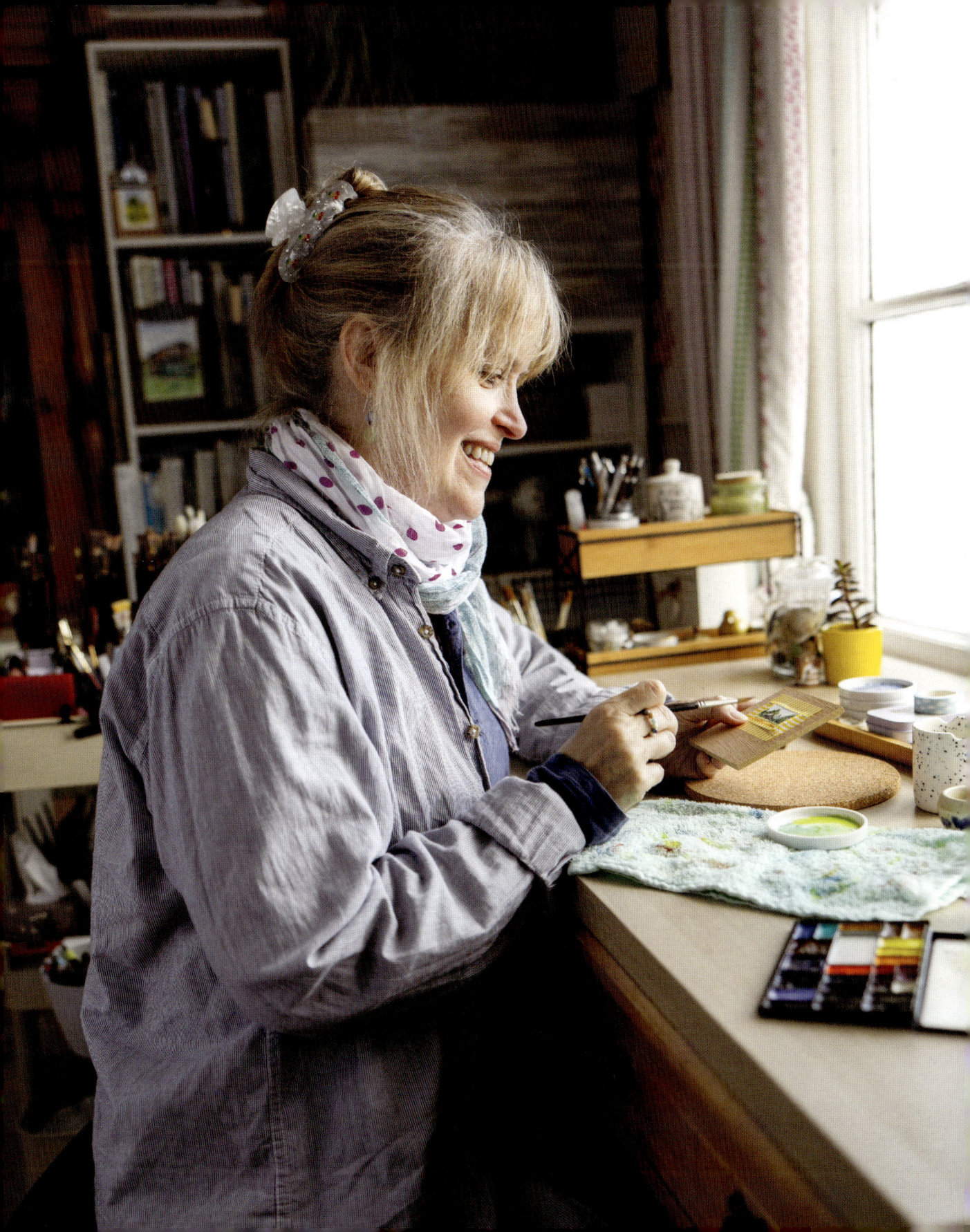

The Elements of Art

In the same way that scientists have the periodic table, mathematicians have formulas, musicians have notes and scales, and dancers have poses, visual artists also have a common language they follow to create successful art – the Elements of Art. These elements can be used to talk about art, but, more importantly, all successful art of any medium displays a keen understanding and demonstration of them. The elements are: Line, Value, Shape, Form, Texture, Colour, and Space. I'll delve briefly into each of these here, especially as they pertain to creating tiny art.

Give yourself the gift of learning the basic Elements of Art. You will later enjoy drawing and playing with colour MUCH more because you will understand the materials and be able to achieve effects intentionally.

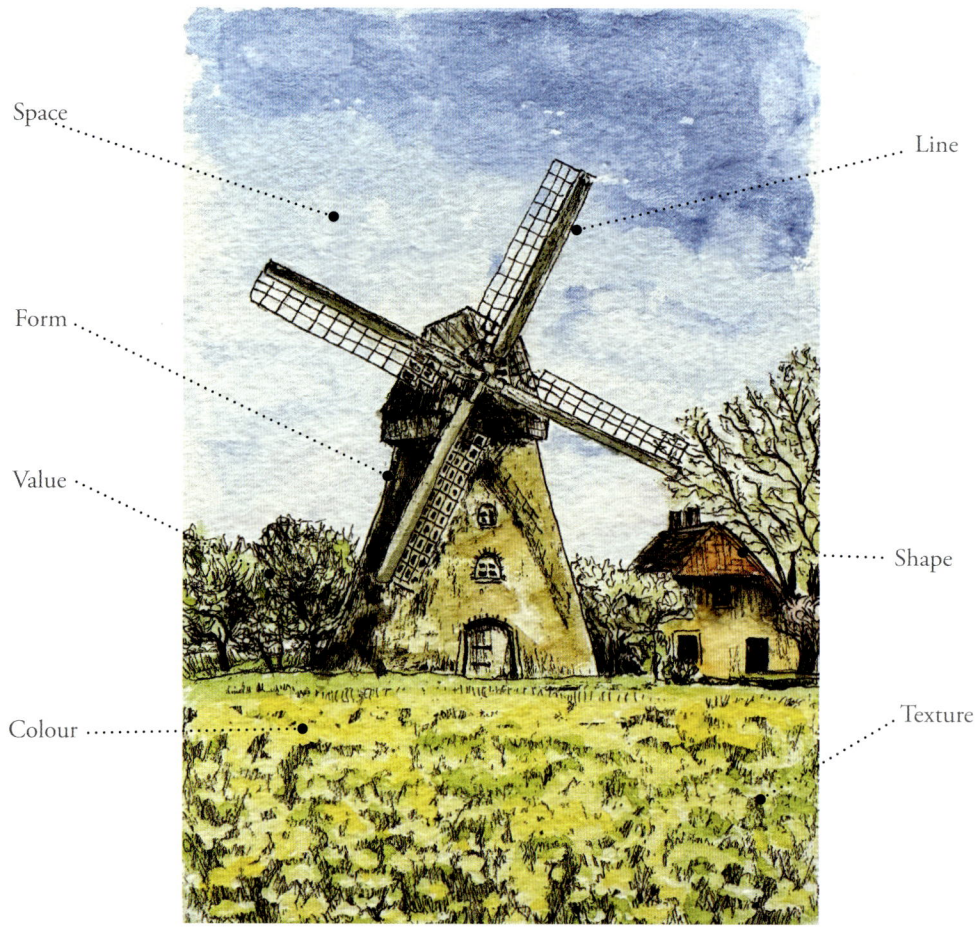

THE BASICS

Line

The most basic of all the Elements of Art is Line, which is sometimes referred to as the path left by a moving point. One of the first things that children do from the moment they can hold a crayon or pencil is create fresh, expressive lines. In fact, if you've ever seen a toddler draw, you'll know that young children are fearless at producing fresh, expressive lines. This ability becomes curtailed as people age and begin writing. After all, expressive lines don't make for legible penmanship.

The trick for making interesting lines in drawing lies somewhere in the in between… creating lines that are intentional and yet expressive. Sound complicated? It doesn't have to be.

CREATING EXPRESSIVE LINES

Many beginning students are taught to work on large pieces of newsprint, which is inexpensive and thus alleviates the fear of making mistakes. It's also because art students are taught that creating expressive lines is easier when you move your entire arm. With handwriting, more focus is spent on controlling the wrist, since lines and curves need to be shorter and more predictable. Therefore, the best way to break that habit is to work larger and looser.

With tiny painting, it's tempting to revert to the old habits of handwriting by carefully controlling each tiny line. If you do this, however, your drawings and paintings will look much stiffer. While it might not be realistic to move your entire arm while drawing, it IS possible to keep your wrist and forearm loose and hold your pencil further back on the barrel.

Line is so simple and elemental that its abilities are often under-explored by beginning artists – after all, you probably use lines every day when jotting down notes or doodling. And yet, many people claim that the only thing they can draw is a stick figure. When many

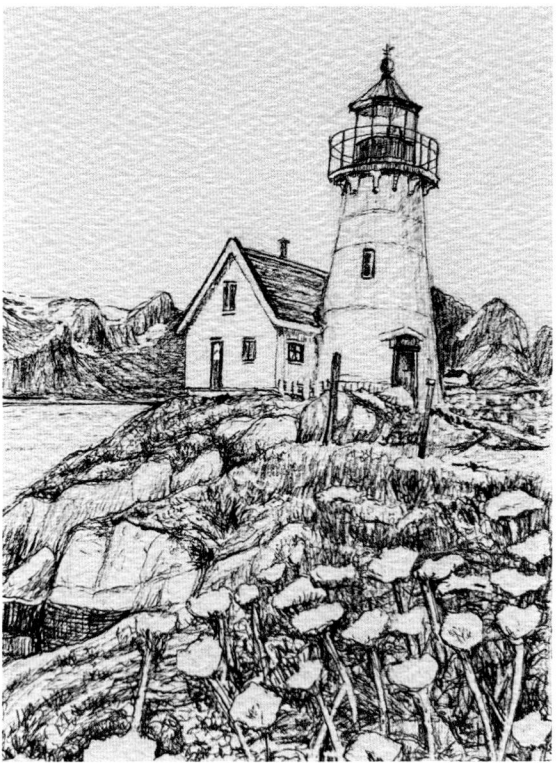

Hatching, cross-hatching, and cross-contour lines indicate the various shapes and textures of the lighthouse, rocks, and distant mountains.

new artists begin to draw, they grip the pencil (or pen) tightly and try to control the line. Or they think that the only purpose of lines is to outline contours of objects. In truth, line can be used in all the other Elements of Art (Value, Shape, Form, Texture, Colour, and Space).

Let's explore some of the ways lines can be used deliberately in art.

Try This: Warm Up Your Wrists and Arms

Do little warm-ups of your wrists and arms before you draw or paint to make sure you are feeling loose and limber. This is often overlooked, but essential. Your fingers, hands, wrists, and arms will be the creators of your lines and will deserve some attention before they are asked to go to work. Create little figure of eights with both wrists (1) and gently clench (2) and unclench your fingers (3). Bend your hands up and down.

Next, cross your arms in front of your body in a hug and then stretch them out to the sides like you're treading water. Repeat each movement a few times.

Feel free to add any other movements that feel natural and organic. A minute or two spent moving your hands and arms will do wonders for your ability to create expressive marks.

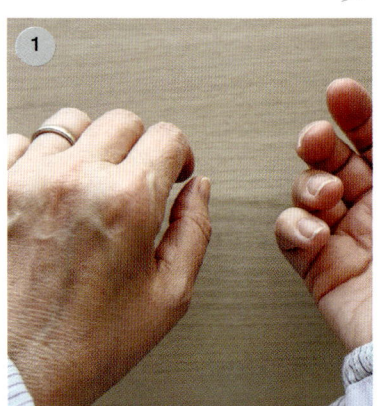
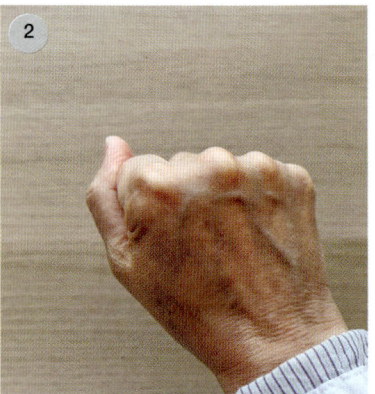
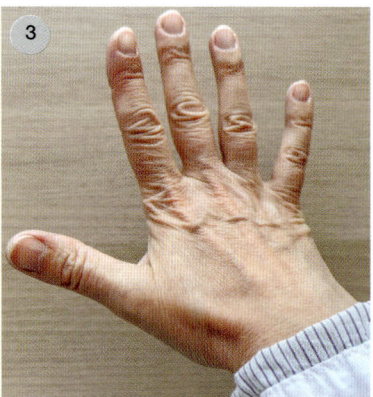

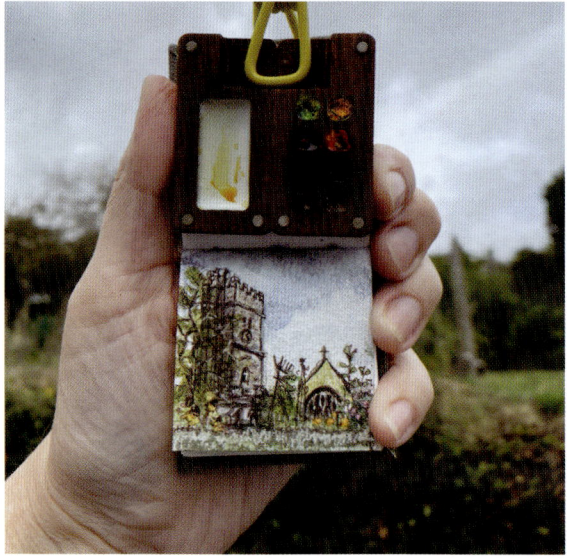

DRAWING TIP

Left-handed? Try drawing from right to left. I know you were taught to write words from left to right, but if you draw that way your hand will always be covering up your work. Drawing (and painting) from right to left will allow you to see what you've already done more clearly.

THE BASICS

Try This: Holding Your Pencil

Hold your pencil loosely (the same applies to a pen or paintbrush). If you grip the barrel of your pencil tightly with your fingers, you will strangle the expressiveness right out of it! Remind yourself to hold the pencil as lightly as if it were a precious feather. Many artists have developed ineffective ways of holding pencils since childhood and are loathe to explore different ways to hold them to create art. You will do yourself and your art a hundred favours if you take the time to learn how to hold your pencil correctly. Your fingers should gently cradle the barrel instead of choking it into submission.

Do not hold the pencil too closely to the tip. Instead, move your fingers further back so that they are closer to the middle of the barrel (1A). Allow the pencil to rest lightly on your middle finger with your index finger and thumb to guide it gently (1B). This may feel strange and wrong at first, but the more you practise it, the more comfortable it will become. You will find that holding your pencil this way actually allows you more control when you need it, while still allowing the pencil to glide expressively when required. Soon, it will feel like second nature.

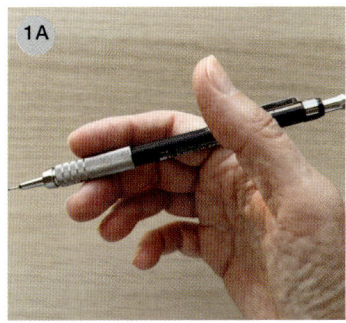

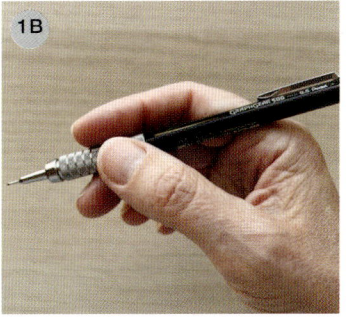

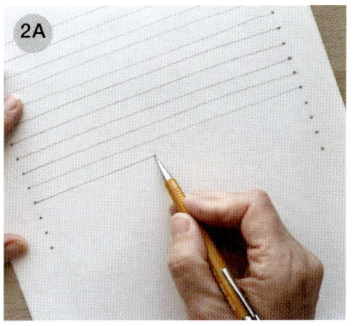

Try This: Drawing With Confidence

On a large sheet of paper, create a column of dots in the left margin and a corresponding column of dots in the right margin. Practise connecting the dots from left to right and then right to left (2A). Hold your pencil as described above and move your entire arm as you do this. Keep your movements quick and assured (even if you miss the dot altogether!). A pro tip is to keep your eye on the destination and not the journey… your hand will naturally follow where the eye leads. So, if you want the line to end on a certain point, keep your eye on that point while drawing it.

Once you've mastered horizontal lines, try adding vertical ones and diagonal ones (2B). This is a simple exercise that will increase your hand–eye coordination and confidence.

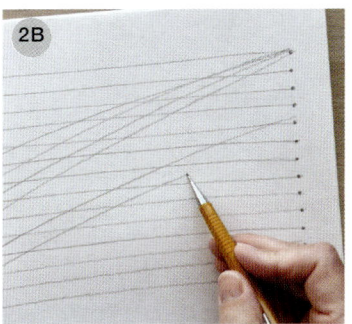

This simple exercise will help you develop confidence in your lines.

Value

Value (also called "tone") refers to how light or dark a colour or hue is. White is the lightest value, black is the darkest, and there are variations of grey in between. Artists may vary the amount of each value they include in a particular drawing or painting, but all successful drawings and paintings use a RANGE of values in their work.

UNDERSTANDING VALUE

The longer I teach and practise art the more convinced I am that value is one of the most important elements. Paintings that lack a range of values – or don't represent them all in some way – are less interesting to look at. That's because everything you see, whether it's a portrait or landscape, is revealed through a combination of light and shadow. If you look at a selection of some of the most famous artworks in history, you can see that even though the styles might be different, they all have a range of values.

Look around you right now and find three items that are the lightest values, three that are the darkest values, and three that are somewhere in between. SQUINT if you have trouble seeing the different values in colour. Your eyelashes will act like the shutter on a camera and partially block the light, allowing you to see the range

of values more distinctly. This is something you can practise at any time, even if you're not drawing. It's easy to see the lightest and darkest values, but many new artists have trouble seeing the mid-values in colour. The more you practise looking at the values around you, the more you will learn to recognise them.

If you have a good range of values in your artwork, it will more closely resemble what the human eye sees and will look more realistic. An easy way to see if your painting has a range of values is to take a photo of it and convert it to black and white.

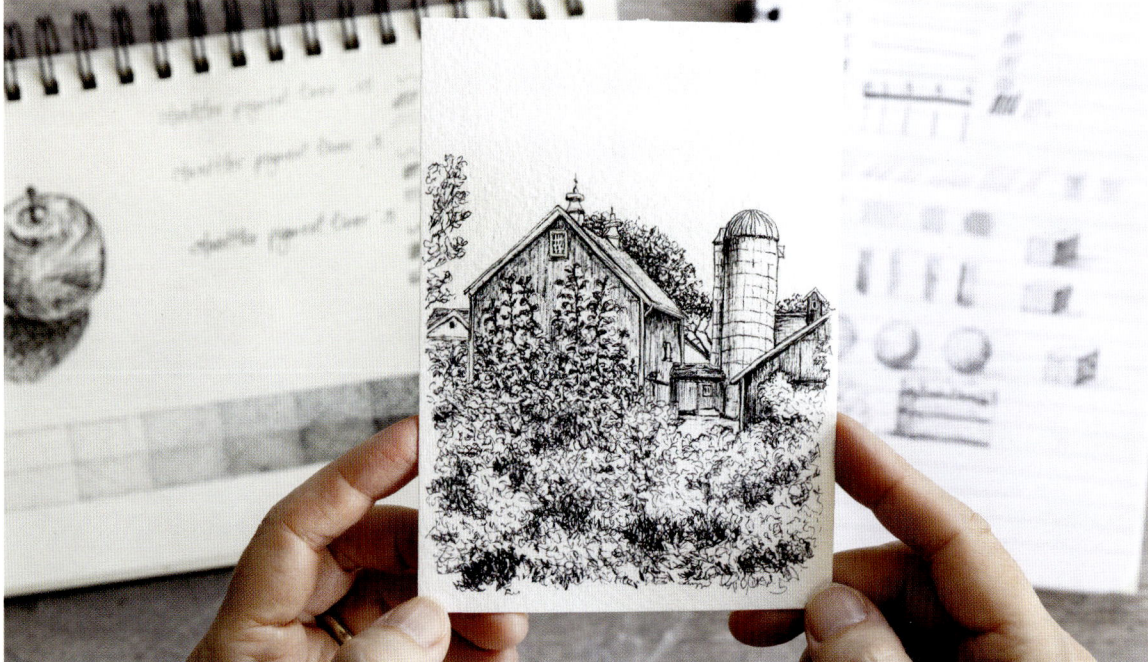

Cooler tree
in distance

Shadowed
side

Variation of
values in foliage

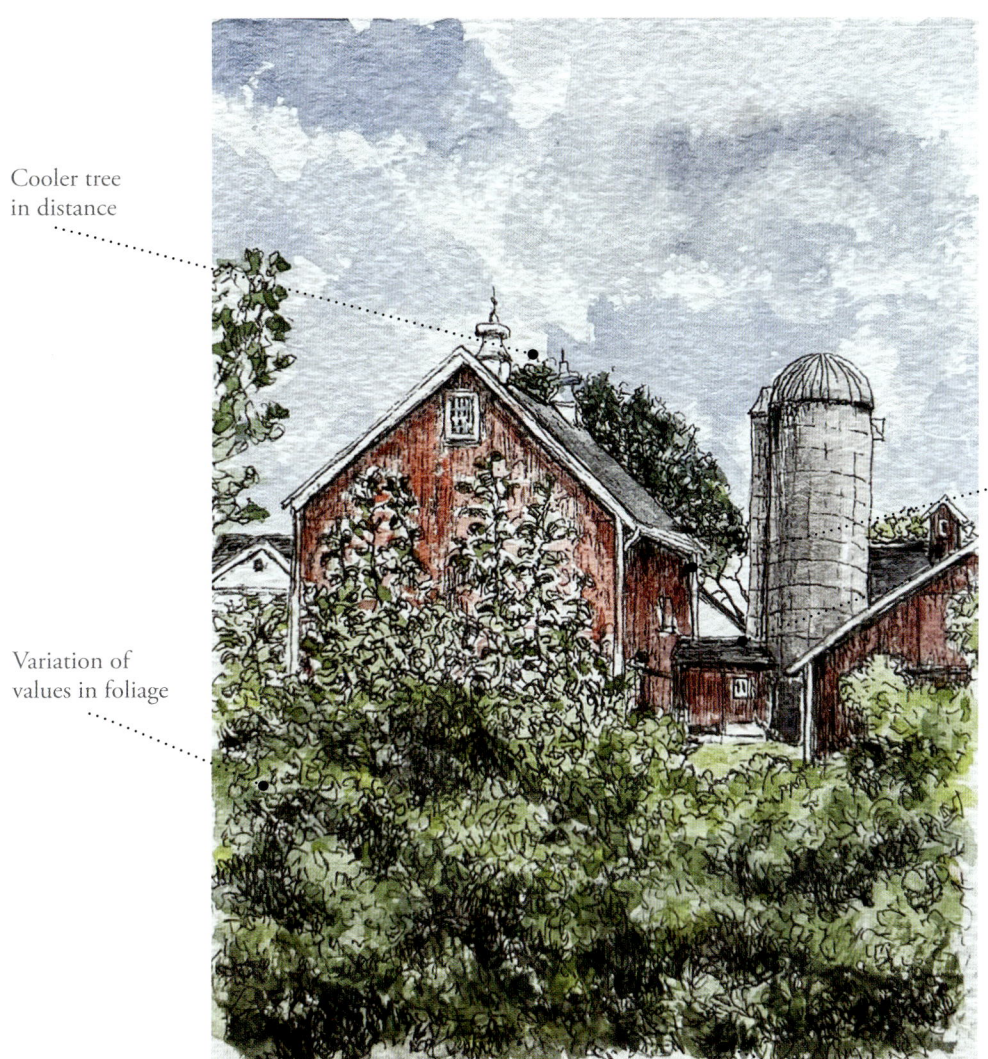

Darkest values
in foreground

Try This: Create a Value Scale in Pencil

Measure a strip containing seven equal-sized squares – 1 x 1 inch (2.5 x 2.5cm) works well for this. The first square should be the white of the paper and the last should be as black as you can get it. In the middle square create a mid-grey. Starting with these three basic values first makes the process easier.

In the two squares between the white and mid-grey, create two values that are darker than white but lighter than mid-grey. In the two squares between the mid-grey and black, create two values that are darker than mid-grey but lighter than black. The different jumps between each value should be equal – like the tread of steps in a staircase. SQUINT to see if the flow looks gradual like a waterfall or if there are areas that feel too light or dark, and adjust the values as needed.

I have found that most people have a natural tendency to create either dark or light values. It's rare that somebody is equally skilled at creating a range of both light and dark values without practice. If you find it easier to create a variety of light values, you'll know that you need to practise creating darker ones, and vice versa. Create as many value scales as you need until it is perfect. You can later cut out your value scale and place it beside you as you draw to make sure you represent each of the values (see Drawing Mistakes and How to Fix Themin Chapter Three). It seems simple, but this little reminder truly does make a difference in prompting you to use all of the values.

You can do several of these value scales using different shading techniques: unblended pencil, blended pencil, hatching and cross-hatching, and stippling. You can use different pencils to make this easier. H leads create harder and thinner lines (the higher the number, the harder and lighter the mark). B leads produce darker and thicker lines (the higher the number, the softer and darker the mark). The traditional value scales include 10 shades of white, greys, and black, but I have found that seven shades are enough to understand the concept and represent the values you see in the world around you. Sometimes I even do five-shade value scales. The point is that you should perfect your ability to recognise various values and create them with whatever medium you are using.

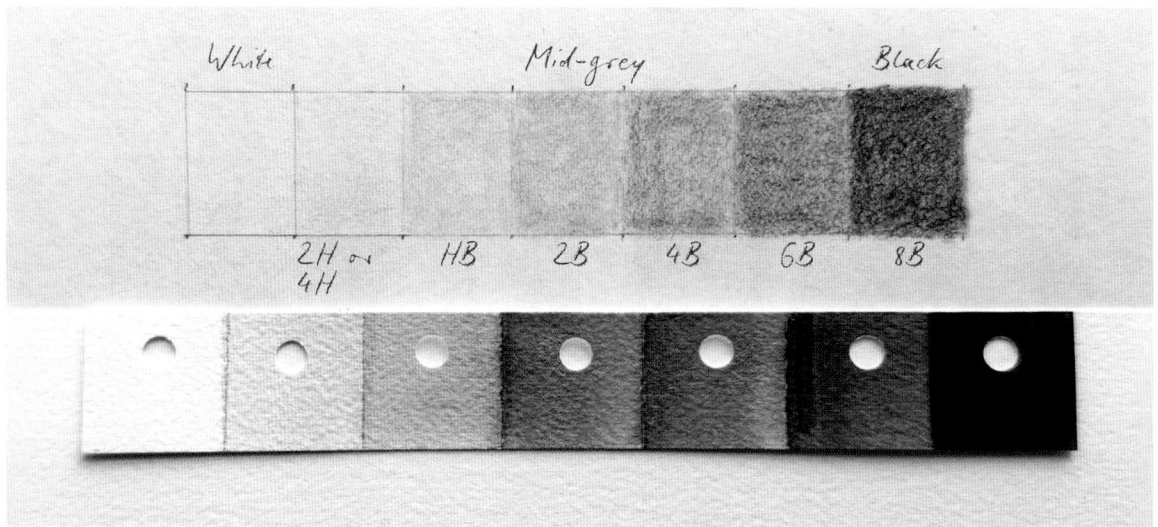

THE BASICS

Try This: Create a Monochromatic Value Scale in Watercolour

Choose any colour (one that is darker, like blue, will be easier) and create a strip containing five or seven equal-sized squares – as above, 1 x 1 inch (2.5 x 2.5cm) is a good size. For watercolour, I find it easiest to start with the darkest value. Then, using a palette with multiple wells, place a bit of the darkest value in a clean well and add a drop of water using a pipette or the tip of a clean brush. Repeat this process to create each subsequent value: place a bit of each new value into a clean well and add a drop or two of water. It takes a bit of practice, but doing this will not only help you understand how to create different values in watercolour, it will also help you learn water control.

Now, create a monochromatic painting that represents all of the values in your value scale. You can use a single colour for this like Payne's Grey or French Ultramarine, but I find that it's helpful to mix my own dark colours. I recommend using French Ultramarine and either Transparent Red Oxide, Burnt Sienna, or Burnt Umber. This has the benefit of teaching you how to mix your own dark grey without needing to rely on a pre-mixed colour (see below).

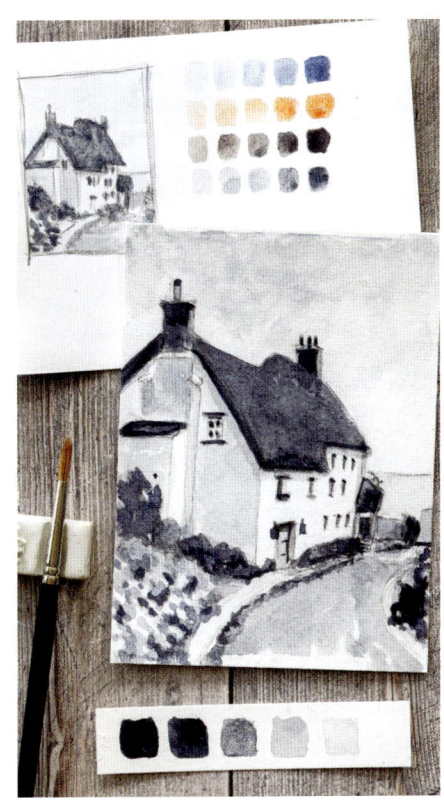

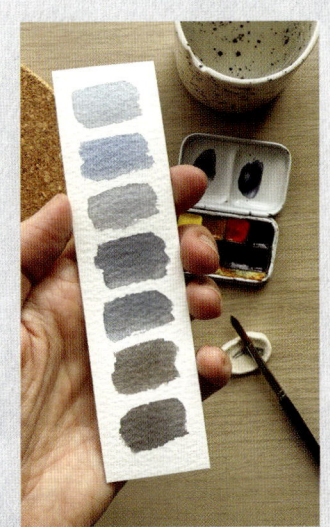

PAINTING TIP: BEWARE OF PRE-MIXED GREYS!

Payne's Grey, Neutral Tint, and other pre-mixed greys can be lovely if you want to create a monochromatic painting, but these paint colours often contain multiple pigments that are not part of your normal palette and can therefore look out of place or too dominant. There are many benefits to mixing your own grey: it's easy; it provides colour harmony with the rest of your painting since it shares the same pigments; and you can slightly vary the colour in different areas, shifting it more towards blue or brown depending on how much of each colour you add (see photo). This will make your paintings look more dynamic and lively. If you ditch the shop-bought greys, you will also be less tempted to add them to your mixes whenever you need to darken a colour, which will risk muddying your palette.

Shape

Everything you want to draw can be broken down into simple shapes and lines. Many shapes are GEOMETRIC like circles, squares, rectangles, and triangles. Others will be ORGANIC, meaning they are more free-form. When you're outside drawing in nature, it's helpful to be able to quickly identify and sketch these shapes and lines before you begin to add ink or paint.

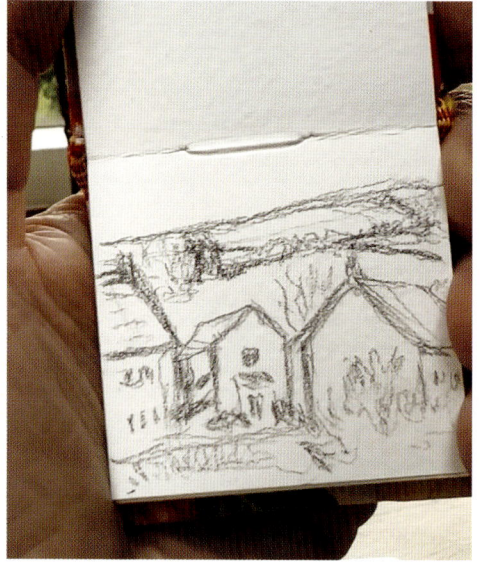

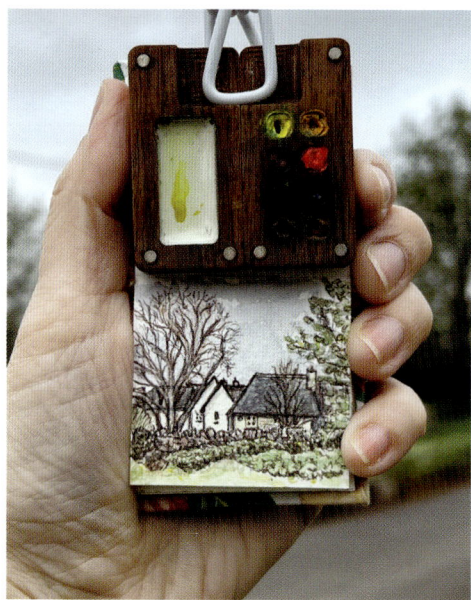

FINDING SHAPES

When you're painting outside, find simple shapes and quickly put them down. All it takes is finding one shape. Once you've found that, it's easier to locate the surrounding shapes and put them in. Ask yourself the following questions about each subsequent shape:

(1) Is it larger or smaller than the first shape?

(2) Is it higher or lower than the first shape (or both)?

After the main forms have been placed, you can sketch in other details like the windows and doors.

Try This: Simplify a Scene

Try to simplify a scene into a few basic shapes and lines. Take any landscape photo that is cropped to the same ratio as your paper (square, 2:3, etc.) or isolate a scene from life. I find it is easiest to start with the horizon line and then place dominant objects first. You might be surprised that with just a few shapes and lines you can give an impression of the scene before you. Here is a sketch of a collection of buildings with moors in the distance (top left). I started by placing the smaller house in the centre and worked out from there. The front of the buildings are simple squares with triangular gables. The sides of the middle and right buildings are rectangles, and the rooftops are parallelograms. I denoted the placement of the horizon line and distant hills with curved lines and used scribbly lines to show where key vegetation would be placed.

THE BASICS

LIGHT AND SHADE

Here are a few terms that will help you to understand how light and shadows work on forms. Taking the time to learn and understand how light and shadows work together will help your work look more realistic.

TINY PAINTING TIP

The key for fitting multiple, complex objects on a tiny surface is to first break everything down into simple shapes and lines. This will help you visualise the scene and know where to place things without making them too large.

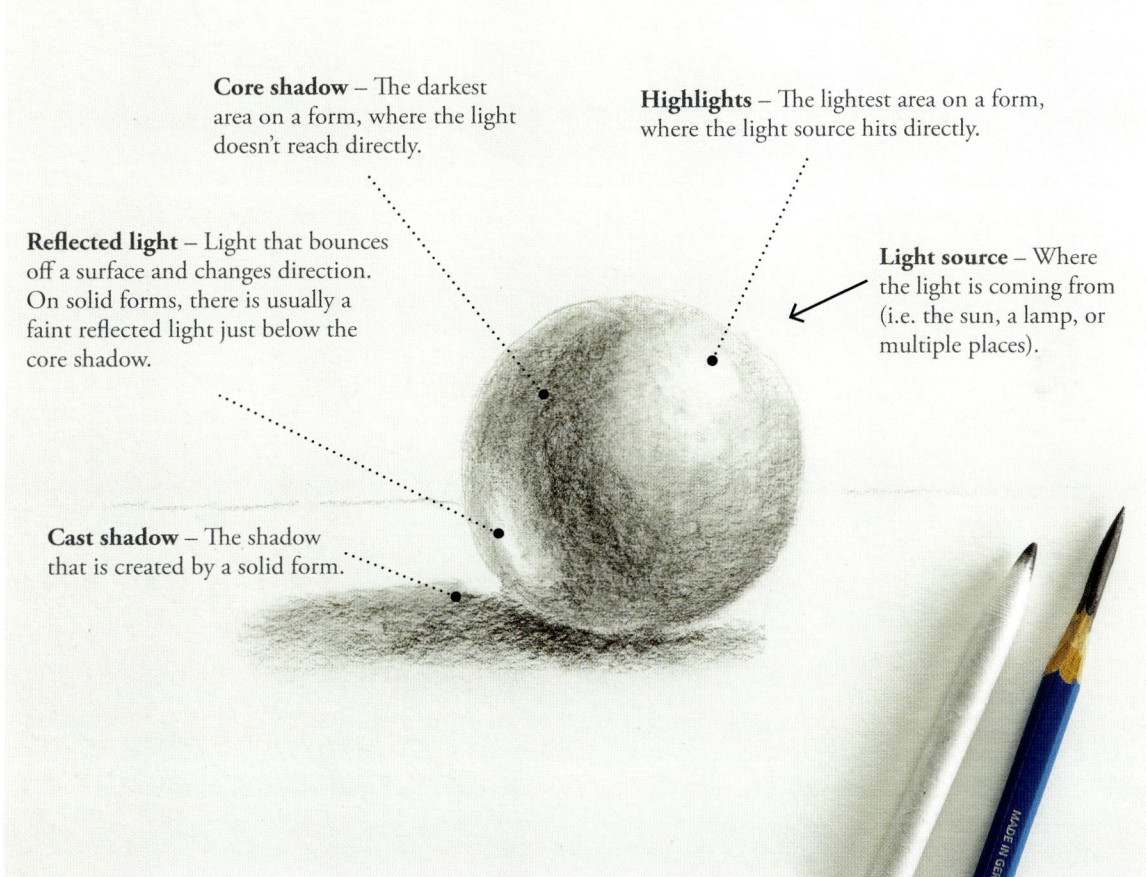

Core shadow – The darkest area on a form, where the light doesn't reach directly.

Highlights – The lightest area on a form, where the light source hits directly.

Reflected light – Light that bounces off a surface and changes direction. On solid forms, there is usually a faint reflected light just below the core shadow.

Light source – Where the light is coming from (i.e. the sun, a lamp, or multiple places).

Cast shadow – The shadow that is created by a solid form.

Form

Form is a shape that is three-dimensional. The way to convey the width, length, height, and volume of a three-dimensional shape on a two-dimensional surface is through shading. For this reason, it's incredibly helpful to understand the basics of how to shade simple geometric forms. There isn't a one-size-fits-all for shading because all objects are slightly different, and shadows will constantly be changing depending on the light source. Rather, the illusion of form can be created by using a variety of all of the other Elements of Art to shade forms.

SHADING FORMS

When you are painting outside during the day, your light source is the sun, and since the sun is constantly moving throughout the sky it's important to be able to quickly find the forms and place the shadows where you see them. Plein air artists often find themselves "chasing the light", which means that the scene they started out drawing or painting often changes completely as the sun shifts position or clouds obstruct it. For these reasons, it's helpful to practise shading simple forms in an environment where you can control the light source.

Try This: Draw Objects Inside a Light Box

Take an old box (or make one) that you can set on your desk and place different objects inside. Try to find white objects if you can, since it's easier to see a variety of values on them. Then, take a desk lamp (or even the torch/flashlight on your smartphone) and shine it directly at the object. This will allow you to more accurately control the light source. It's helpful if the sides and surface of the box are white, but plain cardboard will also work.

Notice how the light hits the object and slowly fades to darker values as the object turns away from and is further from the light source. Also, notice the many subtle variations of values that flow over the surface. Next, move the light to a different area and notice how the shadows and cast shadow are different.

Repeat this exercise with different objects of various shapes: circles, cylinders, cubes, and so on. The more you do this, the better you will understand the subtle variations of light on even the simplest of forms.

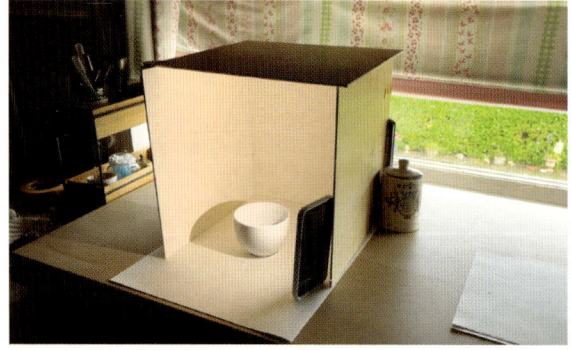
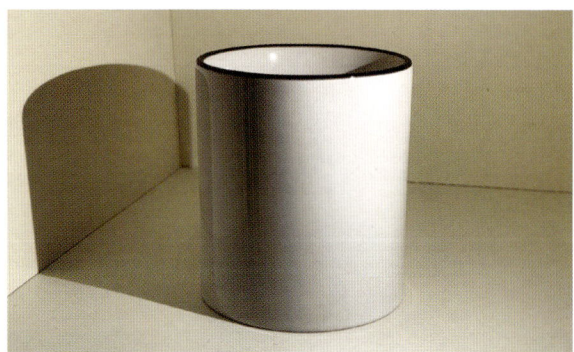

Texture

In a three-dimensional work of art like a sculpture or woven textile, texture is tactile – you can reach out and feel it beneath your fingertips. In a two-dimensional work of art, the illusion of texture can be simulated in a variety of ways. The beauty of line-and-wash is that you can create wonderful textures with the ink and allow the watercolour to bring it to life.

A Few Drawing Terms to Know:

Hatching – Creating value by drawing closely spaced, parallel lines.

Cross-hatching – Creating value by drawing closely spaced, parallel lines with intersecting parallel lines.

Scribbly Lines – A technique used to indicate wild or undefined areas of a drawing.

Stippling – Using dots to create various values.

Cross-contour Lines – Using lines to define the form of a three-dimensional object by following its curves and contours.

Try This: Create Value Scales

Use pencils or fineliners to create value scales with hatching, cross-hatching, and stippling. Once you understand the basics of building value with those simple techniques, you can begin to loosen up. Try varying the direction of your hatching, for example. There are many ways to vary your lines with hatching or cross-hatching. You can start by hatching a series of horizontal lines and then cross-hatch over them with vertical lines, diagonal lines, or even curved lines. Combine hatching, cross-hatching, and stippling.

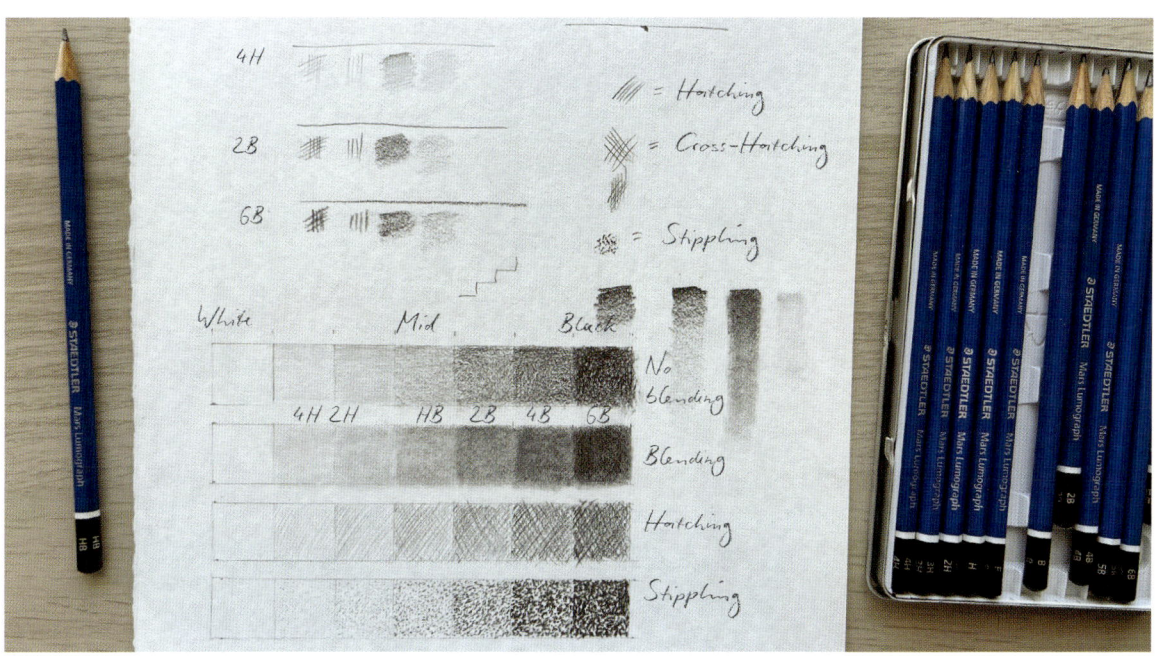

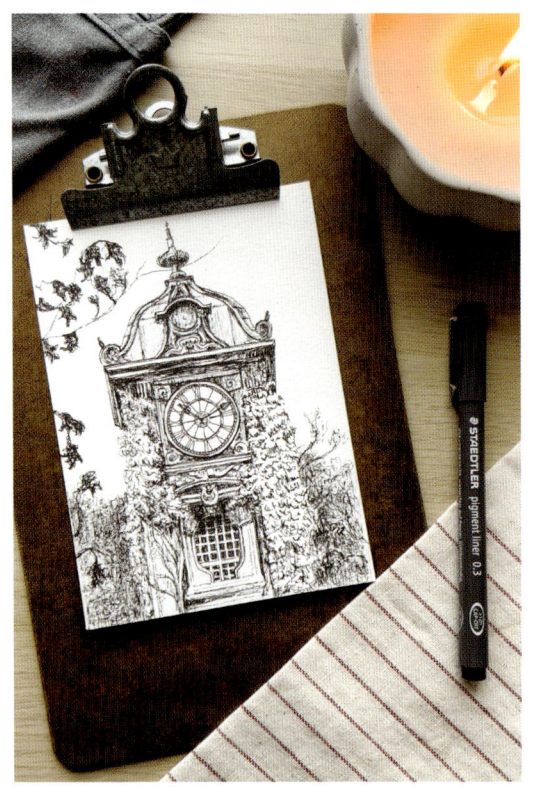

Try This: Create a Library of Textures

Make value scales with each new texture to see how you can create different values with a single texture. In time, you will develop your own unique language of textures that you can use in your drawings.

Keep in mind that in tiny painting every single line is important. Practise making some smaller strokes that can still indicate things you might see: leaves in the wind, a brick or stone wall, tall grasses, and so on.

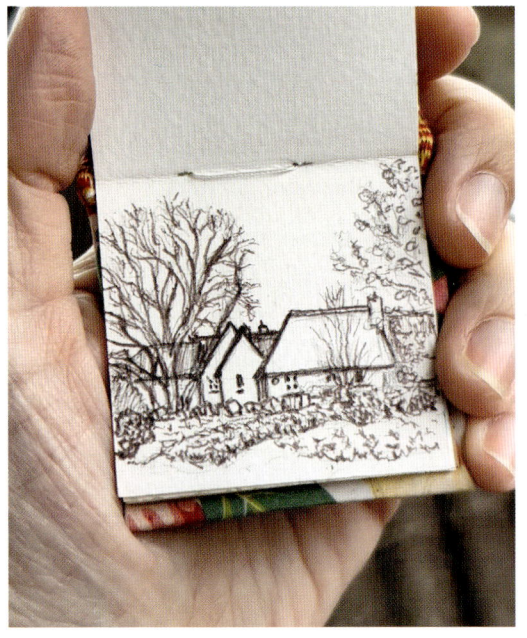

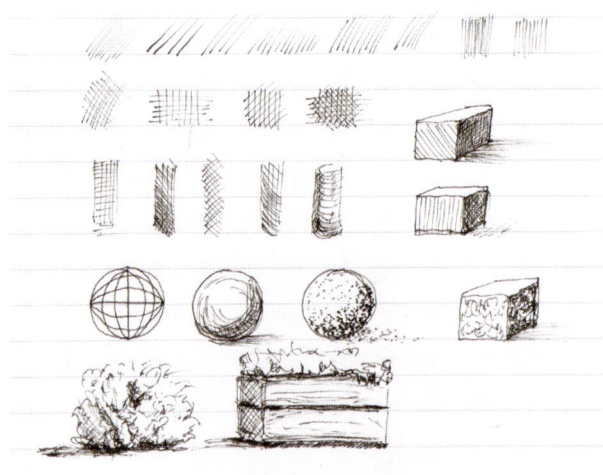

Here, hatching, cross-hatching, and stippling were used to create shaded forms. I used a size 005 fineliner for the thinnest areas, size 01 for thicker lines, and size 03 for the darkest areas.

Try This: Make a Master Copy

It is a centuries-old tradition in art for students to copy the works of the Old Masters to learn their techniques. The Ancient Romans were known for copying the statues of the Ancient Greeks. Artists in the Middle Ages had apprenticeships where they learned through copying and repetition, and this continued through the Renaissance and into the twentieth century. This tradition continues today in ateliers, and some art museums set up special days for artists to come and copy master artworks.

If you think about it, the idea of creating a master copy makes sense. Babies learn to talk by imitating sounds, musicians learn by repeating scales and reading sheet music, athletes follow routines, teachers train in classrooms, doctors undergo internships, and people from all walks of life complete apprenticeships. Learning how to paint or draw is no different. Making a master copy helps you learn new skills and try things you might not think to try on your own, and it will take your work to the next level.

Search for drawings created by the Old Masters and find one that appeals to you. Copy it. Notice the variety of different marks used to indicate forms. Two artists who are known for their beautiful and varied use of lines, value, and texture in their drawings are Rembrandt van Rijn and Albrecht Dürer.

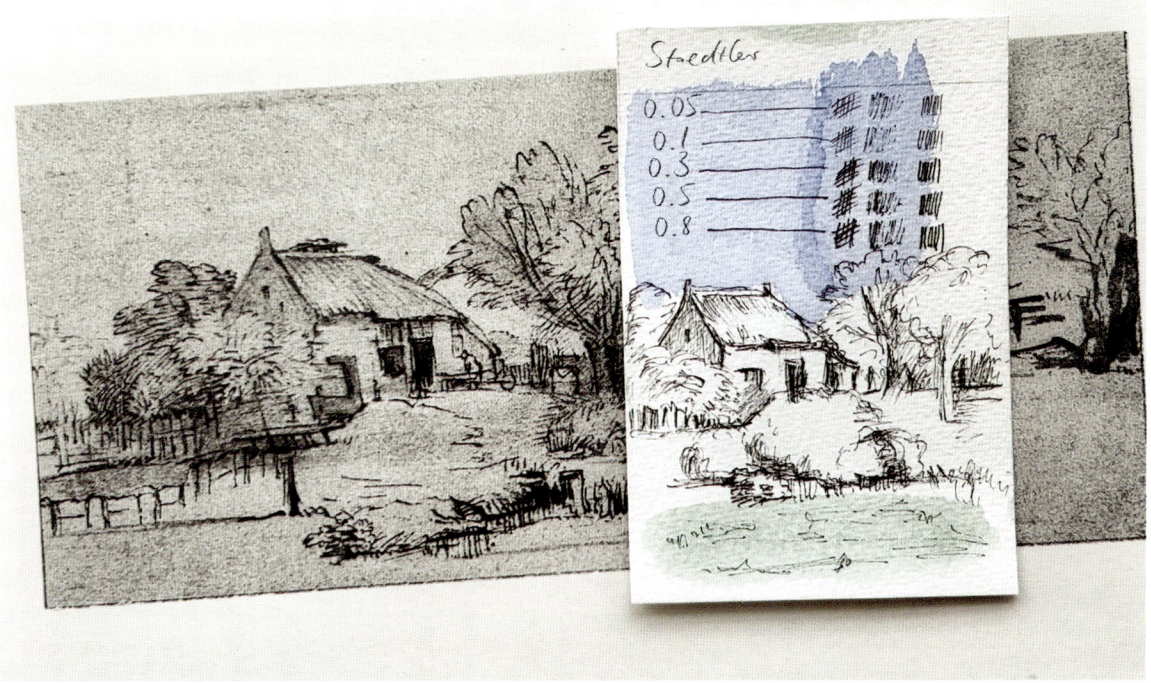

This master copy of one of Rembrandt's drawings was made using 0.05 and 0.1 black fineliners.

Colour

Colour is something that has fascinated artists, philosophers, and scientists for centuries. The Ancient Greeks believed that colour was a result of the struggle between light and darkness. Aristotle theorised that the gods sent colour from the heavens as celestial rays, and the four colours white, red, yellow, and black corresponded to the elements fire, earth, air, and water. You can see the dominance of these colours in Ancient Greek pottery and frescoes.

DEMYSTIFYING COLOUR

This theory was accepted for more than two thousand years, until the late seventeenth century when Sir Isaac Newton used a glass prism to divide the white rays of sunlight into the seven-coloured spectrum. He represented this by drawing a closed circle that artists today refer to as the colour wheel (see following page). This new theory was hotly contested, but it helped artists see colour relationships and develop techniques for colour mixing and colour schemes that are still widely used today. It is often referred to as the RYB model (or red, yellow, blue).

Contemporary scientists have since made tremendous progress studying the physics of light and how the human eye perceives it. Modern printers have developed a printing method that uses a CMYK model (cyan, magenta, yellow, and key, meaning black) to mix all colours. Many artists today prefer to use these colours as their primary colours instead of the more traditional RYB, but it's important to note that most printers use dyes, which are a different chemical composition to the pigments found in most traditional watercolour paints. Because of that, Sir Isaac Newton's colour wheel still makes the best sense for artists learning to mix colour.

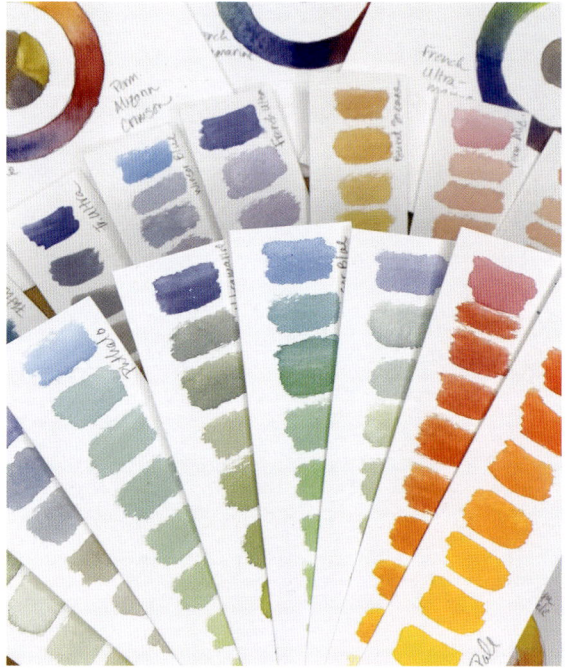

THE THREE MAIN PROPERTIES OF COLOUR

All three properties are important to consider when mixing colours, although many beginning artists only think about the hue and occasionally the value. Colour mixing is a fascinating subject that can take a lifetime to learn and perfect, but this is one of the things I love about painting – it's always exciting!

1. Hue – This is the name we give a colour, like blue, green, or yellow. It's the universally recognised name from the primary and secondary colours on the colour wheel (red, orange, yellow, green, blue, and violet).

2. Value (or Tone when it refers to colour) – This is the lightness or darkness of a colour. Lighter colours are referred to as TINTS, while darker ones are referred to as SHADES.

3. Intensity (often called Saturation or Chroma) – This is how bright or dull a colour is. The closer a colour is to being a pure, single pigment colour (meaning that it was created using one pigment instead of two or more), the brighter it is. This differs from Value because it's possible to have a colour of any value that retains a bright intensity.

MORE ABOUT HUE

It can get confusing when people talk about "hue" and "colour" because sometimes when they say "colour" they mean the colour of a tube of paint (like Ultramarine Blue) and not the colour of the spectrum. Colour can mean either of these things depending on the context. When in doubt, you can use the term "hue" to be more specific.

All manufactured paint is made from a combination of pigments and a binder to hold them together (in watercolour the binder is often gum arabic, and sometimes honey or other additives that preserve the paint). Some pigments are natural, others are chemically manufactured. When mixed with a binder, these pigments become paint.

For the purposes of colour mixing, HUE refers to the 12 general colours of the spectrum. These can be divided into three categories:

1. Primary Colours (Red, Yellow, and Blue) – These are the three colours that can't be mixed by using other colours. They exist in their pure form.

2. Secondary Colours (Orange, Green, and Violet) – These are the three colours that can be created by mixing the three primary colours with one another. Yellow and red make orange, red and blue make violet, blue and yellow make green.

3. Tertiary Colours – These are the six colours in between each of the primary and secondary colours. We often see these colours in the world around us… the yellow-greens and violet-reds and red-oranges, for example. It's helpful to practise mixing them so that you understand how to create them.

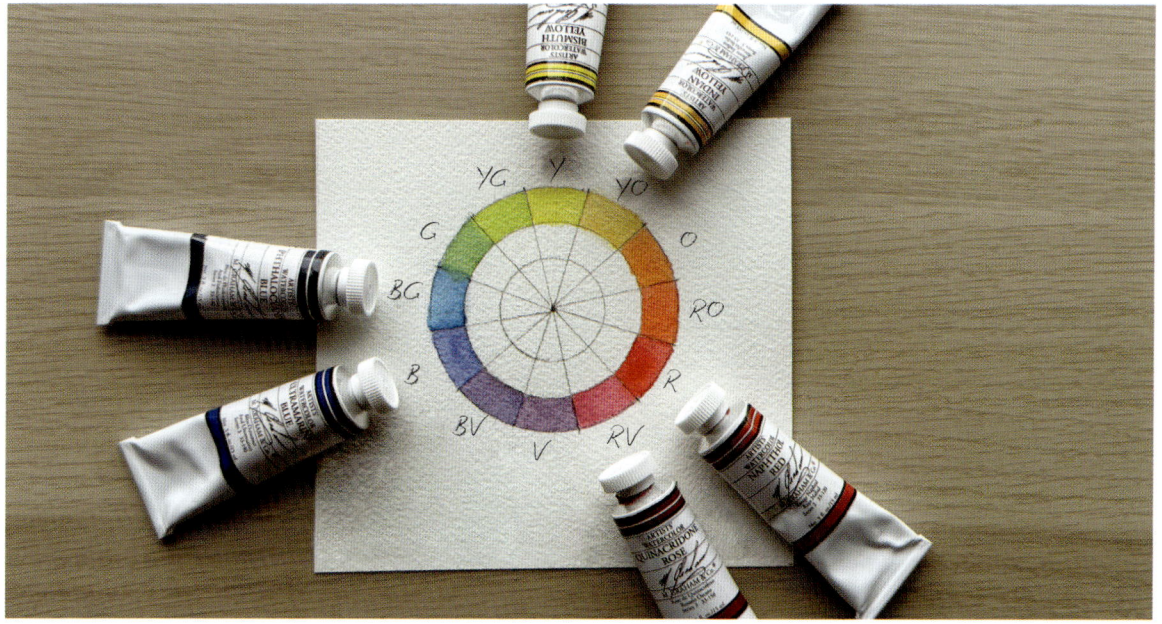

HOW TO KNOW IF A COLOUR IS WARM OR COOL (COLOUR TEMPERATURE)

A good rule of thumb is to understand that yellows, oranges, and reds are traditionally considered to be the "warm" colours, and blue, violet, and green are "cool" colours. So how can a yellow or red be cool, or a blue be warm? An easy trick is to look for the nearest primary or secondary on either side of a colour on the colour wheel and ask yourself which one it leans towards more. If a yellow leans more towards green, for instance, it will be a cooler yellow, because green is a cool colour. If it leans closer to orange, it will be warmer. The same is true for reds. If it leans more towards orange, it will be warmer, whereas if it leans more towards violet, it will be cooler.

Blues can be a little bit trickier, as they often contain chemical properties that enable them to mix both cool and warm colours. In general, however, a blue that leans more towards violet is warmer, since the colour next to violet is red, which is warmer than yellow. If it leans closer to green, it is cooler since green is a cool colour.

Try not to get overwhelmed by these tips. Instead, just start mixing. Create colour wheels and colour charts. Paint outside and experiment with your mixes. The more you paint, the more all this information will become second nature to you. Spending the time to learn the basics and practise at home will help you understand these concepts.

When in doubt, place your paints on a colour wheel to see which way they lean. Compare them to other primaries of the same colour to see the differences. The yellows and reds in this photo are placed closer to the secondary colours they lean towards.

TINY PAINTING TIP

When painting outside, your time is limited. To make colour mixing easier, and quicker, I often use a limited palette with two of each primary colour – one that visibly leans towards warm and the other that visibly leans towards cool (see right). This gives me more versatility when mixing. It also makes it easier to paint with different brands. Instead of asking myself the manufacturer's name for a colour, I can instead ask myself, "Is it warmer or cooler?" If I see a green that is quite warm and earthy, for instance, I'll think, "Okay, I need my warmer blue and my warmer yellow to mix that."

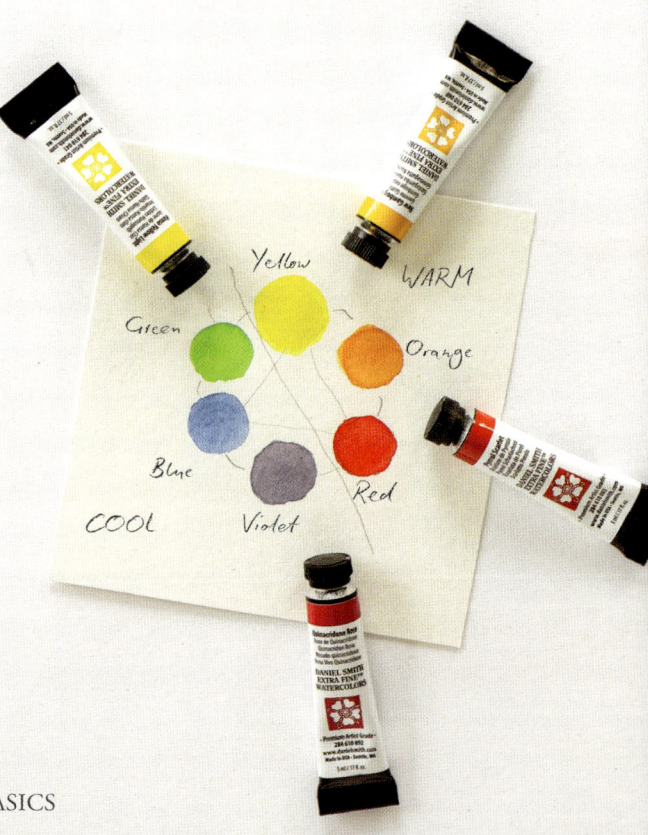

THE BASICS

CHOOSING YOUR LIMITED PALETTE

When you're new to painting, it's easy to think that the more paint colours you have the better your paintings will be, but if you want to get skilled at painting, you'll learn to mix your own colours. This is especially true for painting small, because you have limited real estate on your piece of paper and too many colours can be chaotic.

When choosing your colours, it's best to start with a limited palette of no more than eight colours. With a combination of two yellows, two reds, and two blues, you can mix just about every colour you want. This will also lend a harmony to your paintings because all the colours have been created by the same few pigments. I often use two additional earth colours for convenience (like Transparent Red Oxide or Raw Sienna), but this is purely optional.

I prefer to use a split complement (a warmer and a cooler of each of the three primary colours) in my palette, for the simple reason that all paint colours have a slight bias towards being more cool or warm (see previous page). In other words, it's nearly impossible to find a paint that is a pure yellow, red, or blue. Pyrrol Scarlet, for example, has a slight orange cast to it and so is warmer because it is closer to yellow than blue.

Quinacridone Rose, on the other hand, has a violet cast to it, and is therefore cooler because it leans closer to blue. By including both reds in a palette, you can ensure that you will be able to mix a variety of bright oranges as well as vibrant violets.

You can use any manufacturer of watercolours for your palette. I've provided a list (see Paints in Chapter One), of some warm and cool options for each of the primary colours, but this list isn't by any means complete. As you grow in your painting skills, explore other colours and mixing combinations. It's half the fun!

In these tiny paintings, I mixed most of the colours using warm primaries and earth colours to give them a warmer feeling.

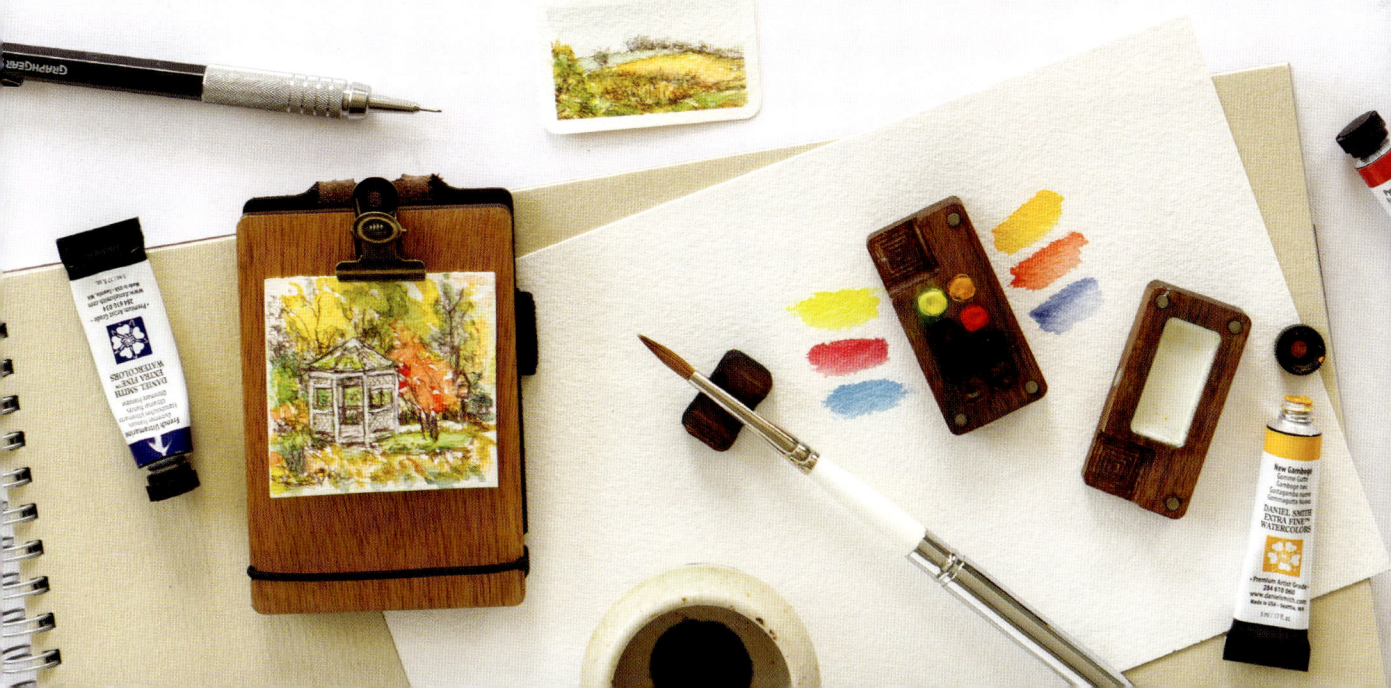

Try This: Make Colour Wheels

An easy way to see how well your colours mix is to create little colour wheels using your primary colours. Experiment with the different primaries to see which ones mix together to create the best secondary colours.

You can trace the lid of a jar or a roll of masking tape to make a circle and then create 12 equally spaced pie shapes for the colours. If you can create a good range of secondary and tertiary colours, you will be able to mix every colour you see. These colour wheels were created using two yellows, two reds, and two blues from three different paint manufacturers.

Try This: Make Colour Strips

Colour wheels and charts are incredibly helpful, but it's possible to create a variety of different hues with only two colours. Make little colour strips where you mix two colours together to show at least six different hues for each combination. Here's how it works: place a wash of each of the two colours next to one another on your palette. Paint a square of the original two colours on opposite sides of a strip of watercolour paper. Then, on your palette, add a tiny bit of the darker or more dominant colour into the lighter one (just the tiniest bit will change the colour) and paint a square of that beside the lightest colour. You may need to add additional water to your mixes as you create the new hues. Continue this process, slowly adding a bit more of the darker colour into the lighter one and then adding it to your colour strip. These colour strips will help you discover the mixing possibilities of any two-colour combinations.

When I make these, I try to place a hue in the centre that doesn't visibly lean towards either of the original colours. Below are three colour strips that each combine two different colours. Notice how the mixes on the left of the strips lean more towards the colours on the left, and the mixes on the right lean more towards the colours on the right.

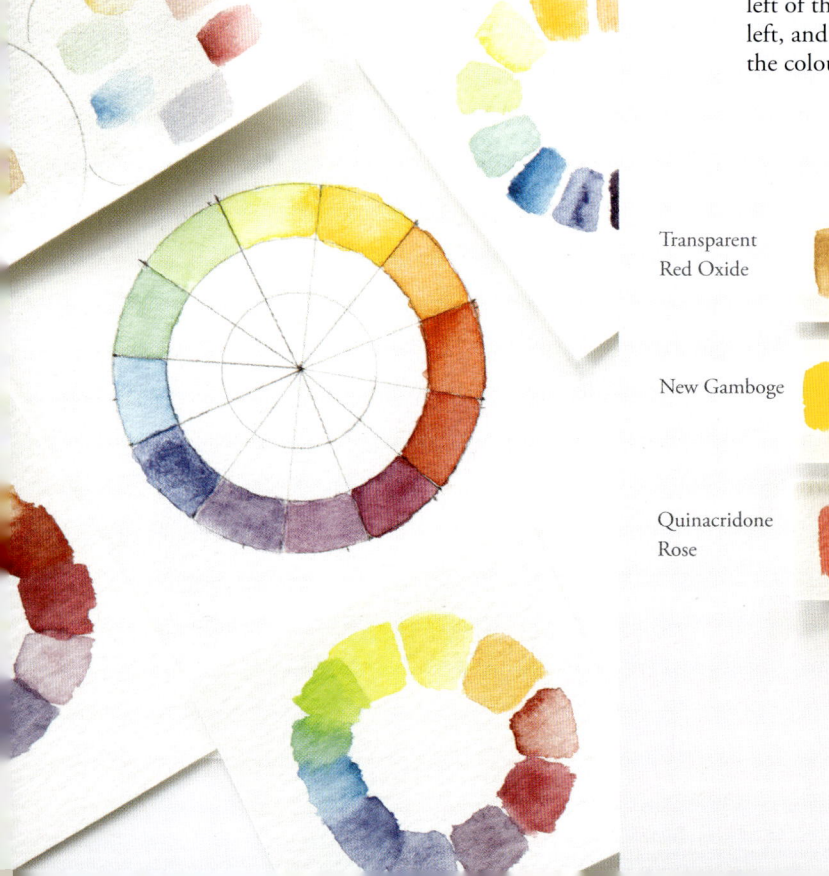

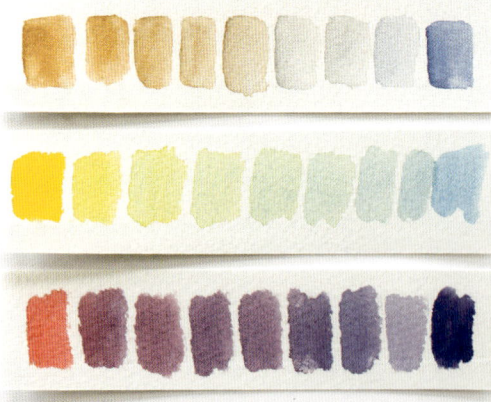

Transparent Red Oxide — French Ultramarine

New Gamboge — Phthalo Blue

Quinacridone Rose — French Ultramarine

WHAT'S IN A NAME?

Paint manufacturers give names to the colours they create. Sometimes these are more universal names, like French Ultramarine, but other times they can be more unique, like Antwerp Blue. Think of these names as a general guide, but don't get tied to them. Instead, look at the pigments that are listed on the tube. A Raw Sienna by one company, for instance, might contain PY42 (pigment yellow 42), while another might contain PY43, and still another might contain PBr7 (pigment brown 8). Some even contain a mix of more than one pigment. It can be quite confusing!

The point is that if you like a colour made by one manufacturer and then purchase a colour with the same name by another, you might be surprised by how different they are. It can seem very overwhelming at first, but if you pay attention to the pigments in your paints, you will soon get to know them. Remember that all paints are created with ground pigments and a binder (like gum arabic or honey) to hold it all together. Two tubes that contain the same pigments can also look different depending on how finely they are ground, how much binder is used, and so on. Don't become obsessed with or overly worried about memorising all this information – just file it away for future thought. Focus on your limited palette to start until the colours are second nature.

PAINTING TIP: AVOID SAP GREEN!

I know it's pretty. I know you probably think it's a shortcut to painting green things in your landscape. But I promise that if you use Sap Green your paintings will look flatter and your colour harmony will be off. This is especially true in tiny paintings. Why? Similar to pre-mixed greys, they likely contain pigments that aren't in the rest of your palette. You will be adding different yellows, blues, and reds than the ones you are using in the rest of your painting, and it will be noticeable. If you try to lighten or darken it, you'll be introducing even more pigments, increasing the chances that it will look muddy. Also, some Sap Greens contain colours that aren't lightfast. It's so easy to mix your own greens, and they will add variety and cohesiveness to your paintings. Have I convinced you yet?

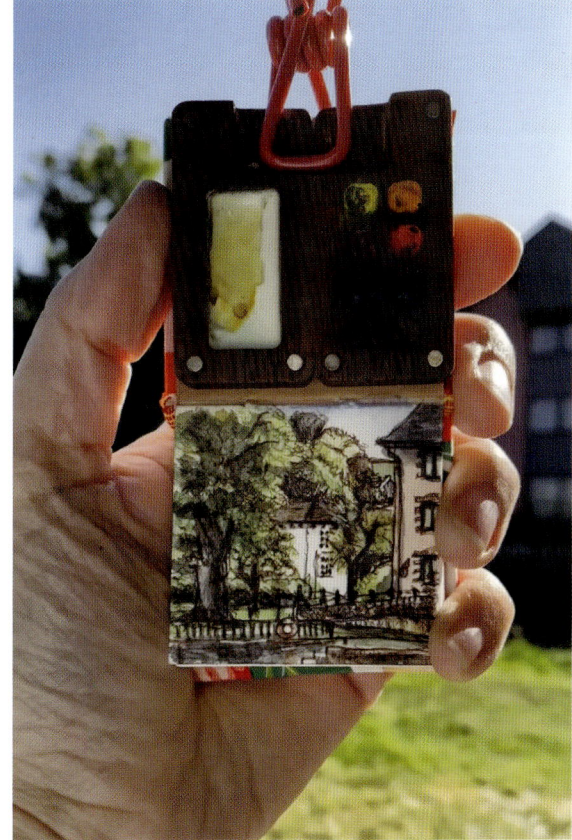

Try This: Make a Colour Chart

Although colour strips can teach you a lot about the capabilities of any two colours when mixed together, they can be cumbersome to carry around or to use as a quick reference. A colour chart, in contrast, will give you a quick glimpse of the capabilities of all the colours in your palette when mixed together. You can hang it on the wall of your studio or carry it with you when you go out to paint. It won't provide the full capabilities of your palette, but it will give you a good indication of the possibilities. As a bonus, they're beautiful to look at and fun to make!

1. Create a Grid – To start, create a grid of squares on a sheet of watercolour paper – these can be any size, but I find that ½ inch (1.5cm) allows you to fill a single page without running out of space. Always include a row and a column for each of the colours in your palette, then add an extra of each.

2. Label Colours – Label your colours down one side of the sheet and then (in the same order) label them across the top of the sheet, leaving the first column blank.

3. Paint Each Colour – Paint the colour in its pure form in the first square beside each name.

4. Mix Colours – Starting with the first row, mix the colour with each of the colours listed above each column. You already know that there are a variety of hues you can create from mixing any two colours, but what I like to do is mix a version that leans slightly more towards the colour listed along the left of each row. If I'm mixing Hansa Yellow Light, for example, each colour that I mix it with will lean slightly more towards yellow.

5. Light and Dark Shades – There will be one square for each colour where it mixes with itself. These will divide your colour chart in half on the diagonal. I like to paint these with one coat and then paint the bottom half with a second coat after the first has dried completely. This provides a nice visual effect and shows you how the colour looks when it's lighter and darker.

6. Colour Spectrum – Eventually, each colour will be mixed twice with each subsequent colour on the chart. Mixing Hansa Yellow Light with French Ultramarine, for instance, will be painted once in the "Hansa Yellow Light" row and a second time in the "French Ultramarine" row. Remind yourself as you paint each row that all the mixes should lean slightly more towards the colour listed on the left. In the end, you will have a full spectrum of colours that can help you replicate what you see in the world around you.

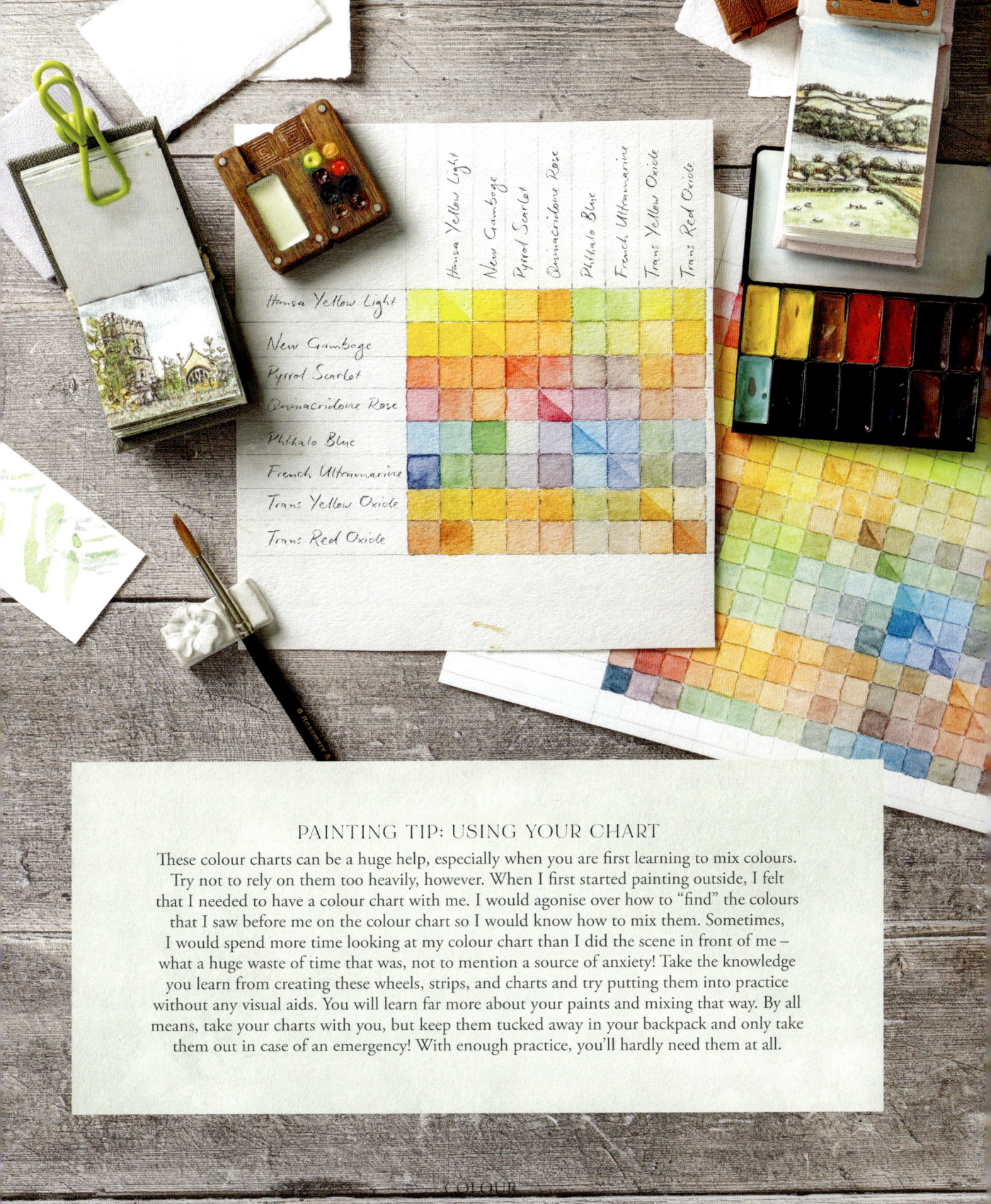

The colour chart shows mixing combinations of the following colours, listed both across the top and down the left side:

- Hansa Yellow Light
- New Gamboge
- Pyrrol Scarlet
- Quinacridone Rose
- Phthalo Blue
- French Ultramarine
- Trans Yellow Oxide
- Trans Red Oxide

PAINTING TIP: USING YOUR CHART

These colour charts can be a huge help, especially when you are first learning to mix colours. Try not to rely on them too heavily, however. When I first started painting outside, I felt that I needed to have a colour chart with me. I would agonise over how to "find" the colours that I saw before me on the colour chart so I would know how to mix them. Sometimes, I would spend more time looking at my colour chart than I did the scene in front of me – what a huge waste of time that was, not to mention a source of anxiety! Take the knowledge you learn from creating these wheels, strips, and charts and try putting them into practice without any visual aids. You will learn far more about your paints and mixing that way. By all means, take your charts with you, but keep them tucked away in your backpack and only take them out in case of an emergency! With enough practice, you'll hardly need them at all.

WORKING WITH YOUR LIMITED PALETTE

I'm going to tell you a secret. Most professional artists use some type of limited palette – meaning they have a certain number of paint colours and they use them again and again until those colours are their best friends and they know everything about them.

Today there are more paint colours than ever, and paint manufacturers are always coming out with new exciting ones. But, especially if you're new to painting, it's helpful to pick a small selection and start with that. As I've stated, I recommend having two yellows, two reds, two blues, and two earth colours, but it's possible to use even less than that. One of each primary is enough to create an array of hues. In the classroom, I always have students start first with only one of each primary colour and create a painting using only those three colours… and then create another painting using a different set of primaries. Doing this is a mini master class in itself.

Mix your colours together. Make colour wheels, strips, and charts. Don't purchase secondary colours at first. The greens, oranges, and purples sold in tubes will usually be made with different blues, yellows, and reds than the ones you're using and can make your painting look cluttered.

Your paintings will have more harmony if you create your own mixes from just a few primary colours. Having multiple pigments in a larger painting is much easier than in a tiny one, so keeping your paints to a minimum will result in more unified and natural-looking paintings. In Chapters Five and Six, I'll take you along with me as I paint a few different scenes. I'll show you how I go about putting it all into practice on a tiny surface, and by using only one small mixing well!

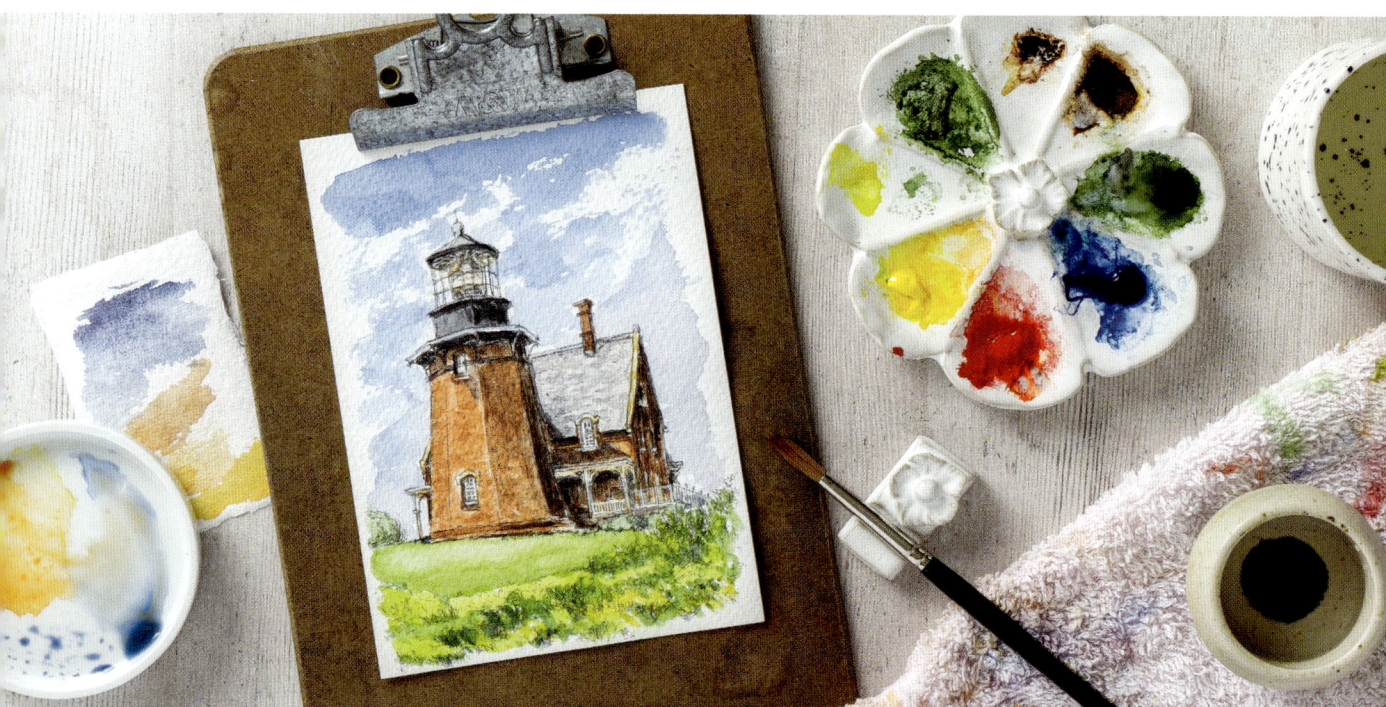

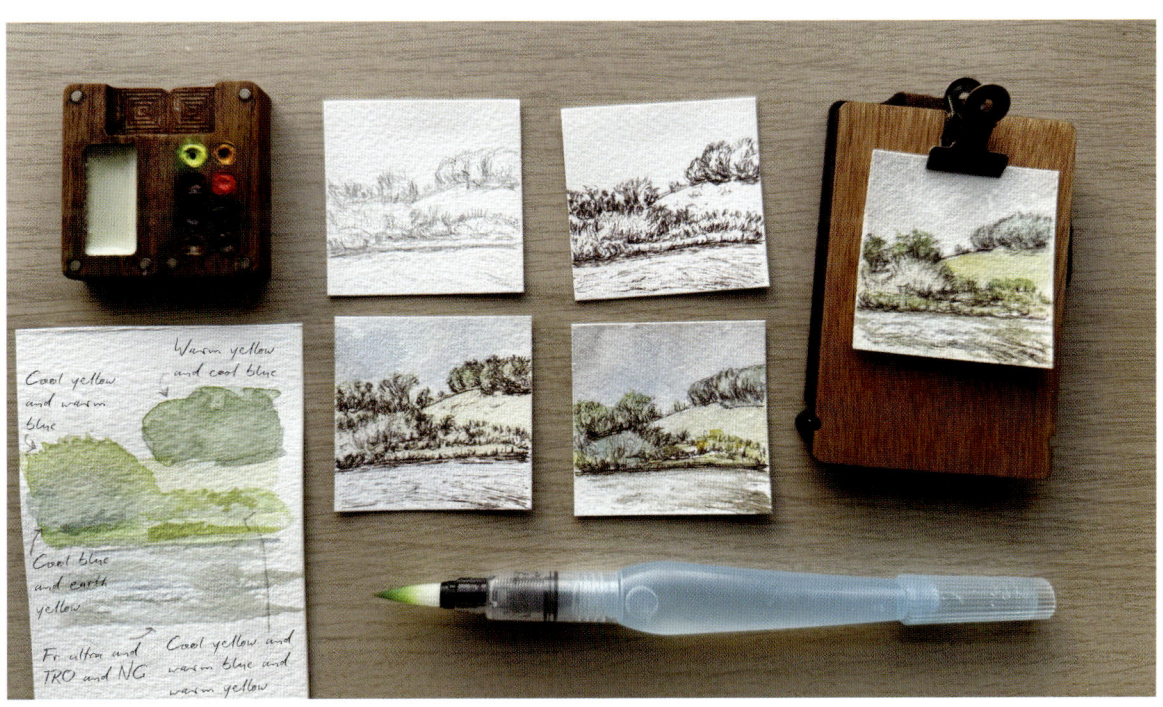

PAINTING TIP: MIXING COLOURS

While it's possible to create secondary colours by mixing ANY two primary colours, certain combinations will produce secondary colours that look brighter, while others will look more earthy. This has to do with whether the two primary colours lean more towards warm or cool. For pure, vibrant secondary colours, mix two primary colours that lean towards each other on the colour wheel (for instance, a yellow-leaning red and a red-leaning yellow make a vibrant orange). For duller, more earthy colours, choose colours that lean AWAY from each other on the colour wheel (for instance, a yellow-leaning red and a blue-leaning yellow).

Space

When we talk about space in art we are referring to the area around, between, and within different elements in a scene. The room you are sitting in right now is a space. You are one element in that space, but other elements are the objects, furniture, people, or animals, and even the air surrounding you. In a two-dimensional artwork there are several ways to convey the illusion of space. In tiny painting, all these techniques are applicable, perhaps even more so because the surface of the page itself is limited and so each brushstroke is an opportunity to tell a story.

HOW TO CONVEY SPACE

When talking about space in a painting there are a few terms to know. POSITIVE SPACE is referred to as the main object or objects in your composition. NEGATIVE SPACE is the area surrounding your positive space. Sometimes this is empty space, but other times it might be an area of less importance that you choose not to emphasise.

Creating the illusion of space on a two-dimensional surface can be tricky at the best of times, but with a tiny painting it is even more essential to remember some of the skills for making your composition look like it has depth.

A few general tips when you're painting:

- Think of your page as having three different zones. The top of the page will contain things that are furthest away (the BACKGROUND, or distance), the bottom will contain things that are closest to the viewer (the FOREGROUND), and the middle will contain the things somewhere in between (the MIDDLE GROUND). The size of each section will vary depending on the scene, and sometimes the zones will overlap depending on what is in the foreground, but it is helpful to be aware of these zones.

- Too often, beginning artists put all their efforts on the FOCAL POINT (or the main object) of their scene and ignore everything else. They will sketch a house or tree or even a single object like fruit in the centre

of the page, and forget to anchor the scene with a HORIZON LINE and shadows. This can be fine if your goal is to create a design, but if you're painting a scene, you need to think about the entire space.

- Don't forget to place your objects in space. If you see a horizon line, place it in your painting. If your object is the close-up of a still life, anchor it by showing the edge of a table or shadows for where that object meets the surface.

- Use overlapping to create a sense of depth or space in your painting.

- Remember – objects that are further away are smaller and have less detail than those that are closer. It's these little nuances that will help the viewer understand your scenes. Every aspect of the blank page is an opportunity to tell your story.

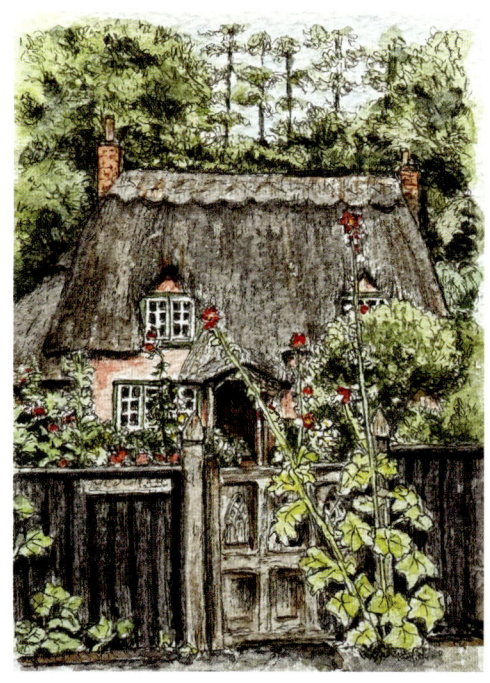

DON'T FORGET AERIAL PERSPECTIVE

If you want to paint convincing landscapes it helps to understand the basics of aerial perspective, which is also called atmospheric perspective. Whereas linear perspective deals more with mathematical ideas (see Drawing Mistakes: Faulty Perspective in Chapter Three), aerial perspective is about how light travels through the atmosphere (or air). Aerial is from the Latin *aerius*, which means "airy" or "in or from the air". Because blue light is scattered the most, objects tend to look bluer as they recede into the distance. This is why objects that are further away have a bluer or even a reddish-violet tint to them. When we look into the distance, we are looking through particles of water, dust, and gasses and it affects the way we see things.

Artists use aerial perspective to emphasise this phenomenon in their paintings. Although it's important to paint what you see, it's helpful to understand the basics of aerial perspective so that you know what to look for. With tiny paintings, I will often emphasise these concepts to create a greater sense of depth.

Here are the basics:

• Objects in the distance are bluer, cooler, and paler (lighter in value).

• As things recede in the distance, they have less contrast and the details are often fuzzy or imperceptible.

• Objects in the foreground are warmer, have greater intensity (saturation), are darker, and have more contrast. The details are more noticeable and varied.

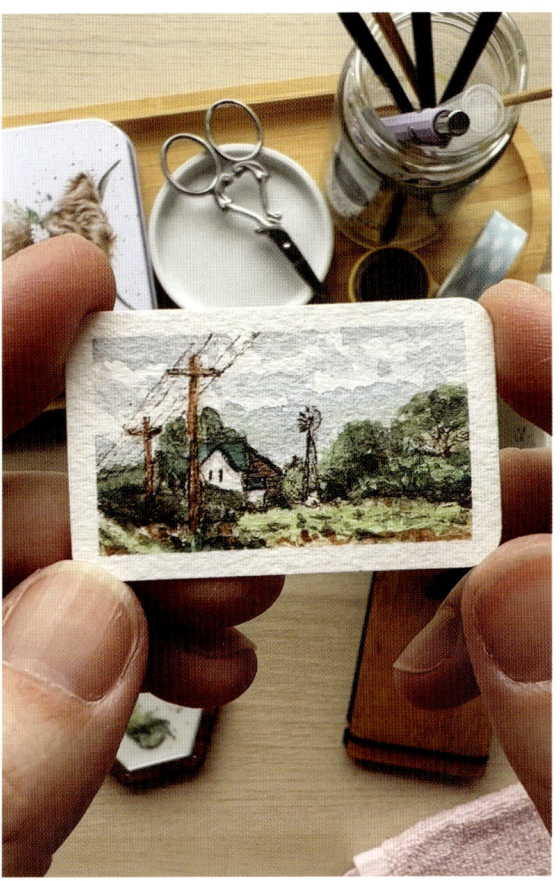

Try This: Paint a Landscape with Far-reaching Views

It's best to do this from life because photographs distort colours and lack the nuances that you can see when you are looking at a scene in real life. Spend time examining the landscape in front of you. Notice how the things that are furthest away are paler and have fewer details. Examine how the objects closer to you are much warmer and brighter. Practise painting what you see.

Chapter Three

BEYOND THE BASICS
(Game-changing Tips)

At first, painting small can feel a bit like trying to write a novel on a postage stamp. This is especially true when you are painting outside. You have the whole world in 365 degrees around you – clusters of buildings, towering trees, winding streets. Distilling it into something tiny takes a little brain rewiring and it will feel strange at first, but I promise: it gets easier and much more fun with practice.

In this chapter, I'll share some of the game-changing tips that will make your tiny painting experience easier and more intuitive. These are the little tricks that will help you avoid some of the common pitfalls, simplify your process, and allow your personality to shine through. Before you know it, you'll be creating your own little treasures.

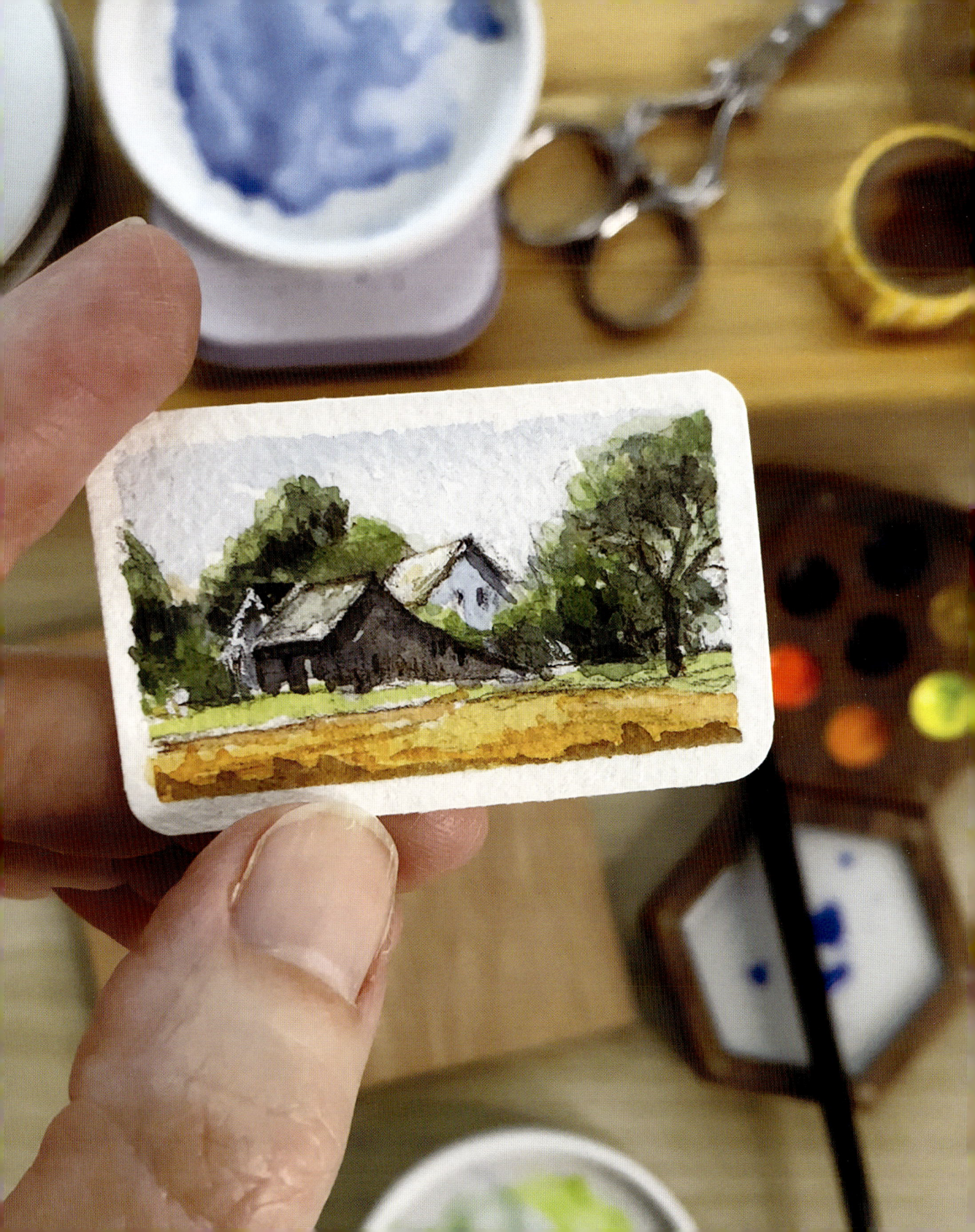

COMPOSITION

One of the most important things to consider before you draw or paint is the composition, or how you place everything within the frame. Your composition is like the foundation of a house – if it's not solid the whole thing can come crashing down. It's also like music – it needs to have an appealing rhythm and balance. Here is a summary of the tips that will help you to plan your composition and go small.

A symmetrical composition with the main focal point in the centre is a lot harder to make interesting than one that's asymmetrical. One with multiple same-sized objects is similarly going to look less pleasing than one with a combination of different sizes. The same goes for making marks that are all the same size and line weight.

You can use the Elements of Art like Line, Value, Shape, Form, Texture, Colour, and Space to make your picture look balanced because a balanced composition will keep the viewer's eyes dancing around the page. If you place objects too close to the edge of the frame, particularly if it's too close to the top of the page, the eye will get stuck there. It's better to have an object go out of the frame entirely or leave some space around it for the viewer's eyes to move around freely.

100 TINY TREASURES

I recently began a personal quest to complete 100 tiny paintings in a year, each one a mere 1¼ x 2 inches (3 x 5cm)! This "Tiny Treasures" project ignited a new fascination with painting rectangular scenes, both in the portrait and landscape format. I invited the public to join me and was delighted to see artists from all over the world painting their own tiny paintings in a multitude of different shapes and sizes. One artist even created octagonal tiny paintings!

RULE OF THIRDS

There are many ways to create engaging paintings, but the rule of thirds is a helpful way to plan a composition. Imagine the grid of a noughts and crosses (tic-tac-toe) board placed over your paper, dividing it into nine equal squares or rectangles: two equally spaced horizontal lines across the length of a page and two equally spaced vertical lines across the width. Plan interesting elements where the lines intersect to ensure that your painting will draw in the viewer. This tip is especially good when you're painting outside because it will help you to imagine where to put all the objects that you see and to stay within the picture frame.

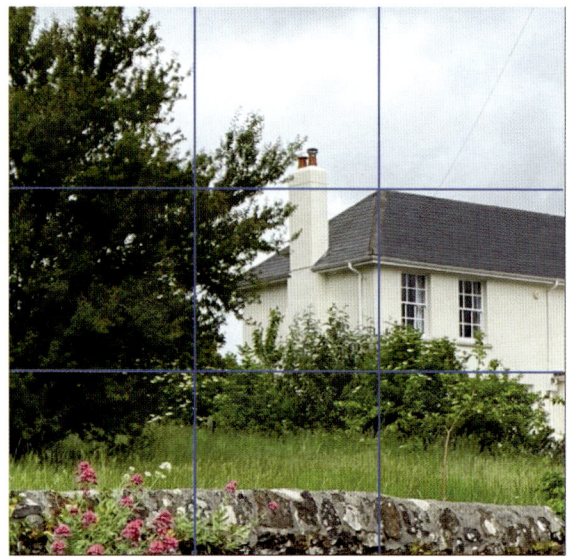

SQUARE OR RECTANGULAR?

A few years ago, I fell in love with painting in
a square format, especially when I was painting
outside. It didn't matter what the medium was
– I was enchanted with square paintings; it felt
like I was painting little scenes that one might
see when looking out of a window. Later, when
I purchased my first tiny sketchbook and all the
pages were square, this preference continued. Then,
I bought a tiny watercolour pochade box that
only accommodated rectangular paper. At first, it
felt awkward, but soon I began to enjoy creating
rectangular compositions too. I'd encourage you to
experiment with both formats. Explore one for a
while and later try another. Mixing things up like
this will help you discover new things and grow as
an artist.

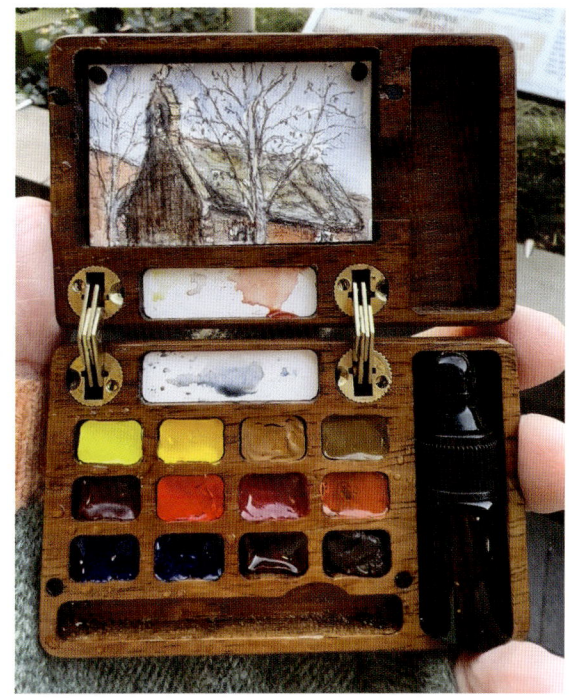

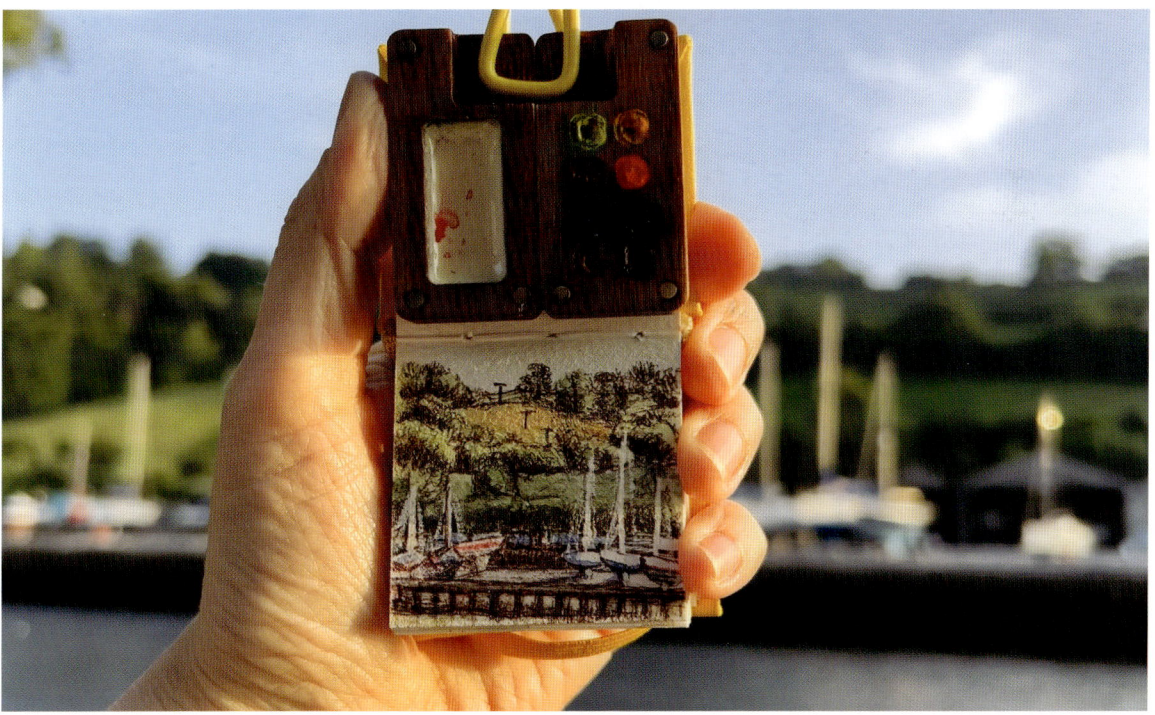

CREATING BALANCE

It's helpful when you're planning your paintings to think about each of the objects in your scene as if they had different weights. Your job as the artist is to "balance the scales". A large object, for instance, will be "heavier" than a small one. To counterbalance things, you could place several smaller objects on the opposite side of the painting. Or you could balance things with colour. Darker hues have more visual dominance, so a large object that is white would be balanced by a smaller object that is dark.

Tips for planning engaging compositions:

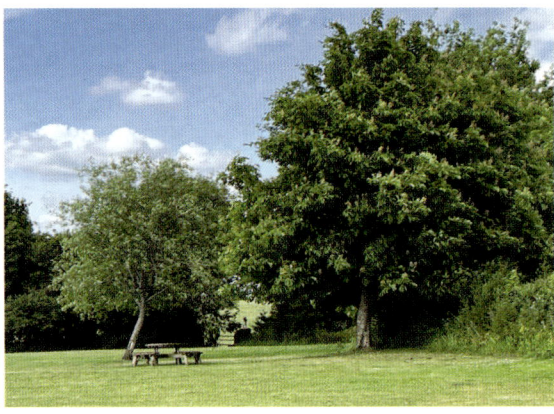

DON'T…
Place two equal-sized objects (like trees) in the centre of your painting, as this will look far less interesting to the viewer.

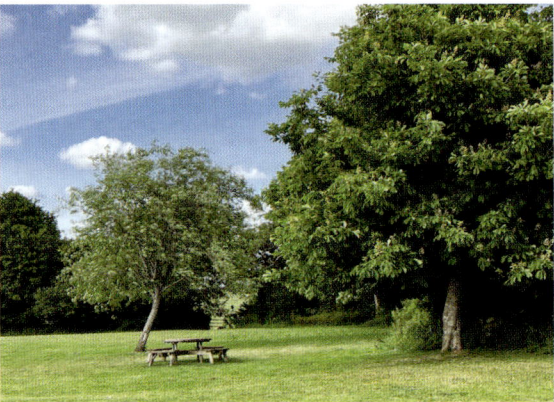

INSTEAD…
Try placing two different-sized trees asymmetrically.

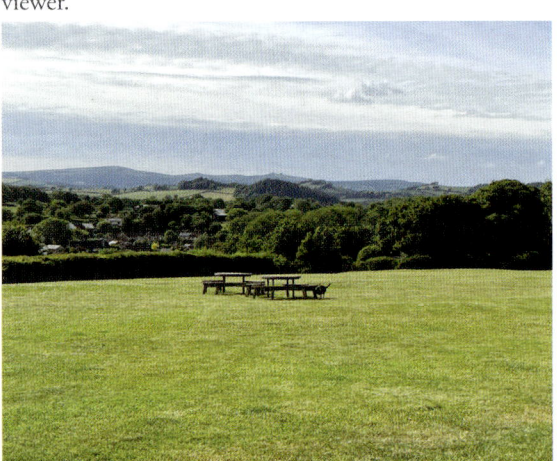

DON'T…
Place your horizon line in the centre of the page, dividing the paper into two equal halves.

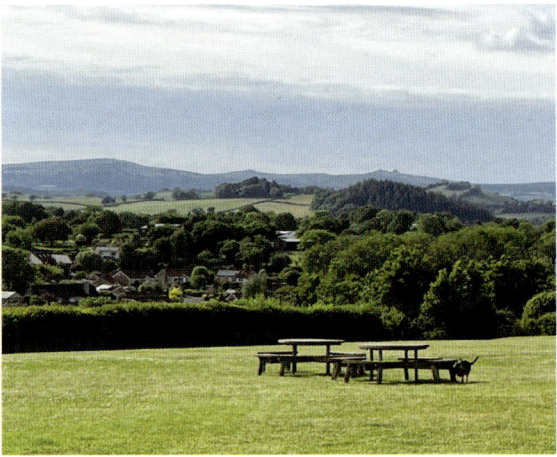

INSTEAD…
Try placing the horizon line either above or below the centre to keep your painting engaging and direct the viewer's eyes where you want them to go.

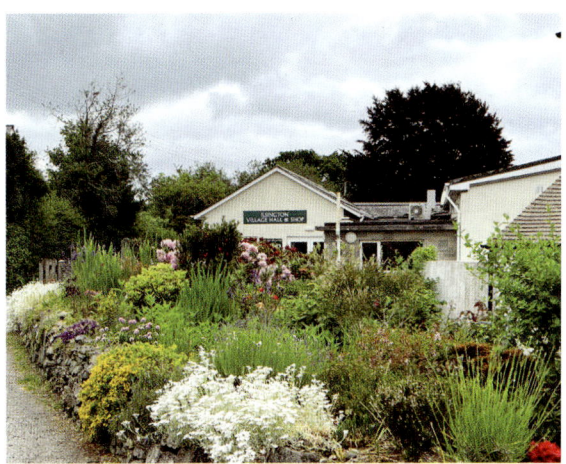

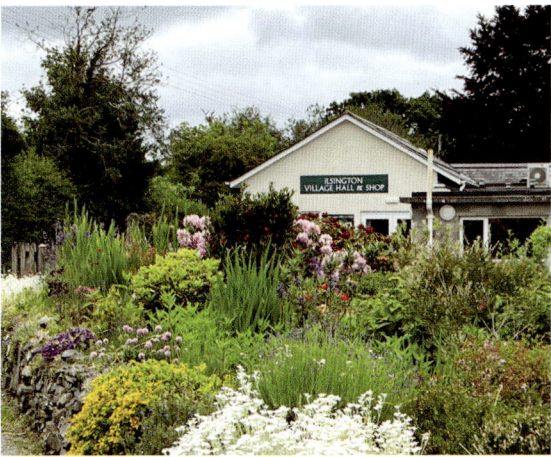

DON'T…
Place your focal point directly in the centre of the page.

INSTEAD…
Place it slightly off centre and use the other objects, colours and lines in the scene to lead the viewer's eyes towards it.

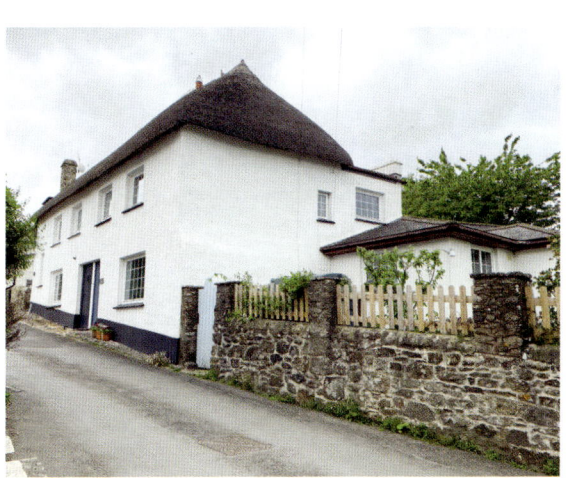

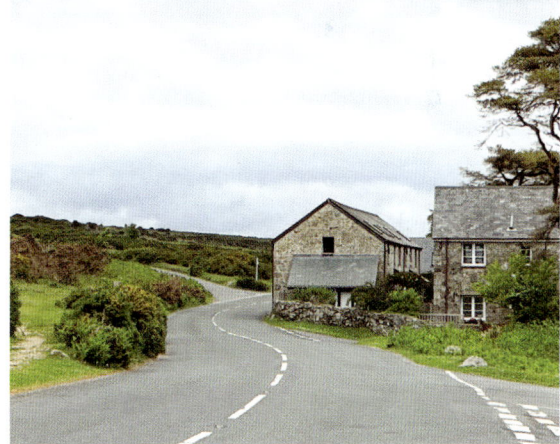

DON'T…
Place a road that starts at the bottom of the page and leads the eye off the page to the right or left.

INSTEAD…
Place a road that leads the viewer's eyes directly into your painting.

USING A VIEWFINDER

Figuring out a way to capture the three-dimensional world on a two-dimensional surface can be overwhelming. Using a viewfinder (see Extra Essentials in Chapter One) will help you to isolate an interesting scene by putting a little frame around it, which then makes it easier to draw or paint.

I use a View Catcher, which has a sliding window that can vary the shape to match that of your paper. It's the mid-grey colour of the value scale and has a hole in the centre that acts as a colour isolator – you can look through the hole with one eye closed to determine the value of the colours you see through it, asking yourself if each colour you see is lighter or darker in value.

The technical way to use a viewfinder is to stand in the same spot each time you use it with your arm fully extended and one eye closed. In this position, you can rotate your arm to the right or left to find a scene that is balanced and interesting. Sometimes I tell students to clip their viewfinder to the side of their canvas or sketchbook, so that they can see the scene through the window and paint exactly what they see. This can help when you are new to painting outside because it tricks your brain into thinking that the scene through the viewfinder is two-dimensional.

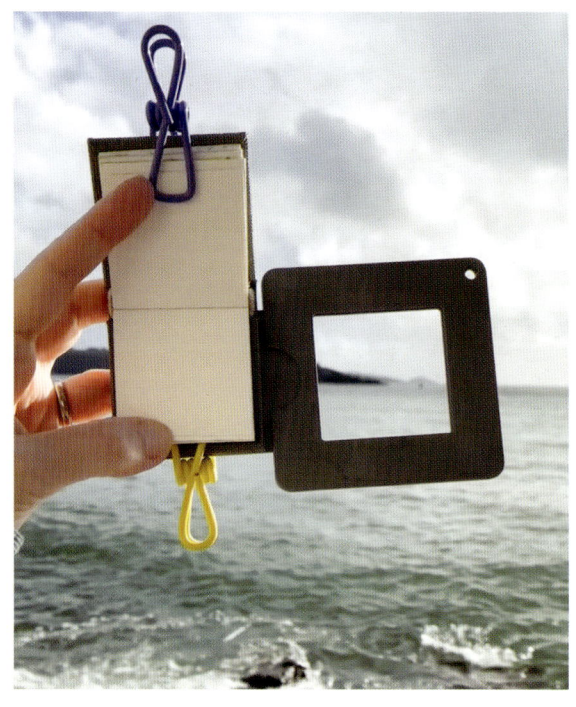

PAINTING TIP

You don't need to spend a lot of money on a viewfinder. You can also make your own from scrap cardboard by cutting out a few different sizes that are the same shape as your paper or canvas.

TIPS FOR THE BIGGEST FEAR-INDUCING ELEMENTS

Whenever you find yourself feeling afraid to paint something, remind yourself that your fear is caused by your brain telling you that it's too difficult. Your brain has been hard at work since the moment you were born, making decisions about why things are the way they are, and in general keeping you safe. That's what it's designed to do. Big thanks to all of your wonderful brains!

In drawing and painting, however, it's important to remind your brain to take a break and allow your eyes to do the work instead. Your brain wants to tell you, for instance, that a person has two arms and two legs and a curvy torso, and feet that stick out a certain way and that, surely, it's much too complicated to draw. In reality, your eyes might only see an indistinct shadow that has a roundish shape at the top.

If you can temporarily silence the bossy messages from your brain and instead allow your eyes to really look at the scene in front of you – no matter how complicated – you will see that everything can be broken down into simple lines, shapes, and values. Search for them. Put them down as you see them. Give your brain a holiday and let your eyes be the heroes of the day.

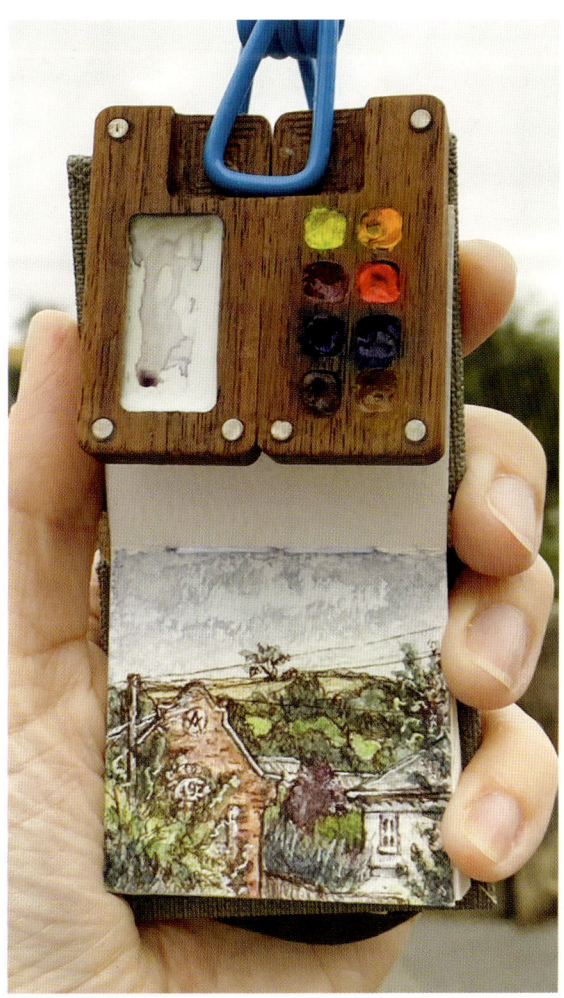

People

I don't often include people in my tiny paintings (I prefer animals), but I know how scary it can seem to draw them, so I'm going to teach you a technique called "the envelope method" which helped my students draw the human figure during life drawing classes. This will help you draw complicated forms very quickly.

Here's a tip for drawing people:

Start by looking at any form and visually imagining an envelope around it using less than six lines. To create this envelope, look for the areas of the form that protrude the most and draw straight lines connecting them until you have a unique shape (1).

Next, draw the shape of that envelope on your paper (2). Check the angles and lengths of each line to make them as close to what you see as possible.

Once you've drawn the envelope, sketch the form inside, paying close attention to the negative space to help you sculpt your image onto the paper (3). Sometimes it's helpful to draw only the negative space so that you don't ascribe a name to the form, like "person", which will awaken your brain and invite it to the drawing party, where it will want to impose unhelpful advice.

In just a few minutes, you can sketch the basic form and later take your time adding shading and details. Keep these details simple. Often, just a few dots of colour that show the relative form of a figure is enough for the viewer to understand that it is a person.

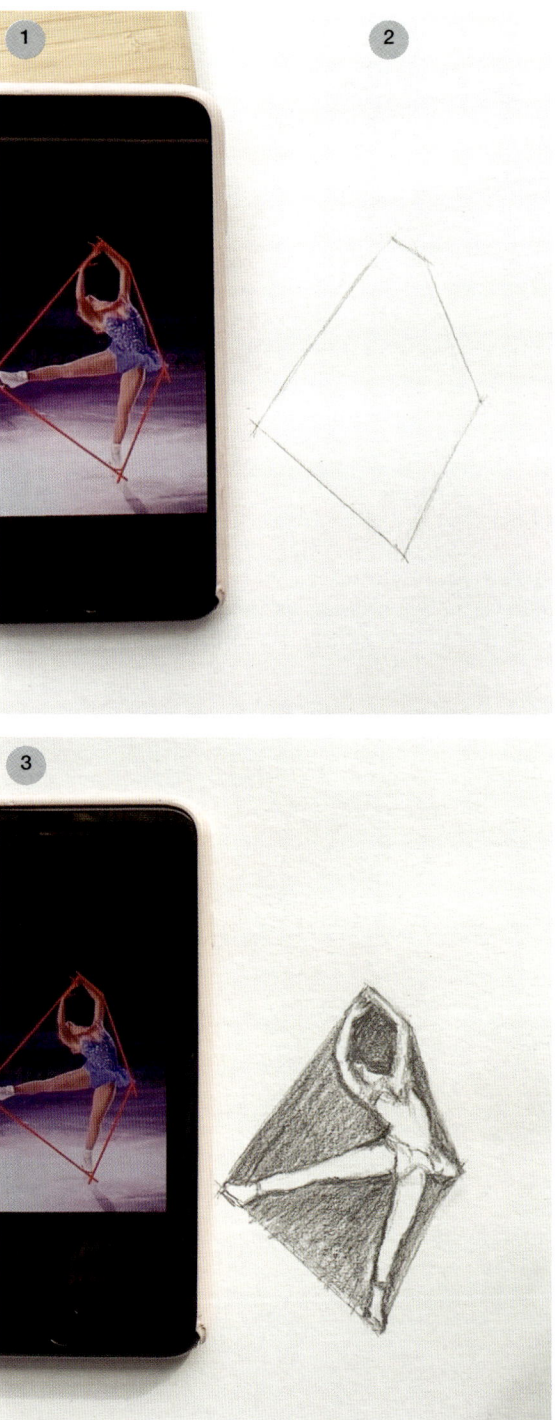

BEYOND THE BASICS

Trees

Many artists are afraid of drawing trees because they are so intricate. The biggest mistake you can make is overthinking it. Let your eyes do all the work and don't allow your brain to get in the way and tell you things like, "Trees have thousands of branches and leaves". The truth is that you can't see all those branches and leaves, so why would you be expected to draw them? In fact, from a distance you often can't see all those leaves and branches, so you shouldn't draw what you can't see.

Trees are rarely in isolation. Often, there are other trees or bushes around or near them. In general, they will be merely a backdrop to the rest of your painting and are the support artists, not the main act. If you fiddle with them too much, they will detract from everything else.

Here are a few approaches for drawing and painting trees:

1. Look at the Contour – Is it round, oval, narrow, square, triangular, or organic? Sometimes trees will be tall and skinny or short and round… each tree is unique. Look for that uniqueness and pencil in the relative shape of the tree before you begin – this will help you capture its essence.

2. Think About the Form – Too often artists look at a tree and mentally flatten it. Imagine what it would look like if you were a bird flying overhead – often, the tree will have a rounded shape to it. Consider this when you're painting and remember how the light fell on the round and cylindrical shapes in your light box (see Shading Forms in Chapter Two). It will be the same with a tree: there will be light tones, mid-tones, and dark tones.

3. Determine the Light Source – If it's midday, the light will be coming from above and the deepest shadows will be underneath the canopy of leaves and deep within. If it's morning or evening, however, the sun will be lower in the sky and the shadows will be longer. You will also see a bigger difference between the side with brighter light and the side that is falling into shadow. On overcast days, the contrast between different areas will be less noticeable.

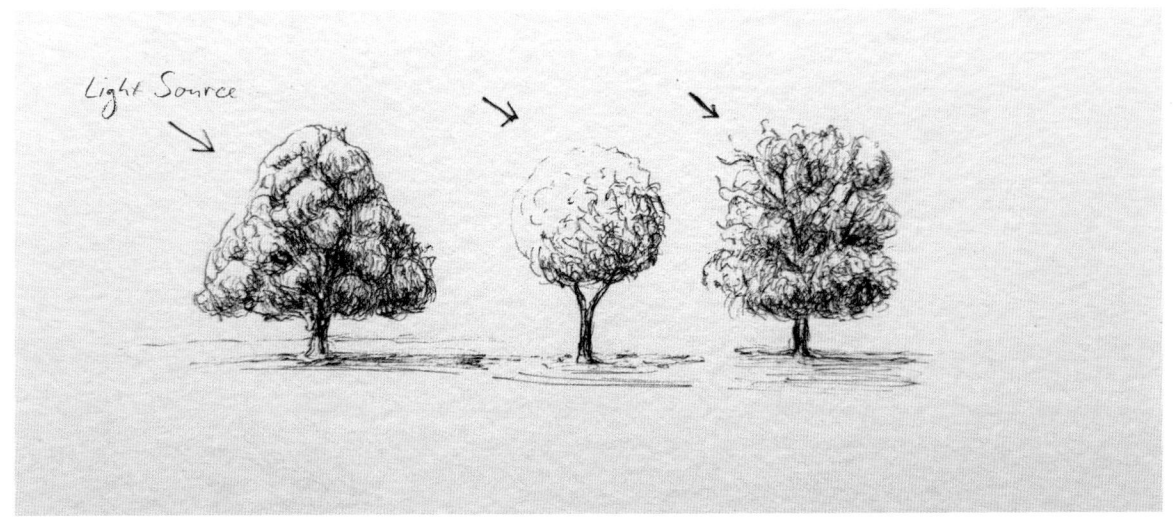

4. Look for Shapes Within a Shape – Each branch will have multiple, smaller branches with leaves that often grow in clusters. Think of each cluster as its own organic shape. If you find the areas of a tree that have deep shadows, you will be able to find these clusters more easily.

5. Notice the Range of Values – Include the full range of values and pay particular attention to the shadows on the ground caused by the canopy of leaves.

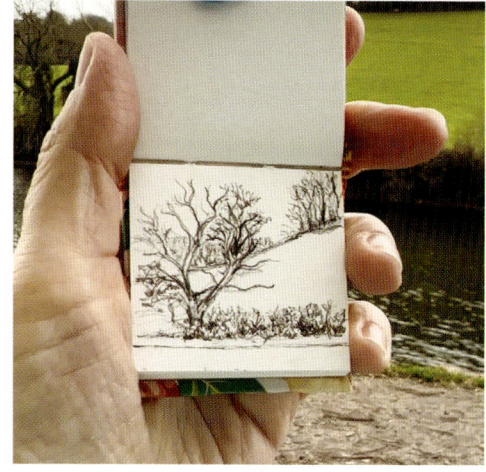

6. Study Trees in Different Seasons – Get to know the skeletons of bare deciduous trees in the winter when they don't have any leaves on them to see how they fill the SPACE that they occupy. Notice how some branches are darker, and others are lighter depending on their direction and how the light is hitting them. This is because they have a round form with branches growing in all directions. Light might hit some branches and not others – take note of this phenomenon and indicate it.

7. Draw the Tree's Essence – If you stop and really look at a tree, you will notice how the leaves are constantly moving. Trees are never completely still, and yet we often think the lines and forms should be orderly when we paint them. I like to stare at the tree and consider all the things I've mentioned above and then decide what type of lines to use to portray it.

If your lines are stagnant and stiff, your drawing isn't going to convey the energy that you see. I find that it's helpful to use curved and even scribbly lines to suggest the energy and movement that you see as a viewer. Every single tree has a different texture or pattern that makes it unique. As the artist, your job is to study your tree and look for those patterns. If the value of a tree is lighter, there will be more space in the pattern, while if it's darker, there will be less empty space.

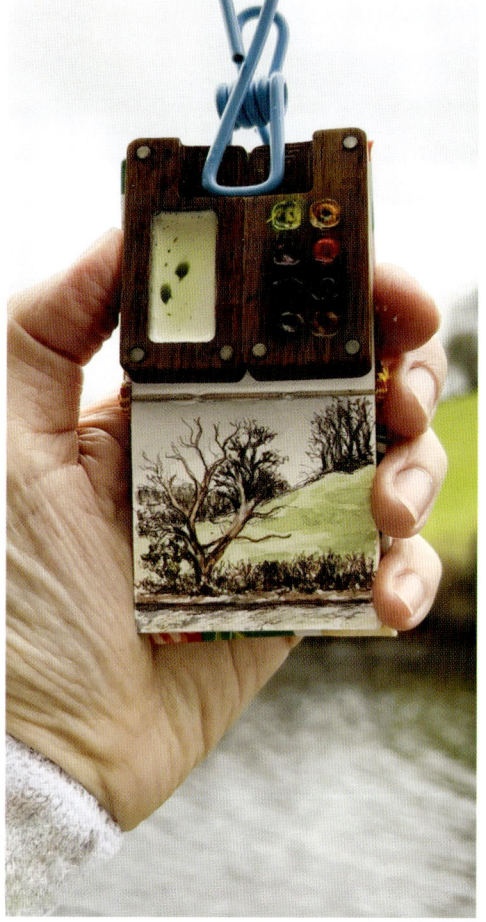

8. Don't Draw Every Detail – Note that in a tiny painting it would look cluttered if you tried to draw every single cluster and shadow as you see it. Choose the main ones and aim for an impression of the tree rather than every detail.

BUSHES

All the tips for drawing trees apply for drawing bushes and other foliage. The main thing to remember is NOT to overthink it! Approach drawing bushes the same way you do when painting the canopy of a tree. Bushes will often be clustered together, so look for the slight variations in colour and texture to differentiate them from one another.

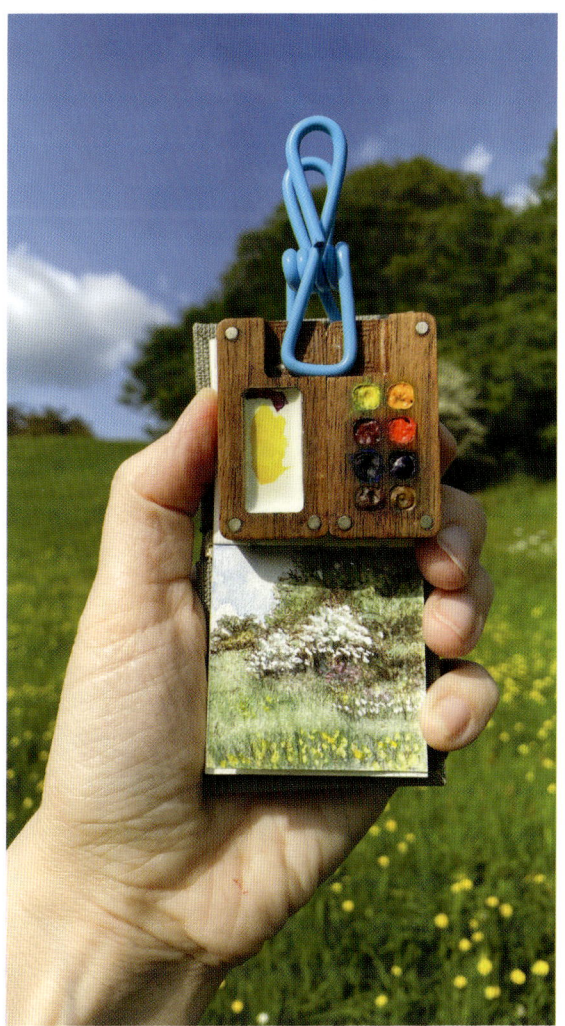

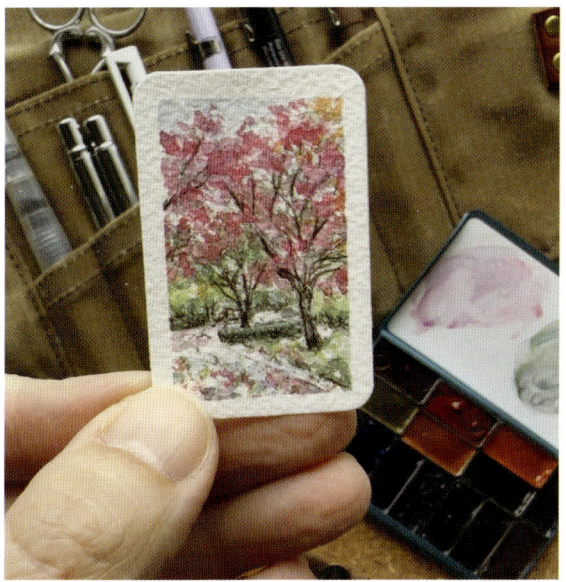

LEARN FROM THE MASTERS

Study the drawings and paintings of some of the master painters of the past to see how they approached drawing trees. You will see how loose and unique the marks were for each tree or bush. There are some amazing ink drawings and etchings done by artists like Rembrandt van Rijn and Vincent van Gogh, to name a few. Copy some of these drawings so you can understand how it feels to create these different marks. Copying the movements of an accomplished artist is like taking a master class in art.

Skies

In large-scale paintings, artists can create intricate skies with clouds of multiple hues and values. In a tiny painting you don't have the space to add that much detail, so it's important to give the impression of layers and clouds with just a few brushstrokes.

Here are a few pointers to help paint tiny skies:

1. Skies are Darker at the Top – Try this the next time you're outside: look straight up and point a finger at the colour you see. With your arm outstretched, slowly lower your finger towards the horizon line, allowing your eyes to follow. You will notice that the sky is deep at the top and gradually fades as it reaches the horizon. Often, the colour will shift too, from a deeper, Ultramarine Blue to a Pale Cerulean. This is a result of atmospheric perspective and the position of the sun shining through a domed atmosphere. To make landscape paintings appear more realistic, it's helpful to indicate a sense of this colour shift, even if it is subtle.

2. Skies are Lighter Near the Sun – The brightness of the sun creates an optical effect that makes the sky appear less intense and paler in the area around it. Repeat the same exercise as above, but this time point your finger at the blue of the sky closest to the sun and slowly turn, rotating your arm until it is facing 180 degrees away from the sun. Observe how the sky darkens and appears more saturated as it shifts away from the sun. In a sweeping landscape, it's helpful to indicate this effect with a dash of darker colour in the area furthest from the sun.

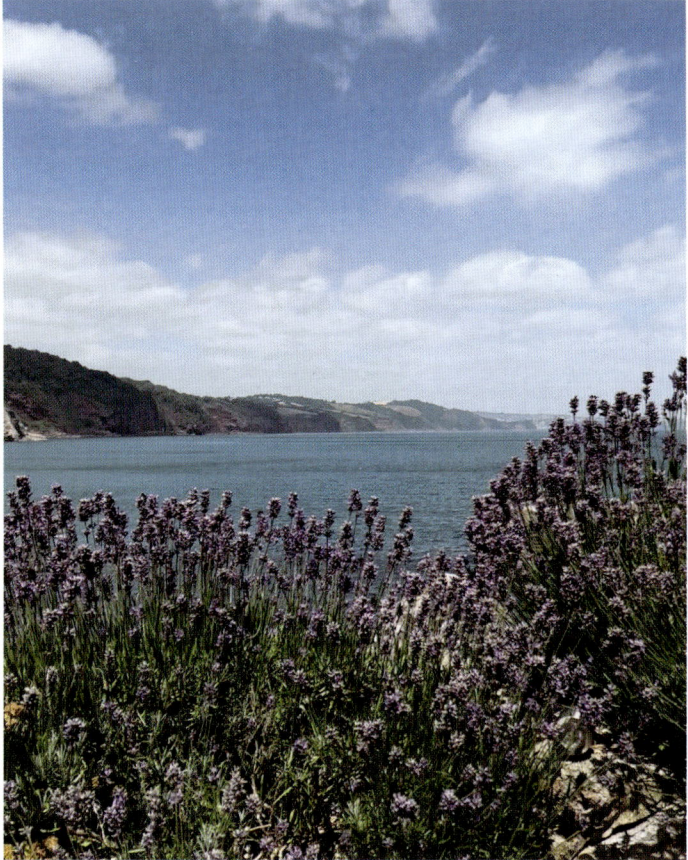

3. Paint Clouds Quickly – In a tiny painting, your sky will often be represented on a strip of paper the size of a single brushstroke, so the opportunity to add details is limited. If I'm painting a scene with white, fluffy clouds, I generally dot in areas of the sky and leave the white of the paper where the clouds are. If the clouds are softer, I will paint the sky and then dab little bits with a tissue to indicate the clouds.

4. Clouds Nearest the Sun are Darker – When clouds are near the sun, or completely block it out, they will appear darker in the centre with a ring of light around them. When they are further away from the sun, they are darker at the bottom with light and mid-values at the top. Look for this occurrence. I often skip these details in a tiny painting because I don't want my skies to be too cluttered or detract the viewer from the focal point, but if you would like to vary the clouds, adding a darker value with the tip of your brush to them can indicate depth.

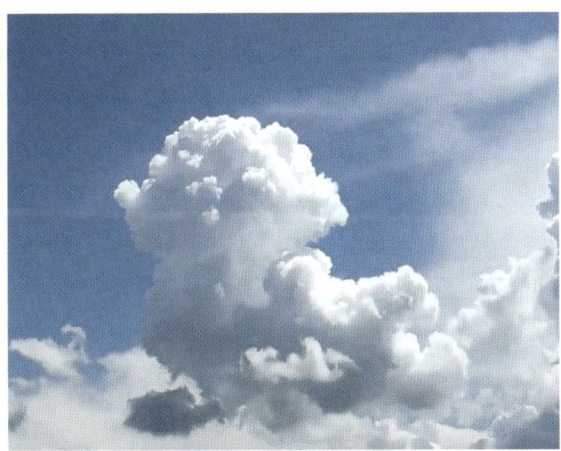

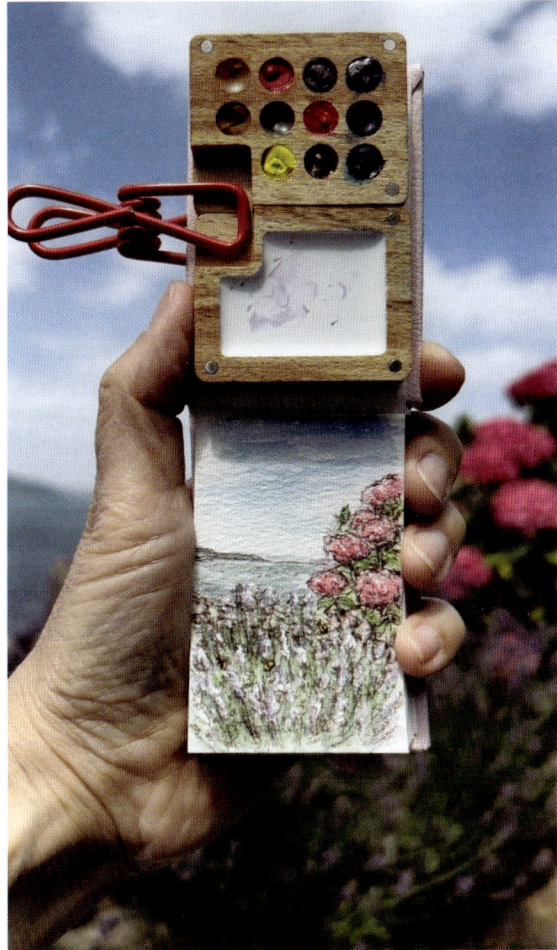

TINY PAINTING TIP
Remember that clouds in the distance appear smaller and closer together. The way this translates on a tiny painting is that the clouds that are closer will be at the top of the page and the clouds that are further away will be near the horizon.

Bodies of Water

It's uncanny how something so seemingly simple can provide endless opportunities for study! Painting the sea, a lake, a river, or a stream will all offer different challenges.

Here are a few tips for painting water:

1. Choose a Strong Composition – One of the biggest challenges that comes when painting the sea is finding a compelling composition. Merely painting the sky and the sea with nothing else will lead your viewer's eyes off the page in both directions. Look for things that can add visual interest: an inlet of land in the distance, a sunrise or sunset that casts a glow of golden colour across the water, a turbulent sky, crashing waves, or even a boat. I often turn my body to create an angle where the sea meets the beach so that the waves are diagonal to break up the horizontal nature of a seascape (1).

2. Add an Interesting Foreground – If you can find some rocks in the foreground, or a boat or figure on the beach, it will give the viewer something to keep their eyes looking within your painting instead of drifting off the page. If you don't want to show the beach, think about some of the things that obstruct the view of the water – a tree, some wild flowers, or even a boat can all add appeal (2).

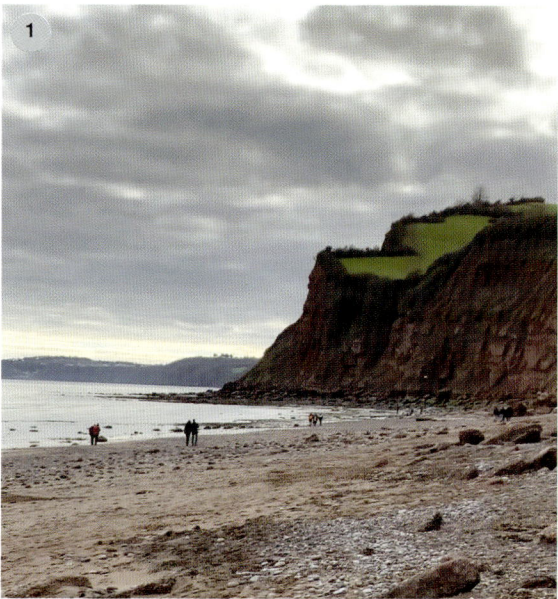

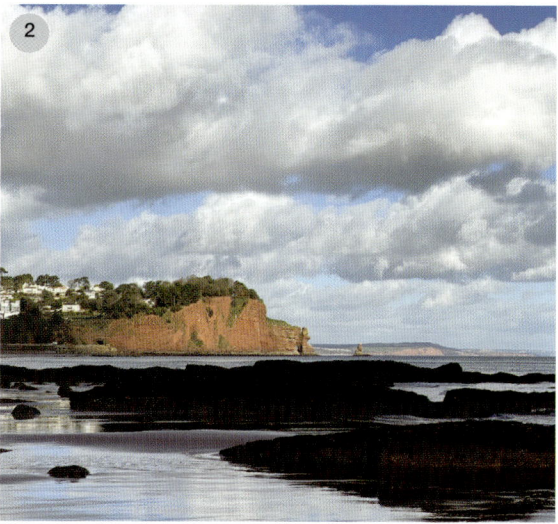

3. Study the Colour Patterns – Many different factors can alter the colours you see in water: the position of the sun, the season, the cloud patterns above, and ripples from a passing boat. Bodies of water with a distant shoreline will often be still and will contain reflections from the objects on the shore. These reflections will have undefined edges due to the movement of the water.

When painting tiny, I find it works best to isolate the many different colours in the water and dot those onto the paper with small, broken strokes. Allow areas of the palest values and the white of the paper to shine through and give an indication of movement and the sun sparkling on the surface. Look for bands of colour. The rules of atmospheric perspective (see Space in Chapter Two) will apply, but trust your eyes to lead you (3).

Where I live, the sea often looks like a stripe of deep blue or indigo in the distance. Other times it looks cerulean with a pale stripe on the horizon. Still other times, there are dark stripes somewhere in the centre. Many times, the water is an incredibly pale colour and is lighter in value than the sky.

4. Make Colour Notes – Spend five or ten minutes examining all the colours before you paint. Making little colour swatches of what you see and labelling them, will not only help you know how to mix those colours, but it will also alleviate your anxiety (4).

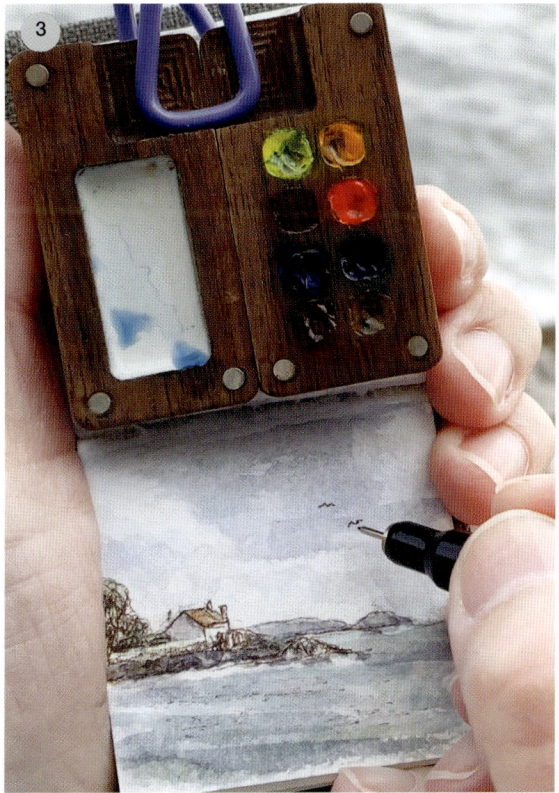

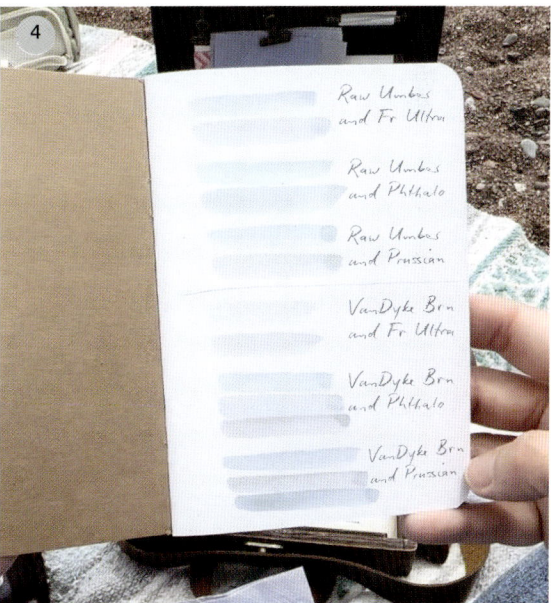

BIGGEST MISTAKES

After more than 30 years of teaching drawing and painting, I've noticed that certain challenges tend to show up again and again, especially for beginners. If you're new to studying art, there's a chance you've struggled with some of them too. The good news? Each one has a relatively simple fix.

A solid understanding of the Elements of Art (see Chapter Two) will steer you in the right direction. But there are other things that separate a student's work from that of a more seasoned artist; these may seem immediately obvious to a more trained eye, but elusive to a beginner. When I was an art student, I was often disappointed in my drawings and paintings, but didn't really know how to improve them. I have made it my mission as a teacher to ensure that I always teach my students the skills they need to ensure they can achieve everything they want.

It's worth noting that for every "rule" there is an artist who breaks it with deliberate flourish. Pablo Picasso made a name for himself by bending some of these rules, but only after he had mastered them. Like many Expressionists, he began with a strong foundation in realism and classical techniques.

Learning the rules doesn't mean you're locked into them – it means you have the power to bend them on purpose, with confidence. And if you've picked up this book, I'm guessing that's exactly what you're aiming for.

In the following pages, I'll share with you the most common drawing and painting mistakes – and, more importantly, how to correct them.

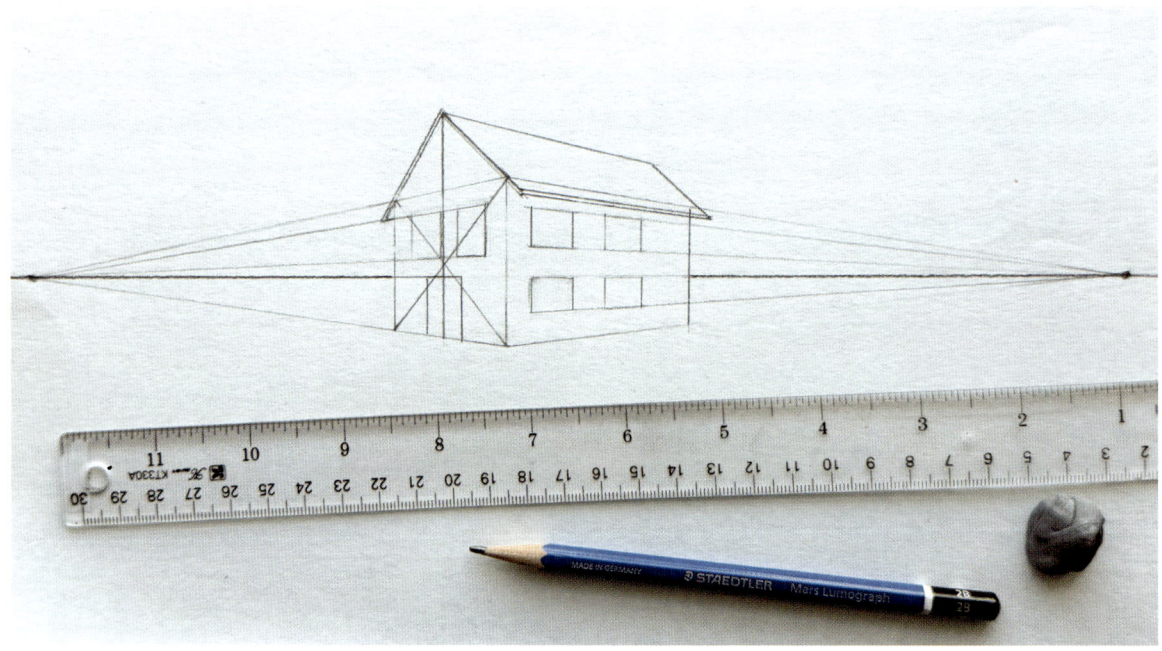

BEYOND THE BASICS

Drawing Mistakes
(and How to Fix Them)

FAULTY PERSPECTIVE

A drawing of a building by a beginning artist often stands out as having an improper understanding of linear perspective. One of the biggest things you can do to improve your art is to get your perspective correct.

The Basics of Perspective

In ONE-POINT perspective all lines converge at a single point on the horizon. These lines should be horizontal, vertical, or diagonal. Most diagonal lines will converge and meet at a VANISHING POINT on the horizon line (1). The angles of rooftops are an exception and will be addressed later.

In TWO-POINT perspective the rules are similar, but there are two vanishing points on the horizon line instead of one (2). Often, the vanishing points will extend so far to the right or left that they won't fit within the borders of your paper.

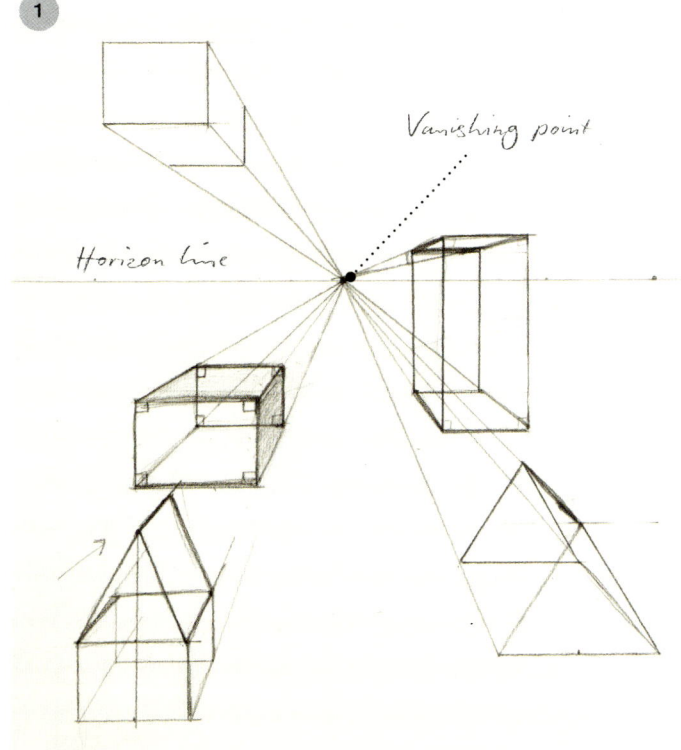

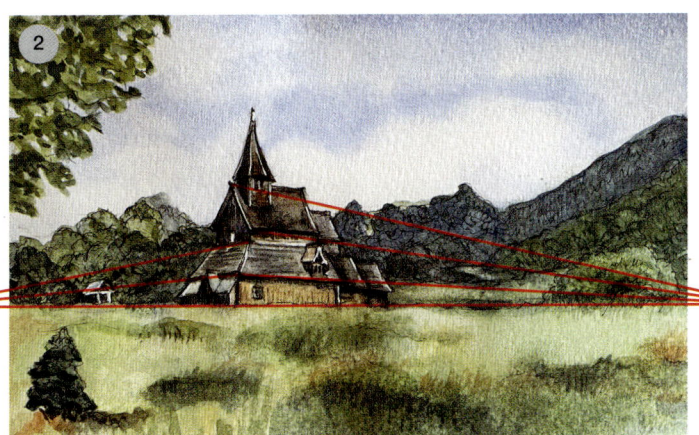

With THREE-POINT perspective, as you look up at a building, the vertical sides will slightly slope in towards one another to eventually meet at a single point far off the top of your paper (3). Unless you are sitting lower on the ground and the building is towering above you, however, this is barely perceptible.

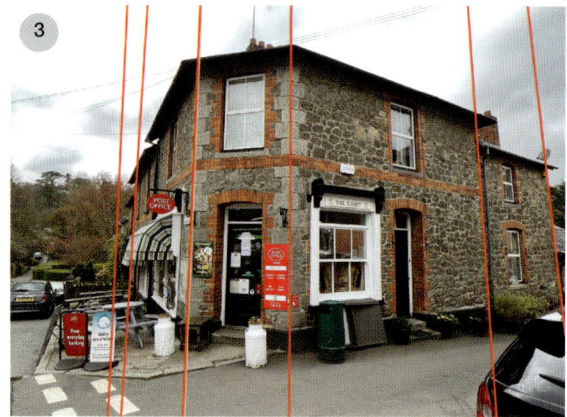

DRAWING TIP: CHECK YOUR ANGLES

These rules can be tricky to apply, especially if you're drawing structures in a hilly region, but the easiest – and quickest – way to approach them is to check your angles. Hold up a measuring guide such as a ruler, knitting needle, or bamboo skewer to determine the angle of the building, and then transfer that angle onto your drawing surface. As long as your surface is parallel to the scene you are viewing, your angles will be the same.

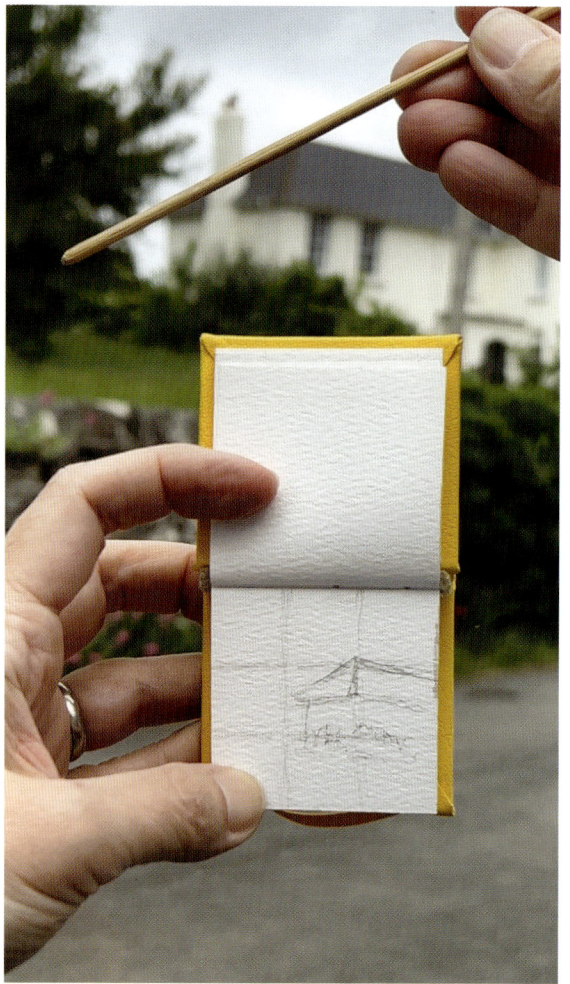

TINY PAINTING TIP

Looking straight at a building is a simple vantage point that works particularly well in tiny painting because you don't have to worry about difficult perspective issues.

DRAWING CROOKED LINES

Many new artists use crooked lines when drawing architecture or architectural elements. It can be difficult to understand which lines should be angled in a perspective drawing, but here is a good rule of thumb: when you look straight at a building, most of the time all the vertical lines – the windows, roofline, doors – will be parallel.

If you line up a T-square along the bottom of the paper, all the posts and vertical sides of windows and buildings of your drawing should be perpendicular to the bottom of the page and parallel to one another (1). Even when there are multiple buildings, the vertical lines will almost always be parallel, unless the buildings or elements have settled in a particularly wonky fashion, but even that's more the exception than the rule.

Many new students, however, will have one side of a building that tilts in and then another that is straight. Or they will have one that even tilts out. These buildings would be structurally unsound, and even if a viewer doesn't understand the rules of perspective, their eyes will notice that something isn't quite right.

This student has drawn the edges of the building angling away from one another and hardly any of the posts or windows are parallel (2).

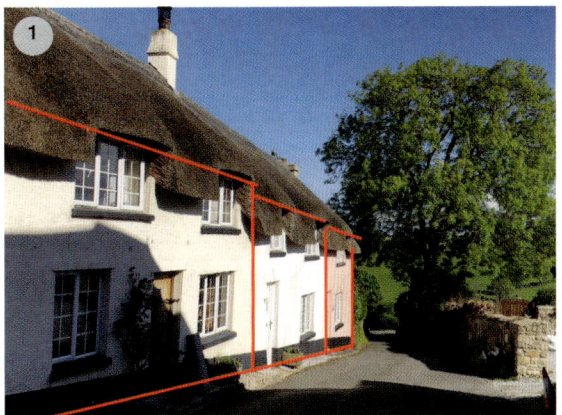

This scene features one-point perspective. Notice how all the convergining lines angle to meet at a point (off the page), while the vertical lines are all parallel to one another.

How to fix them:

Unless you are using three-point perspective or there is an unusual building (like an ancient building that has defied the odds), make sure your vertical lines are parallel (3).

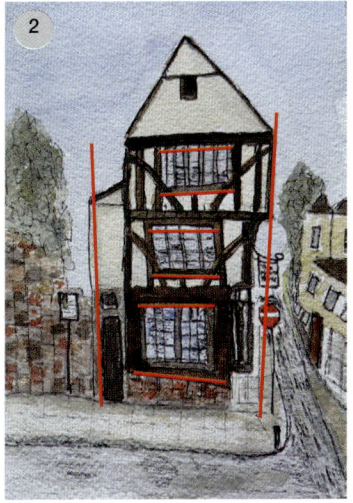

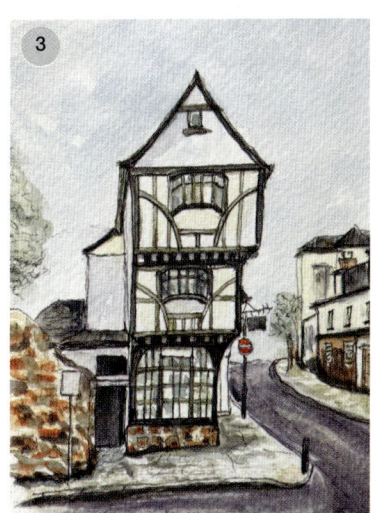

CROOKED WINDOWS AND DOORS

Beginning artists usually understand that when you look straight at a building and don't see either of the sides, all the horizontal lines will also be parallel. This means that the tops and bottoms of the windows and doors are parallel to one another as well as to the eaves of the roof (1). If you take just a few steps to the right or left, however, where you can see the side of a building or buildings, the whole perspective shifts. While the vertical lines will still be parallel, all the horizontal lines that were parallel will now gently converge and will eventually meet at a single point along the horizon line, usually far off the page (2).

Drawing these CONVERGING LINES can be confusing. Your brain will try to override what your eyes actually see and insist that windows and doors have parallel vertical lines and parallel horizontal lines. The drawing often ends up with something where the bottom and top of the house converge, but the windows don't, leaving an awkward space below them. Or there will be some other combination of angles and parallel lines that look wrong to the viewer.

How to fix them:

Place two straight edges along the lines you know are normally parallel (like the top and bottom of a building) and see where they meet (3). This will be a point on the horizon line that is referred to as a vanishing point and will ususally be off your paper. If you keep one part of your straight edge on this point and move the other end above and below the horizon line, you will notice that all the converging lines meet at that point.

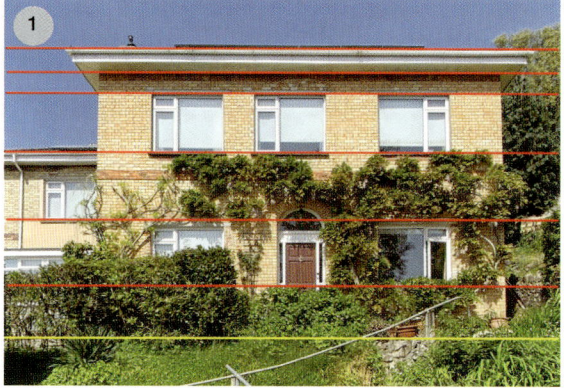

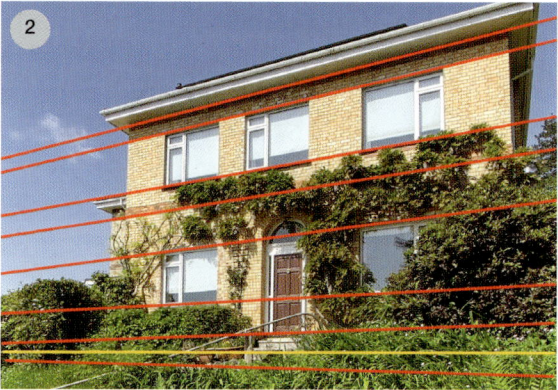

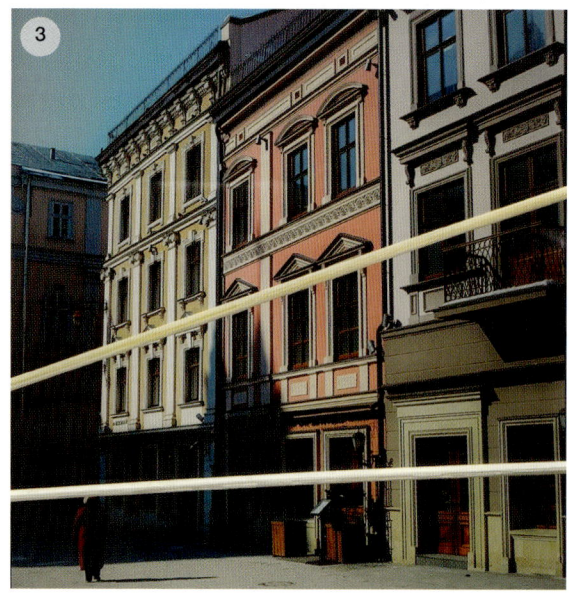

FLAT WINDOWS AND DOORS

Too many new artists draw rectangles to indicate the doors and windows on a building – and that's it. Remember that both features are slightly recessed and will have casing, frames, and shadows. Giving the illusion of depth and details on windows and doors can be challenging, but it's especially so when you're drawing architecture on a tiny surface.

How to fix them:

Study the building before you draw it and put down an indication of what you see. Look for the main lines and decide which ones are darkest. If your building is at a slight angle, you will often see the frame on only one side. There will usually be a ledge below a window and a slight overhang above it.

I have found that less is more in terms of detail. To ensure that my windows aren't too dark and dominant, I use the ink sparingly – putting down as few lines as possible and dotting where any windowpanes are visible. I then rely on the watercolour to give the illusion of depth. I'll place the relevant shadows at the tops of the windows and under the ledges. I'll do the same for awnings on buildings. Placing the shadows will go a long way towards creating realistic buildings.

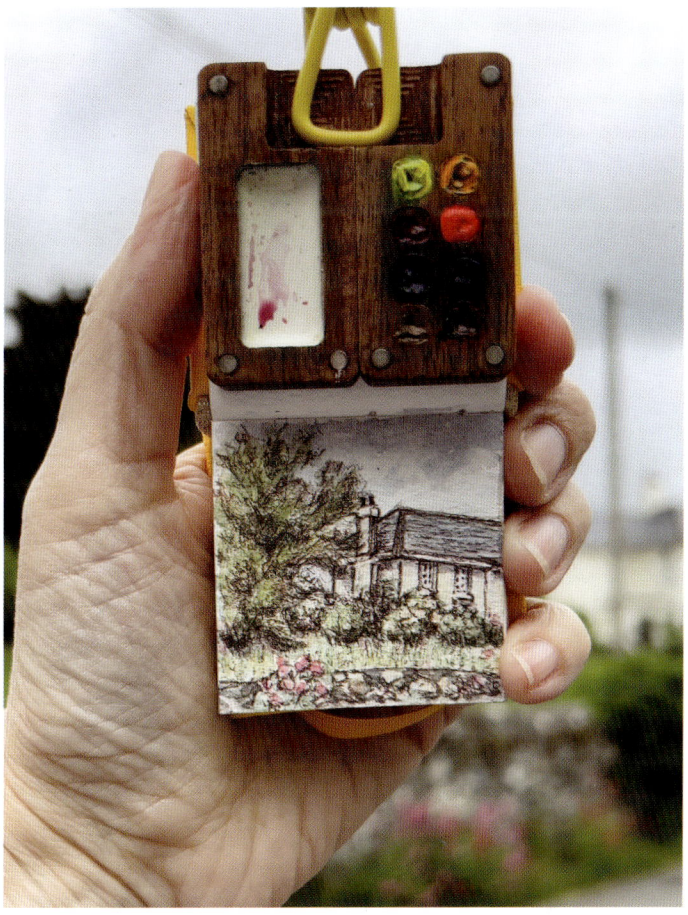

CROOKED ROOFTOPS

A common mistake many new artists make is not getting the pitch of a roof correct. Students will often make them uneven, like in this painting (1).

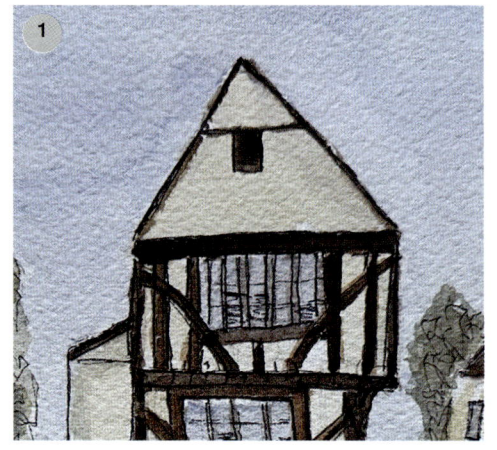

How to fix them:

When you're looking straight at a building, draw a line connecting one corner to another diagonally, and then do the same with the opposite corners, creating an X (2). The middle point of this X shows you where the centre of the building is (3).

Draw a vertical line through the centre point of the X to the highest point of the rooftop (4). This shows you where the peak of the roof is. You can then connect lines from that point to the sides of the building (5). Keep in mind that these points will overhang slightly and will have a depth to them.

In two-point perspective, if the pitched roof is on the side of a building, you can find the centre by using this same method. The back pitch of the roof will usually be parallel to the angle of the front.

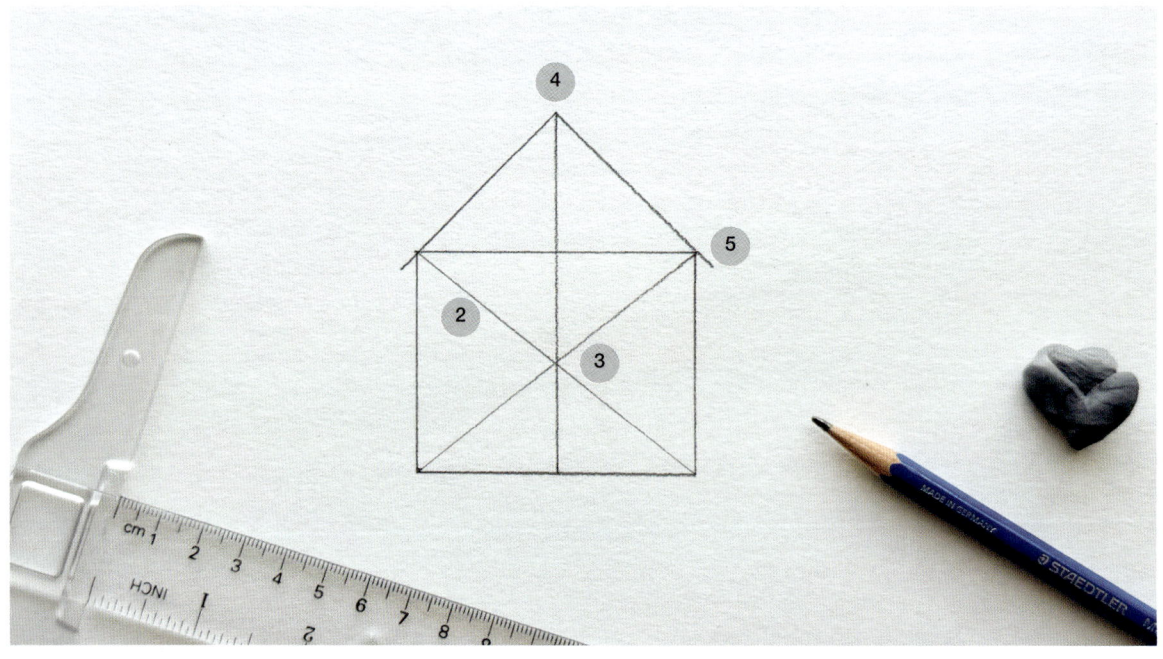

BEYOND THE BASICS

MISPLACED HORIZON LINES

You may have been taught that in linear perspective the horizon line is where the earth meets the sky and that is where you will find your vanishing points. Or maybe you were told that it's really the eye level where all converging lines meet. Or that the horizon line IS the eye level. The truth is that it's a little of both.

In nature, you will see the horizon line at your eye level. Whether you are sitting or standing, your eyes will naturally adjust it (1). Try it. Find a far-reaching view and notice how the horizon line is always at the level of your eyes.

This is one of many reasons why drawing from life is much more accurate. When you draw from a photograph, the horizon line will be level with the camera that took the photo.

In an interior scene or in a closed scene, like this detail of a village (below right), many beginning artists don't know where to find the horizon line and therefore don't know where to place their vanishing points. This can make drawings look crooked and unrealistic.

How to find the eye level:

Use the method described for Crooked Windows and Doors, where you take two straight edges (rulers, skewers, or knitting needles) and line one up along the top of a building. Line the other one up along a feature you know to be parallel to it, like the top of a window or a ledge. Don't use the bottom of a building because it might be built into a hill. By placing two straight edges along lines you know were built to be parallel, you can determine where those points converge (2). This will help you find the true eye level, which is also the horizon line.

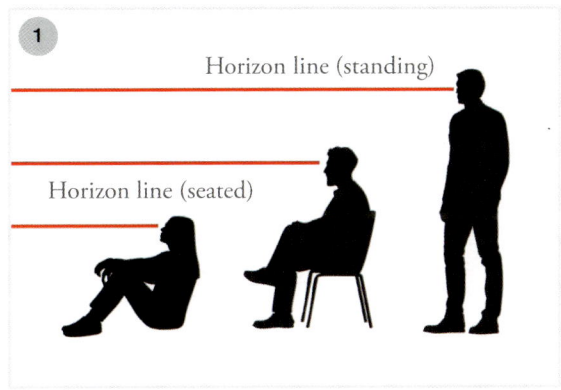

Horizon line (standing)

Horizon line (seated)

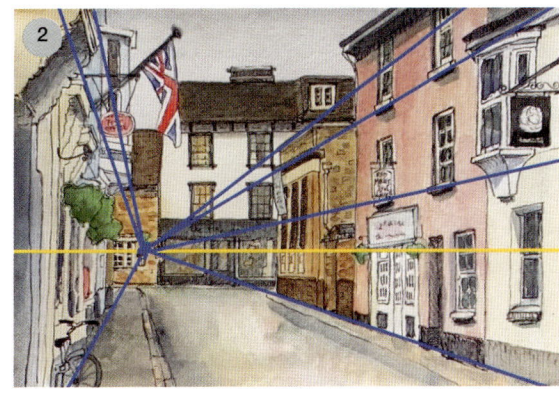

Horizon line

NO RANGE OF VALUES

Most beginning artists are so focused on getting the proportions of their painting correct that they forget to include a range of values. This can make paintings look flat and unrealistic. Wherever you are right now, pause for a moment and look around you. Notice the variety of values that you see in the different colours. It can be tricky to learn how to see the values in colour, but with practice you will.

Here are two ways that will help you train your eyes:

1. Convert a Photo to Black and White – Take a photo of the scene in front of you (1) and change it to black and white in your editing software. You might be surprised to notice how different the values are from what you expected them to be. These days most people carry mobile phones with built-in cameras, so it's easy to find the true value of a colour simply by converting a photo to black and white (2).

2. Create a Value Scale – Follow the instructions in Understanding Value (see Chapter Two) to make a value scale (3). Punch a small hole in the centre of each value square. This will help you isolate the colours you see in nature. Close one eye and hold your value scale in front of you, looking through the different holes and moving it until you find the correct value match for the colour in question. Squinting will help this process. This is an easy way to immediately determine the value of the different colours in a scene.

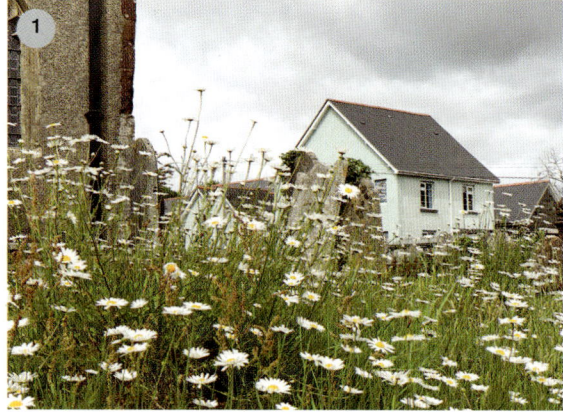

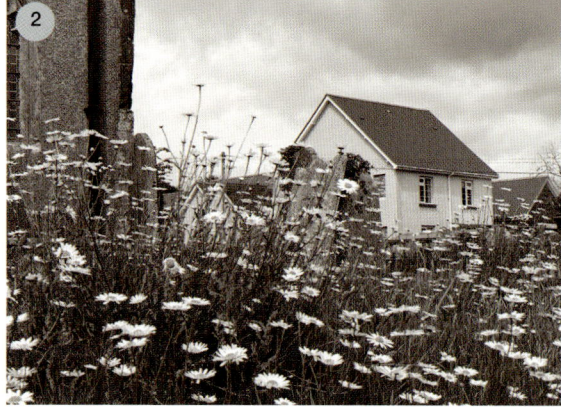

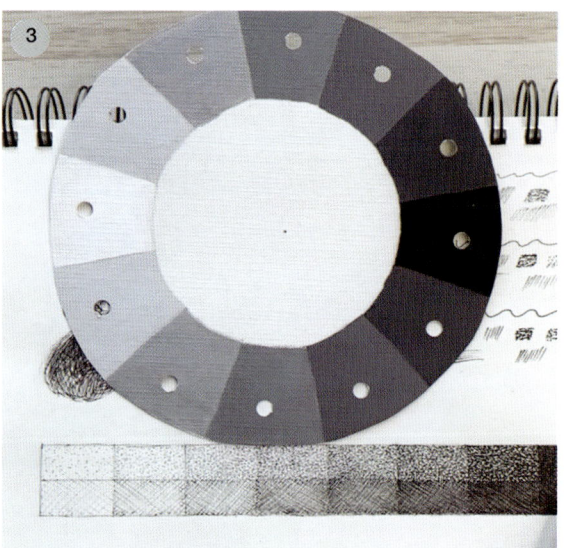

WEAK COMPOSITION

Too many new artists underestimate the value of creating a scene that engages the viewer. The truth is that if your composition isn't appealing, the artwork won't be appealing. Review the section at the beginning of this chapter to guide you as you choose your compositions.

Here are a few tips to help you choose engaging compositions:

1. Select a View – Use a viewfinder or make quick thumbnail sketches before you paint to decide which view is the most engaging (1). Remember that if a scene captures your attention, it will probably capture the attention of the viewer as well.

2. Crop Your Image – Take a photograph of the scene with your phone and practise cropping it in different ways. Although you shouldn't rely on this photograph for drawing or painting the scene, it's a handy way to be able to get an idea of how your chosen composition will look in a tiny format.

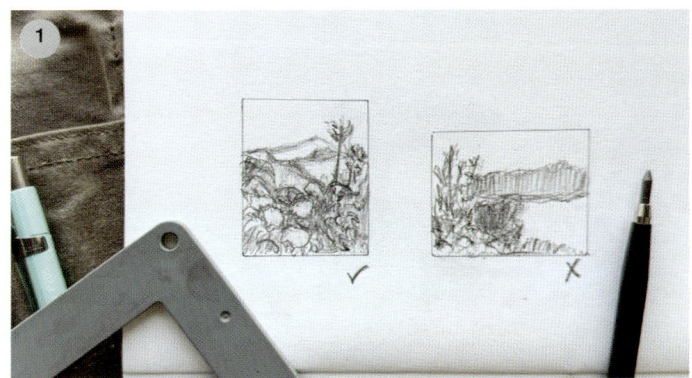

OUTLINING EVERYTHING

When artists learn to draw, they often rely too heavily on the contour of each object and spend less time examining how those objects actually look in their surroundings.

If you want your art to look more realistic, don't outline everything! That's just your brain confusing your eyes with its knowledge. In real life there are soft edges everywhere and the transitions are often blurred or lost in shadows or highlights.

How to fix it:

Pay attention to the negative space – the area around the main subject – to see where some of those edges can blur. This will often be in areas where one thing overlaps another, or where things fall into shadow or bright light. Choose your sharp edges carefully and search for the opportunities where the negative and positive space are a bit hazier and more subdued (2).

Hard edge   Soft edge   Soft edge

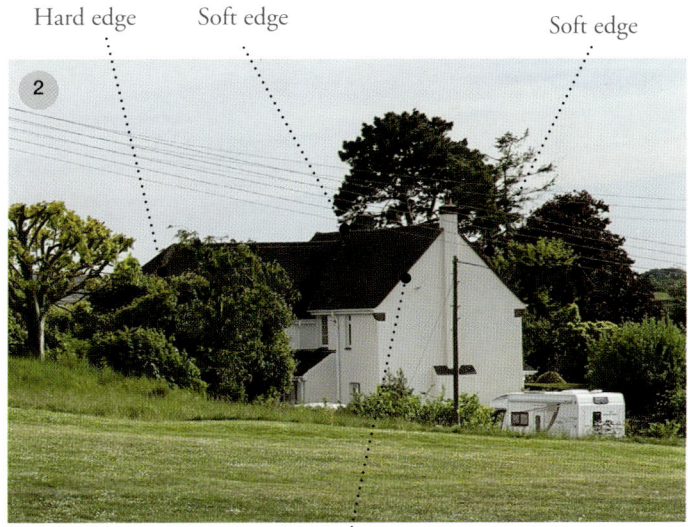

Hard edge

Painting Mistakes
(and How to Fix Them)

USING TOO MUCH PAINT

One mistake I see a lot with beginning watercolour artists is when they use too much paint and not enough water. They dig their brush into their paint pans and apply the paint thickly on the paper. This will not only waste a lot of paint (and be costly), but it will also result in a dull, lifeless finish. The secret of watercolour is in the name. You want to use water to make it flow. It's especially important with a tiny painting to keep your colours vibrant.

Try This:

Before you start, spritz your paint with some water and let it sit for a minute or two (1). This will help reactivate it. Wet your brush and use a mixing well to create a wash of the colour you want to use. Add more water if you want the colour to be thinner and paler, and add less water if you want it to be darker and thicker. Test it out on a separate scrap of paper. When you are happy with the consistency, apply it to the paper in as few strokes as possible.

USING TOO MUCH WATER

Along with using too much paint and not enough water, a common mistake is using too much water when applying paint to the page. Adding too much water on the page, your brush, or in the mixing well, can make colours look dull and washed out. It can also prolong the drying time.

Try This:

1. Create two small squares on a sheet of watercolour paper.

2. In the first square, add a wash of yellow paint using a damp brush and then, while it's still wet, add a few drops of blue with a damp brush. You might be tempted to blend or add more water at this stage, but resist.

3. In the second square, start the same way and then add a few drops of blue into the mix with a brush that is very wet. The colours will immediately begin to separate and look uneven, and the patch of paper will be overly wet.

After both squares have dried you will notice how much brighter the first strip on the left is, while the second strip on the right is duller and less intense (2). Remember that a damp brush will spread colour evenly, while one that is too wet can cause the colours to settle in undesirable ways with dull patches. Practise this often.

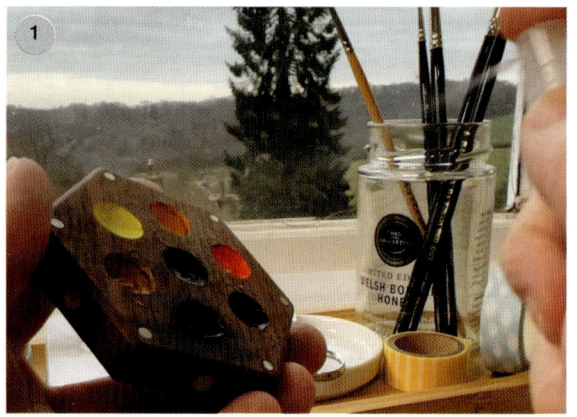

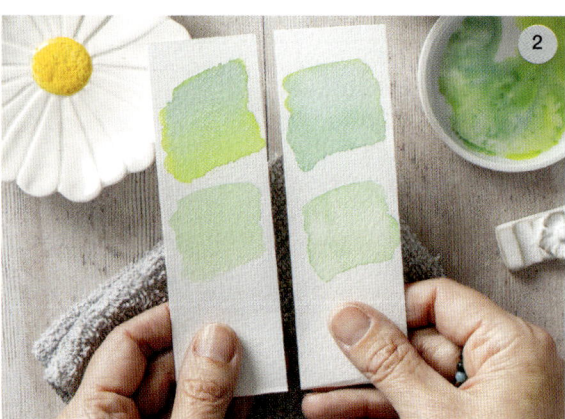

BEYOND THE BASICS

PAINTING DARKS FIRST

It's tempting to rush in with your darkest colours too soon. This can work with certain wet-on-wet techniques, but in general it's not advantageous, especially with tiny paintings. Watercolour is different from other media like oils, acrylics, and gouache because it is less forgiving. You can't easily cover up your mistakes, so if you go too dark too soon you won't be able to add lighter colours on top. Here are a couple of tips to help:

Try This: Paint in Layers

Search for the lightest colours you can find in an object or scene and paint those first (1). Allow the paint to dry and then add the mid-tones, and later the darks (2). Because watercolour is a transparent medium, if you apply each layer thinly, the colours on the lower layers will shine through.

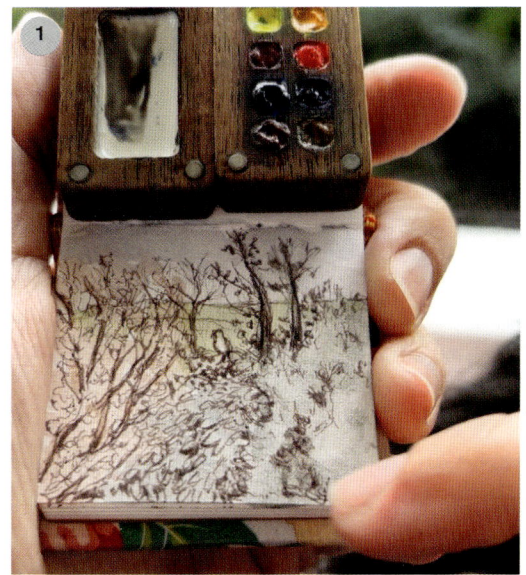

TINY PAINTING TIP

In a tiny painting, I find it's especially important to avoid puddles and overly wet paper. The skill comes in understanding how wet to make the bristles on your brush. If you are creating sweeping washes of colour on a large sheet of watercolour paper, you might want to keep your bristles wet so that the paint flows better. In a tiny painting, however, too much water will make everything bleed together in a muddy patch.

Try This: Create Mixing Charts

Create charts where you layer different colours on top of one another to see how they look when they're dry. Try layering them when the lower layer is dry and also when it's wet to learn which combinations excite you the most. A few quick, strategic combinations in a tiny painting can create a fresh vibrancy (1).

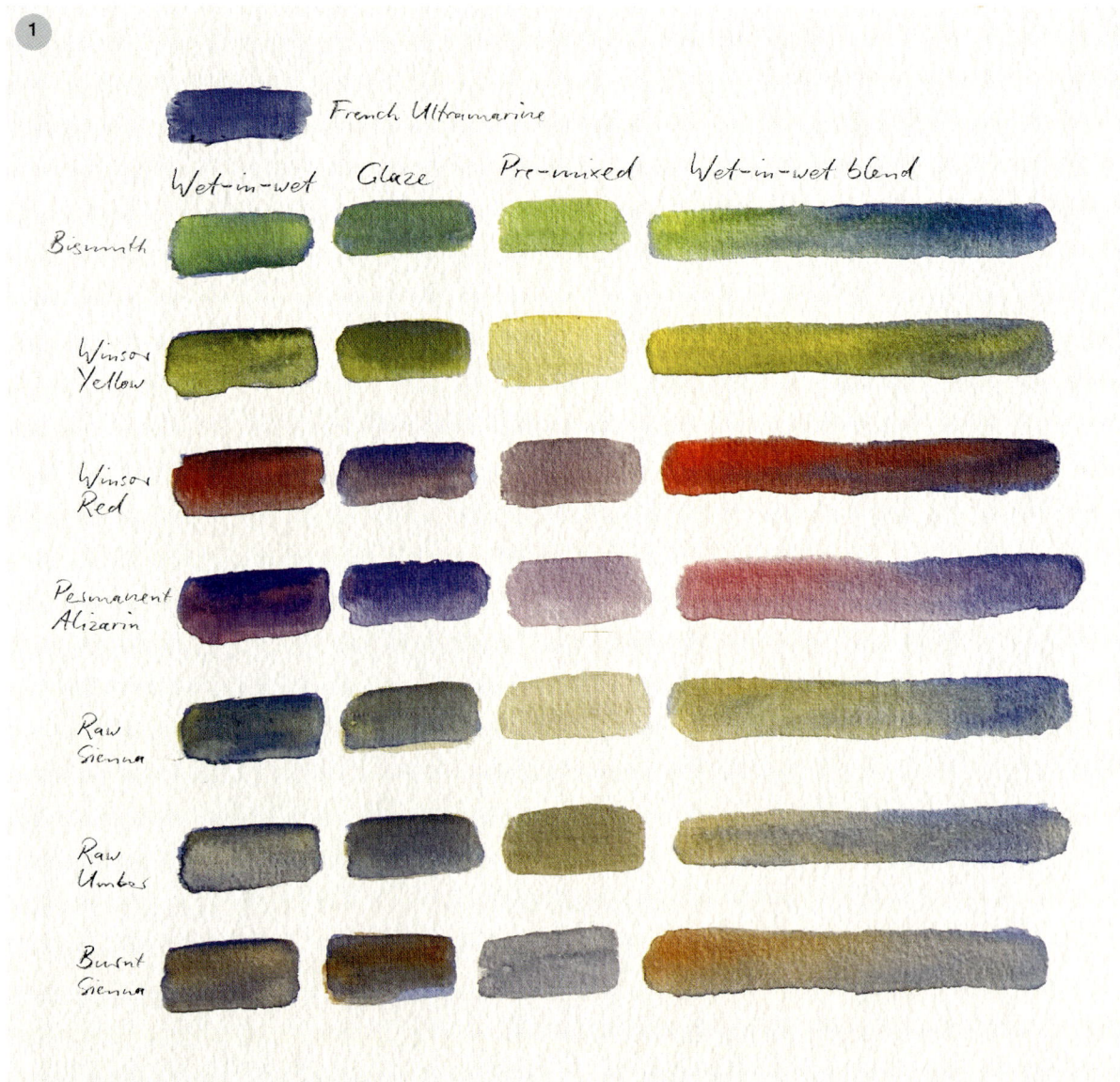

BEYOND THE BASICS

NOT LEAVING ENOUGH WHITE

In watercolour, and especially in tiny painting, it's essential to leave enough white and light values throughout the composition. It's very easy to get too dark too soon, and you can't easily cover or erase it without adding another opaque layer that won't be as fresh and vibrant as the rest of the colours. You have to be an architect in watercolours and plan ahead, or the whole structure can fall apart.

Try This: Practise Painting a Tree

1. Start with your lightest values and leave passages of the painting where the white of the paper is preserved.

2. After it has dried, add a second layer of your middle values, paying attention to where the light source is and leaving enough light areas.

3. Next, add the darker mid-values where you see the deepest shadows to create a sense of form and light. After the painting has dried, add the darkest values sparingly. Notice how the sense of form is created while still retaining enough light passages.

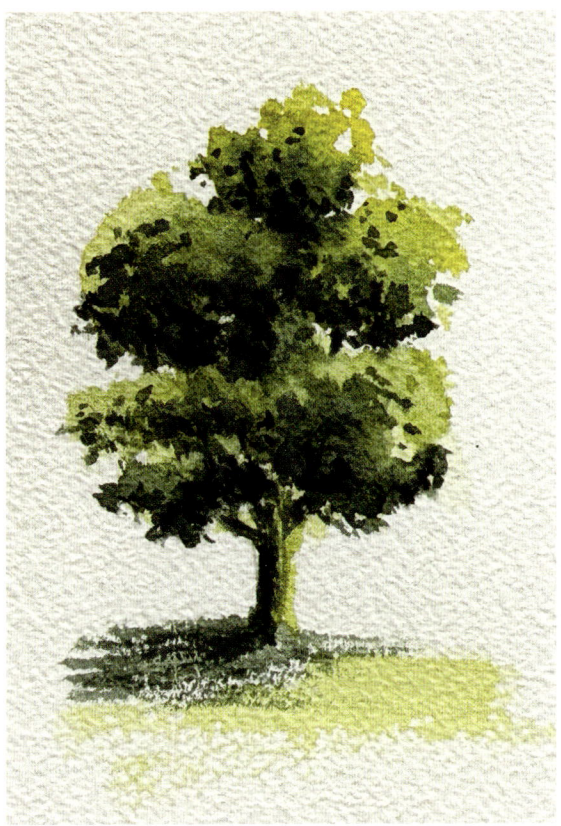

TOO MANY LAYERS (OVERWORKED PASSAGES)

It's incredibly easy to overwork a watercolour painting, especially one that is tiny. It's inevitable that this will happen on your quest to becoming a better tiny painter. There are, however, a few things you can do to try to "rescue" your overworked paintings.

Try This: Rescue Overworked Paintings

1. Use Cotton Paper. This will be able to withstand multiple layers of paint without the colours becoming overly muddy.

2. Lift Colours. Use a flat, damp brush or a damp cotton bud to "lift" colours that are too dark. This is best done as soon as you apply them. This technique doesn't work well on cellulose paper, but cotton paper is more forgiving.

3. Add White. Use white paint to dab onto the areas that need lightening. While this will create an opacity that won't match the transparency of the rest of the painting, it will enable you to salvage your painting and walk away with something that you don't entirely dislike. You can use gouache or an opaque paint such as Dr. Ph. Martin's bleedproof white for this. My favourite is a white Pentel Milky Brush, which dries quickly and even allows me to drop lighter colours on top without blending into the white and becoming pastel.

Chapter Four

PLANNING A TRIP
(Painting Outside)

Painting outside will improve your art! When you're surrounded by nature, you see colours that aren't detectable in a photograph. You might be surprised by how much more vibrant the world becomes when you stop and examine it in detail. Shapes and forms have more depth. It's a visceral, meditative experience.

When I'm painting outside, my heart rate slows, my stress levels dissipate, and I feel calm and relaxed. Each painting becomes a visual diary. When I look back at a painting I created outside, I remember everything about that day – what I ate, how I was feeling, the breeze against my skin, and even who I was with. It's a perfect visual and sensory diary.

Plein air painting also fuels creativity because when you are fully immersed in a subject, you feel invigorated. It makes you feel alive and like you're truly a part of the world, something that can be elusive to many people in our world of screens and distractions. After an hour painting outside, the colours appear brighter, textures feel more alive, and you will be motivated to create even more art.

So, how do you begin? What do you bring? What do you wear? Where should you go? In this chapter, I'll walk you through everything you need to plan your own painting adventures.

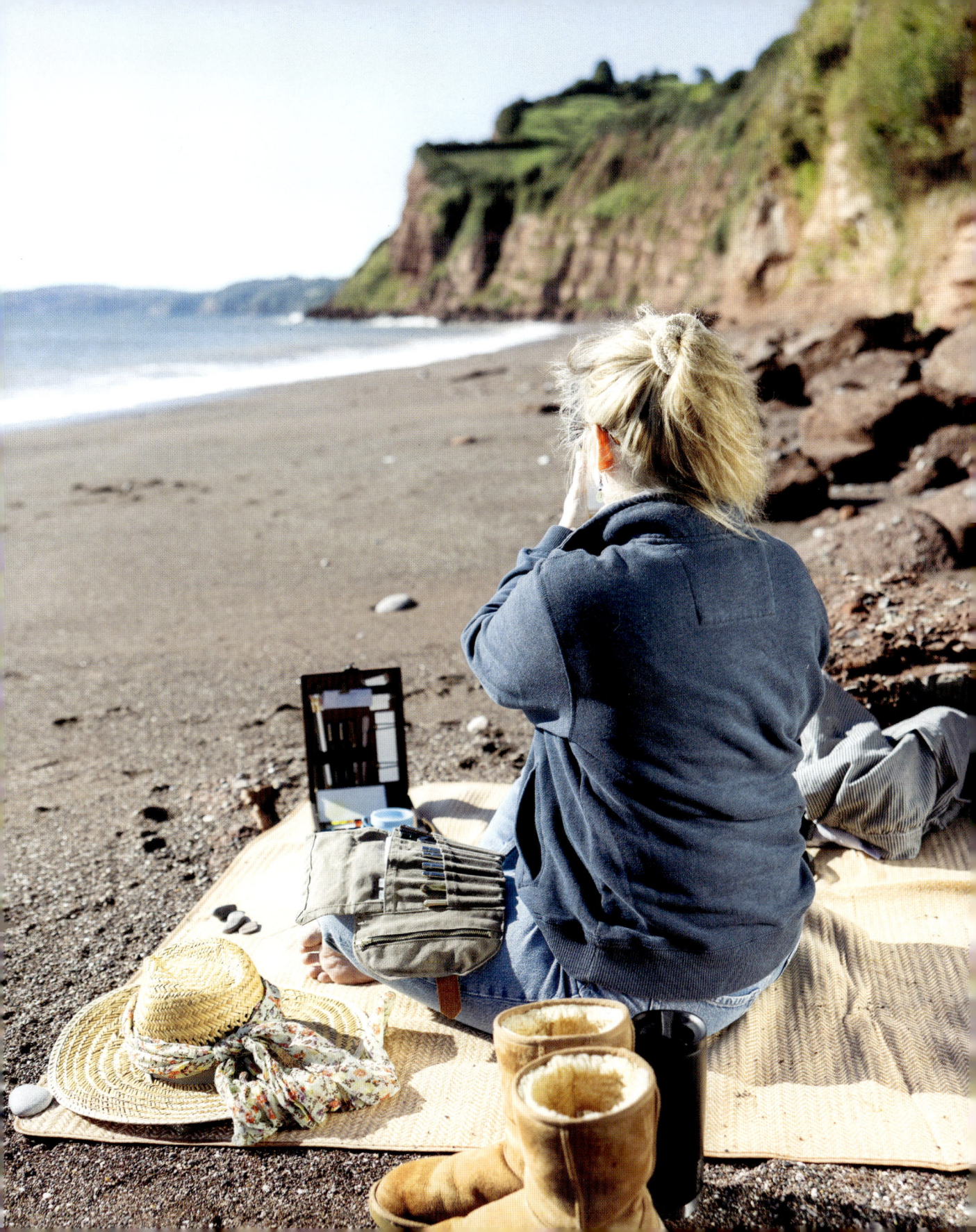

Travel Supplies

Less is more when you're painting outside. It doesn't take much to create a lovely tiny painting. That said, it's helpful to have all the little things you might want so that your experience is as easy and relaxing as possible. Relaxation is good for creativity! For more details about supplies you might like to include in your art kit, refer to Chapter One. To break things down further, here is a checklist of the essentials (plus a few lovely extras!).

PLEIN AIR ESSENTIALS

Watercolour Paint and a Palette – Tiny or otherwise!

Mechanical Pencils for Drawing – I recommend using one with 0.3mm or 0.5mm lead, so that you can sketch more details without smudging.

Fineliners or a Fountain Pen and Ink – Make sure both have waterproof ink! I only use brown, sepia, or grey fineliners for tiny paintings because black is overly dominant on a tiny surface.

Watercolour Brushes – A couple of water brushes with the water in the barrel (one small and one large), or a few travel watercolour brushes, will usually be enough.

Tiny Sketchbook, Pochade Box, or Pre-cut Paper with Tiny Clipboard – You can choose to work in a tiny sketchbook that you can clip a tiny palette to, or use a tiny pochade box or a little clipboard.

Clips – It's always helpful to have a few clips for attaching your palette or paper.

Erasers – These come in a variety of shapes and sizes. I'd suggest taking a kneaded eraser and an eraser pen in your kit.

Water Pot – Unless you're using water brushes, you'll need a pot for cleaning your brushes. Collapsible ones are ideal.

Water – This is essential if you're using travel brushes, but even water brushes need refilling, so it's important to take a bottle of water along.

Paper Towels, Tissues, or a Towelling Athletic Wristband – For cleaning brushes between colours, a towelling wristband keeps things simple, but it's also helpful to have a tissue or paper towel for cleaning your mixing well, or for dabbing out unwanted colours.

Rubbish Bag – A small bag or place to put used tissues is helpful, since you won't always have a public waste bin available.

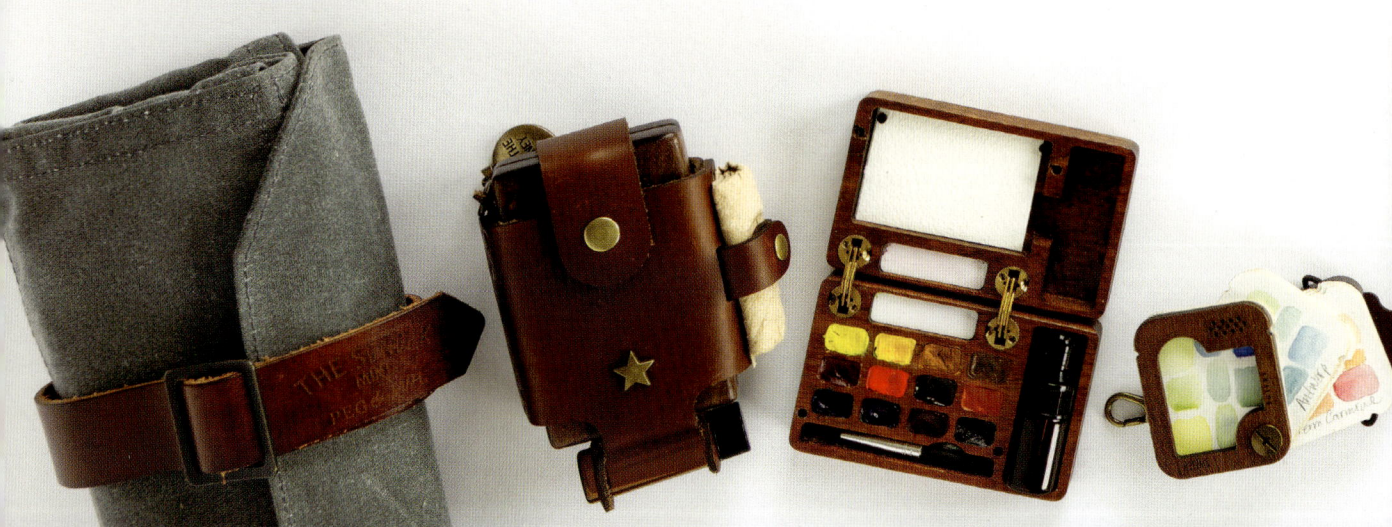

PLEIN AIR EXTRAS

Masking Fluid Marker – These are wonderful for preserving the white of your paper while you paint larger sections.

White Marker or Pen – Sometimes you will go overboard with the paint, so it's helpful to have a way to reintroduce white into your painting. A tube or pan of white, dried gouache will also work.

Pipette – You don't need this to add water to your water brushes, but it makes it easier.

Spray Mist Bottle – This is an easy way to re-wet your paints.

Ruler – A ruler is always a useful tool for art.

Natural Rubber Pick-up – This is the easiest, cleanest way to remove masking fluid. You can cut a piece to size from a larger one for portability.

Cotton Buds – If your paper is too wet or you want to quickly lift a colour, cotton buds are a quick fix.

Academic Divider – These are useful for measuring proportions quickly.

Knitting Needles or Bamboo Skewers – These are helpful for measuring items or checking perspective.

Washi Tape – If you are painting on loose sheets of paper, this helps keep them from shifting as you paint.

Viewfinder – This will help you find the perfect composition and can also help you isolate colours.

Small Scissors – These can cut your washi tape and are also handy for incidentals.

Extra Mixing Well or Palette – Sometimes it's helpful to have an extra place to mix colours.

Larger Palette with Extra Colours – Although I recommend using a limited palette 95 per cent of the time, it's useful to have some extra bright pinks or lavenders, especially in summer when the flowers are blooming everywhere. Sometimes, you may want to try new colours in a particular scene. For some seascapes, I like to replace Transparent Yellow Oxide with Raw Sienna, for example. Or I'll swap one of my blues for a different blue. I use travel palettes made by Art Toolkit because they are as thin as a business card holder and accommodate tiny pans that you can mix and match. They also fit nicely into an art kit or bag.

Extra Lead and Erasers for Mechanical Pencil – It's always handy to have extras in case you run out in the middle of a painting!

Red Filter or Sunglasses with Red Lenses – These will help you see the range of values in a landscape.

A collection of my favourite travel art kits and watercolour pochade boxes.

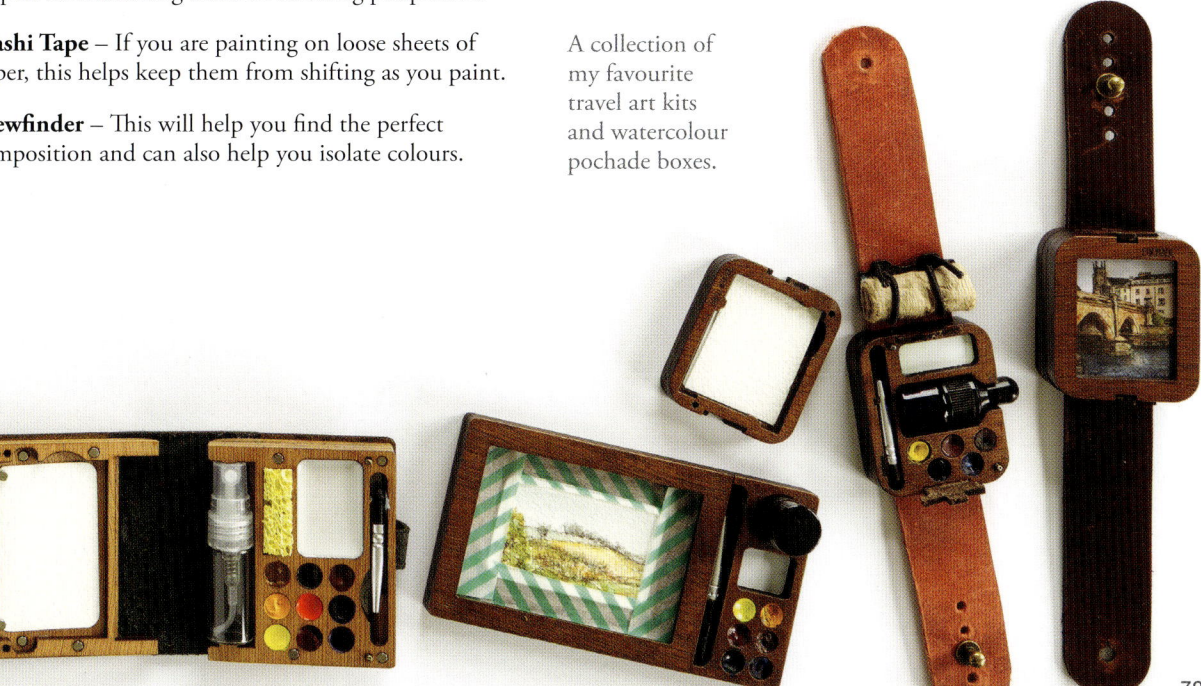

Travel Set-ups

Creating your own custom art set-up is one of the exciting parts of travel painting.

ART KITS

There are many companies that make clever products designed to keep your supplies organised (see Recommended Brands and Supplies), but you don't have to spend a lot of money to have the perfect set-up. I'll share with you some of the travel kits I've used, explaining what I liked and didn't like about each. Use these ideas to create an art kit that is a perfect fit for your own artistic needs.

Pencil Pouch

For about a decade I used an inexpensive, soft pencil pouch that was likely designed to appeal to pre-teens (1). I loved it! When you unzipped it there were two open pouches with a central, zipped pouch in the centre (2). Not only was it affordable, but it was also unique to me. I constantly changed the arrangement of items, but in general I kept my erasers in the middle, zipped pouch, my pencils, pens, and brushes on one side, and a watercolour palette on the other. I took it travelling all around the world, but eventually I yearned for a kit where I didn't have to dig around each time I wanted a new item.

Pencil Case

I found an affordable, green pencil case (3) online that solved the problem of "losing" my supplies in open pouches. This one had mesh and elastic sections and even a "page" in the middle where I could carry extra goodies. This was a wonderful replacement. I could alter it to carry additional supplies and larger palettes for bigger paintings. Everything had a place, which made the painting experience more streamlined. I wasn't the only one who loved this kit – within a year of featuring it in my videos online, I noticed that many other artists had adopted the same one.

When I had a table or surface to place it on, it was efficient. However, when I wanted to stand and paint, it was cumbersome, especially having to "flip" between sections for different items. The elastic held the items in place when it was full, but if I removed a few things, they would shift and sometimes fall out, making it easier to lose precious art supplies.

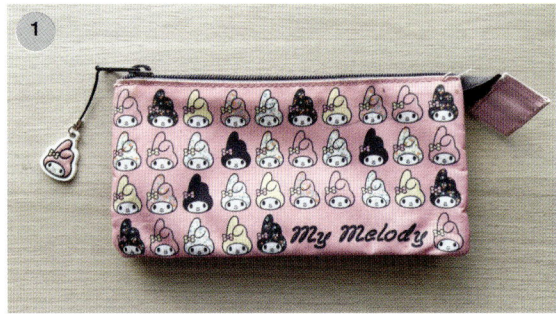

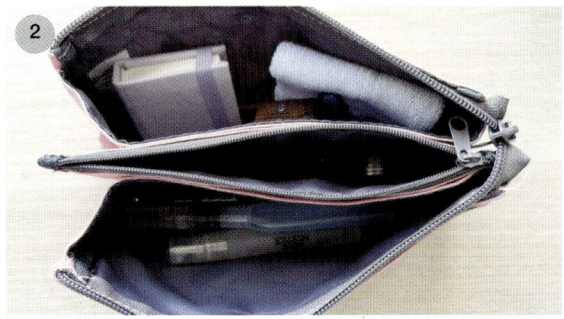

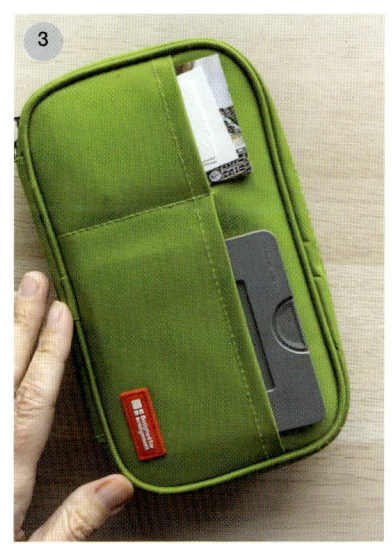

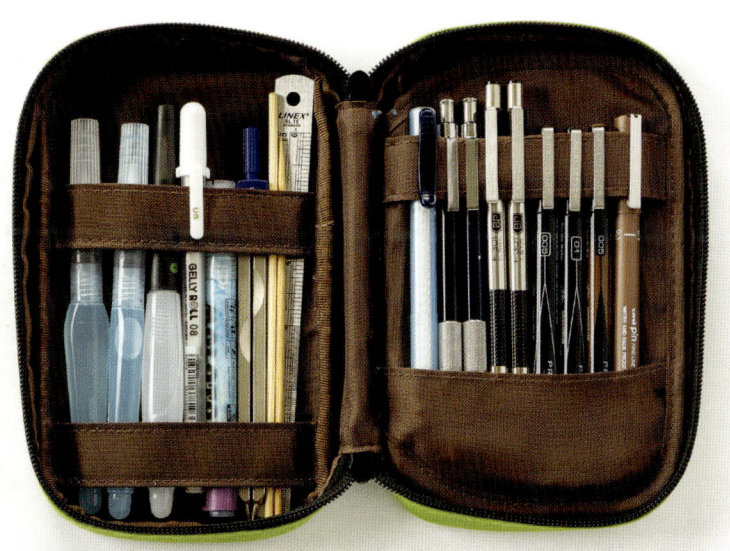

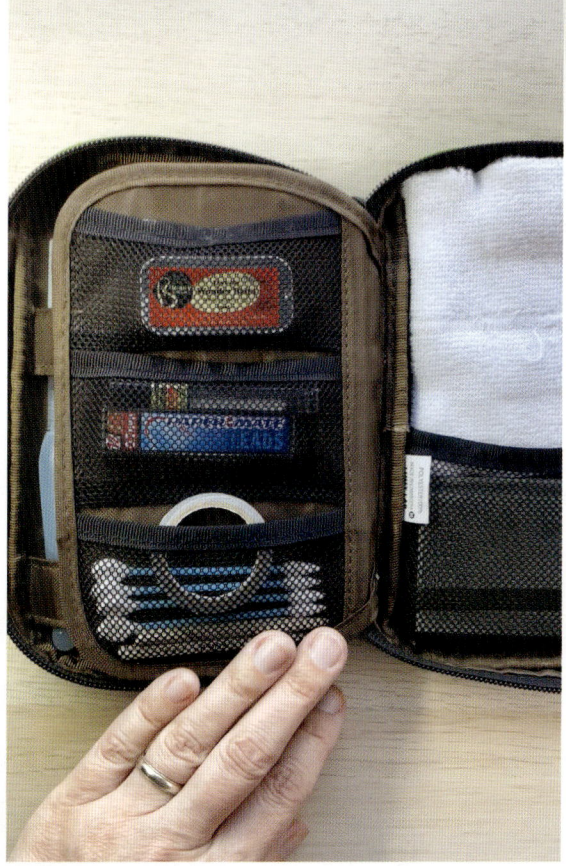

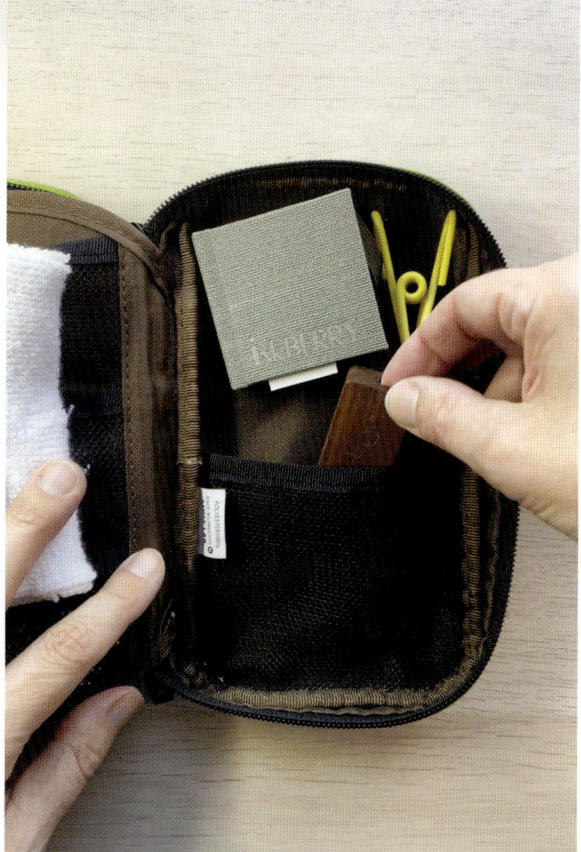

Art Wrap

I was gifted a handmade, waxed canvas art wrap called the Sendak by Peg and Awl. I'd seen other artists use them but hadn't much cared for art wraps in the past, which had many of the same problems as my green kit and were bulky. From the moment I put my supplies into the individually sewn pouches of *this* art wrap, however, I was instantly smitten!

The design features a combination of sewn sleeves for things like pencils and pens as well as deeper pouches behind for larger items, and a zipped section on the side. It even has deep pouches on the back of the art wrap. When it is packed full, I can fold it in half and easily fit it into my bag. The best part, however, is that when I want to sit and paint, I can drape it over my leg and nothing falls out! The pouches are snug enough to hold everything in place.

If I want to stand and paint, I can put the wrap in my bag and easily access everything. I have been so delighted with this clever design that I purchased a "mini" version and use them both. The Mini-Sendak is great for when I want to go out for a quick, tiny painting. The regular Sendak is perfect for when I want to indulge a bit more and have additional supplies at my beck and call. It's also ideal for longer travel holidays and I've found that I also use it in the studio for easy access to all my favourite supplies.

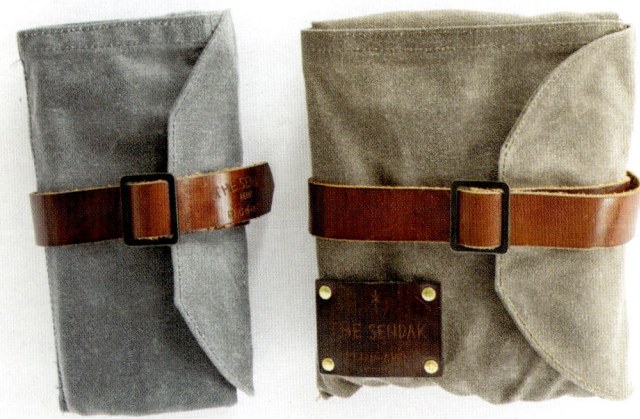

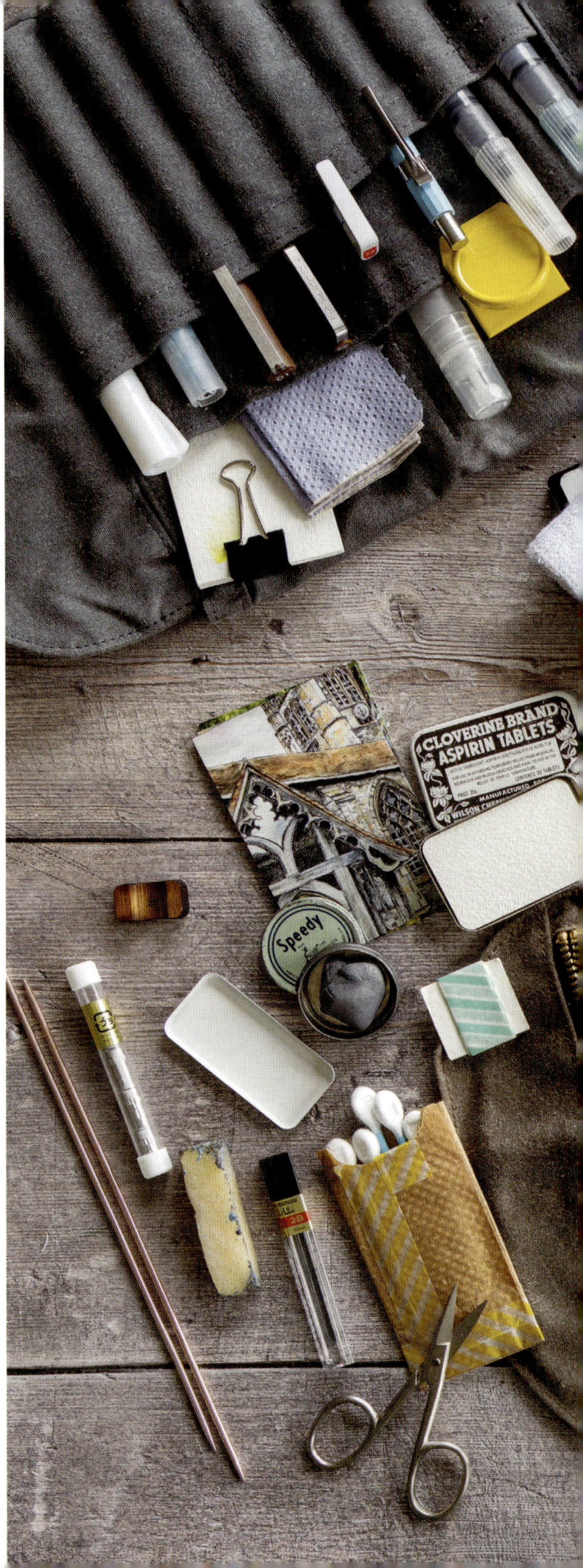

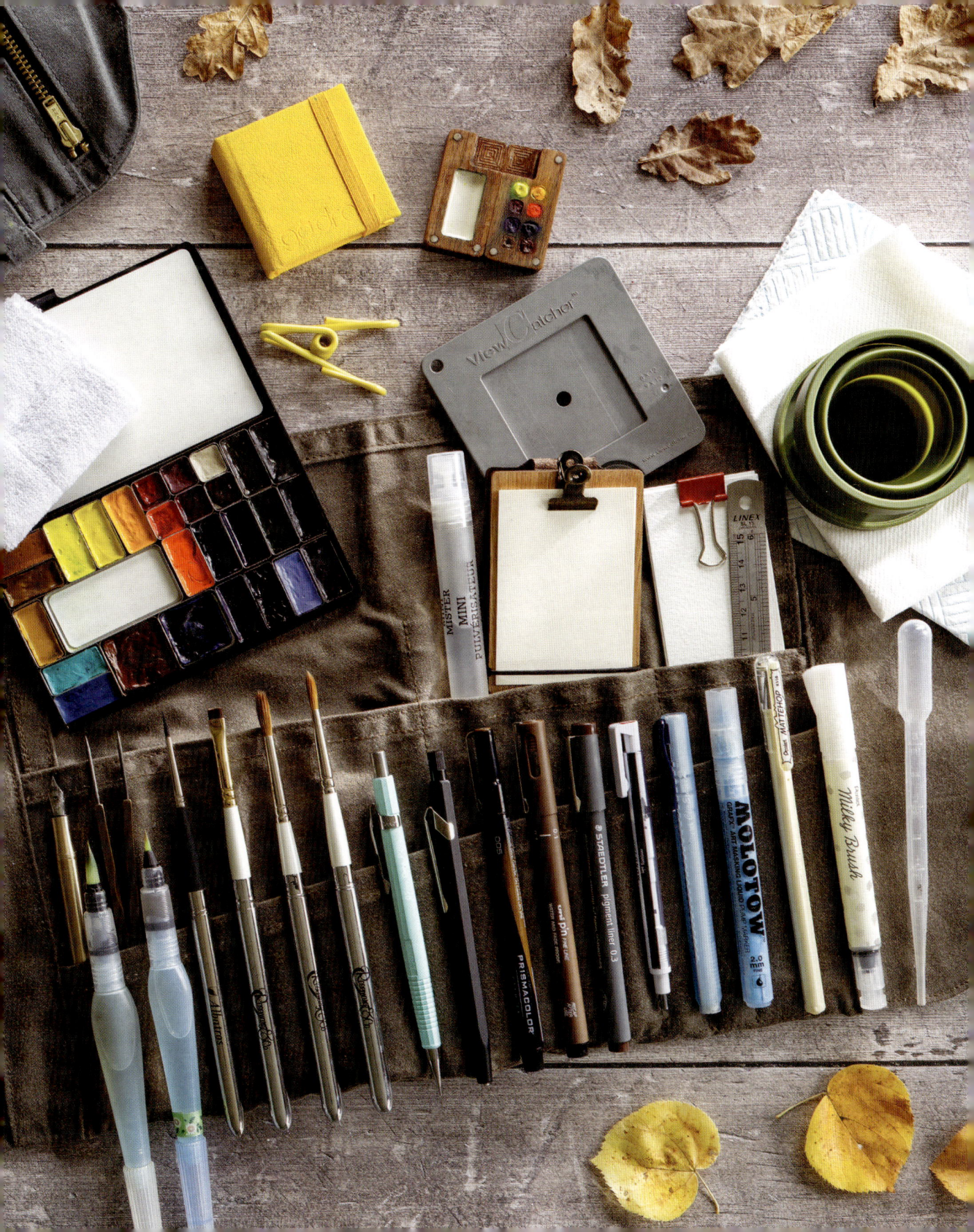

Non-art Supplies

Although the art kit is the most important part of your travel set-up, you'll want to bring other things that will make your painting experience as comfortable and easy as possible. For this, you can be as minimal or extravagant as you like. Here are a few ideas to get you started:

Backpack or Bag – Find a backpack or oversized bag that you can dedicate to your painting adventures. It should be large enough to fit your art kit and all of your extra supplies.

Hat with a Brim – Whether it's a large gardening hat, a baseball cap, or something in between, having a hat that shades your face will not only protect you from the sun, but it will also help shade your eyes so you can see colours better.

Sun Cream – Because you'll be outside for long periods of time, bring some of this to prevent sunburn.

Folding Sit Mat – These are readily available in stores that sell outdoor or camping gear. They're lightweight, portable, and give you a softer seat, especially if you sit on a lot of rocks or hard surfaces. They will also insulate you from cold and wet surfaces.

Picnic Blanket – If the weather is nice and you're in a location that has space, it can be lovely to sit on a picnic blanket while you paint.

Foldable Camping Chair or Stool – If you're going to be in a remote location, or someplace where seating is limited, it's handy to bring your own comfortable chair. Look for one that is small and portable.

Water – You can use it to drink, to keep your water brushes and spray mist bottle full, and to use as paint water.

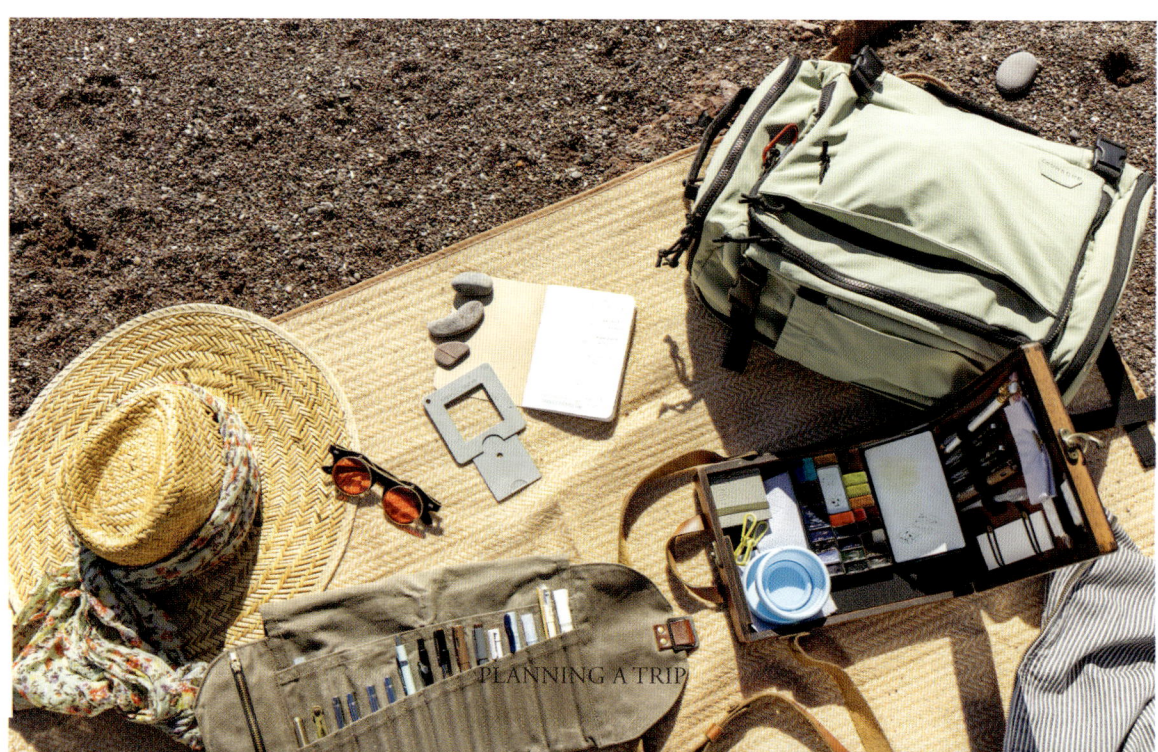

PLANNING A TRIP

Warm Drink – Make sure to stay hydrated by drinking plenty of water when you're out painting, or take a warm drink to keep the chill at bay in colder months.

Paper Towels and/or Hand Wipes – Even with watercolour, you will get messy, especially when you're holding your canvas in the palm of your hand. These will help clean you up!

Refreshments – You may get distracted or busy and it's always helpful to have food. It will also give you much-needed energy.

Camera (or Phone Camera) and Charger/Power Bank – Taking a photo of the scene you are painting is useful for any later touch-ups, and a power bank will keep your gadgets charged when you're out in the field.

Rain Jacket and Umbrella – The weather is unpredictable and it's always good to be prepared!

Sweater, Hat, and Gloves – When you're not moving for long periods of time you can get chilly. Being prepared for weather changes will ensure you can finish your painting without shivering.

Compass – This will help you track the sun and anticipate where the shadows will fall.

PLEIN AIR TIP: PAINT WATER DISPOSAL

Some colours contain pigments that are toxic, and even ones that are marked as safe for humans can be harmful for aquatic life. This means that it's important to dispose of used paint water responsibly. I mitigate this by carefully choosing non-toxic colours when I'm painting outside, but even so, it can be difficult to know what to do with used water after a painting session. I usually carry an empty water bottle and a collapsible funnel, which I can pour my paint water into and dispose of at home. Check the local regulations with the waste management department in your region to see what they suggest. If you visit the websites of the manufacturers of your paints, they also provide information about paint water disposal.

Painting From Your Vehicle

If you have a vehicle, you can create a cosy art nook inside where you can sit and paint in any weather. This can be especially welcoming when it's cold or rainy, or if you're shy and don't want others to know that you're painting.

CAR STUDIO

My old VW Golf doubled as my portable art studio for many years. I had a table that hooked under the steering wheel where I could put my supplies. I created many paintings from that space with my little dog, Poppy, curled up beside me on the passenger seat. I had a tea or coffee in the cup holder, the car heater for chilly days, and perfect views of the landscape. Many days, I opened the window and sat sideways to get an unobstructed view. Sometimes, I even painted from the boot (trunk)!

PLEIN-AIR MOBILE

I enjoyed painting in my vehicle so much that I decided to get a little van that I could kit out as a plein air mobile. I removed the back seats to create an inexpensive painting haven. If you have an SUV, a minivan, or a van, you can do the same for little cost. For the first year, I kept my set-up quite simple – or what they call a "no-build build". I placed a carpet remnant down over the floor, stacked a few cot mattresses on top of one another for a moveable bench seat, and added a portable tray table. This set-up enabled me to paint from any side of the van and to go out for longer excursions. I also added a portable compost toilet for emergencies and a power bank so that I could use a heating pad or electric blanket, charge my phone, and use an electric kettle.

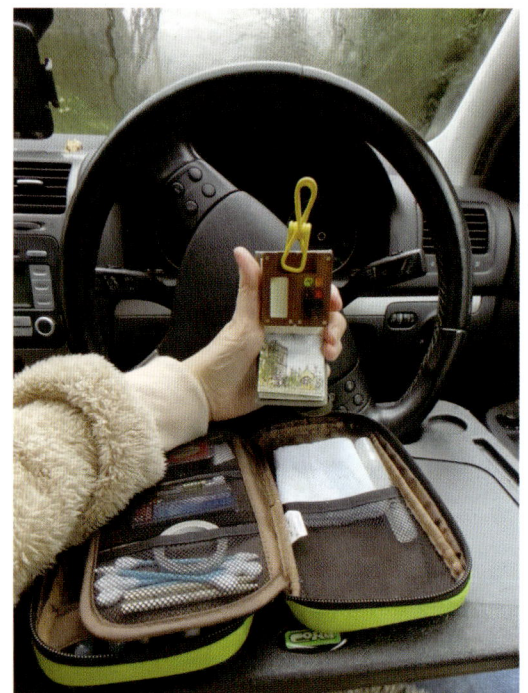

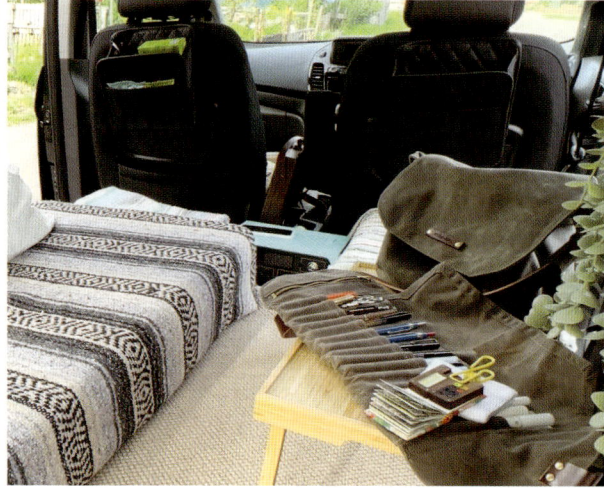

PLANNING A TRIP

CUSTOM PLEIN-AIR MOBILE

After a year of using my no-build build, I worked with a company called Campal that specialises in making custom, removable "boot jump" conversions that you can put into the back of your vehicle for camping. They patiently helped me design the perfect mobile art studio that I could use for shorter day trips or longer, overnight painting adventures.

Because I had painted in my van for a year, I knew which features worked for me and what I needed. It's a bit like a transformer with an "L" extension in the back: I kept the bench seat low so that I could sit up straight, but still have storage underneath and the option to convert it into a wider bed for sleeping, a custom shelving unit with pull-up tables on both sides, and even a bench extension that covers the portable toilet behind the passenger seat. It's a plein air artist's dream!

If you like painting or camping (or painting and camping), you might also enjoy kitting out your van with a more custom design. No matter what size vehicle you have, you can create a little art space for yourself inside. Try it!

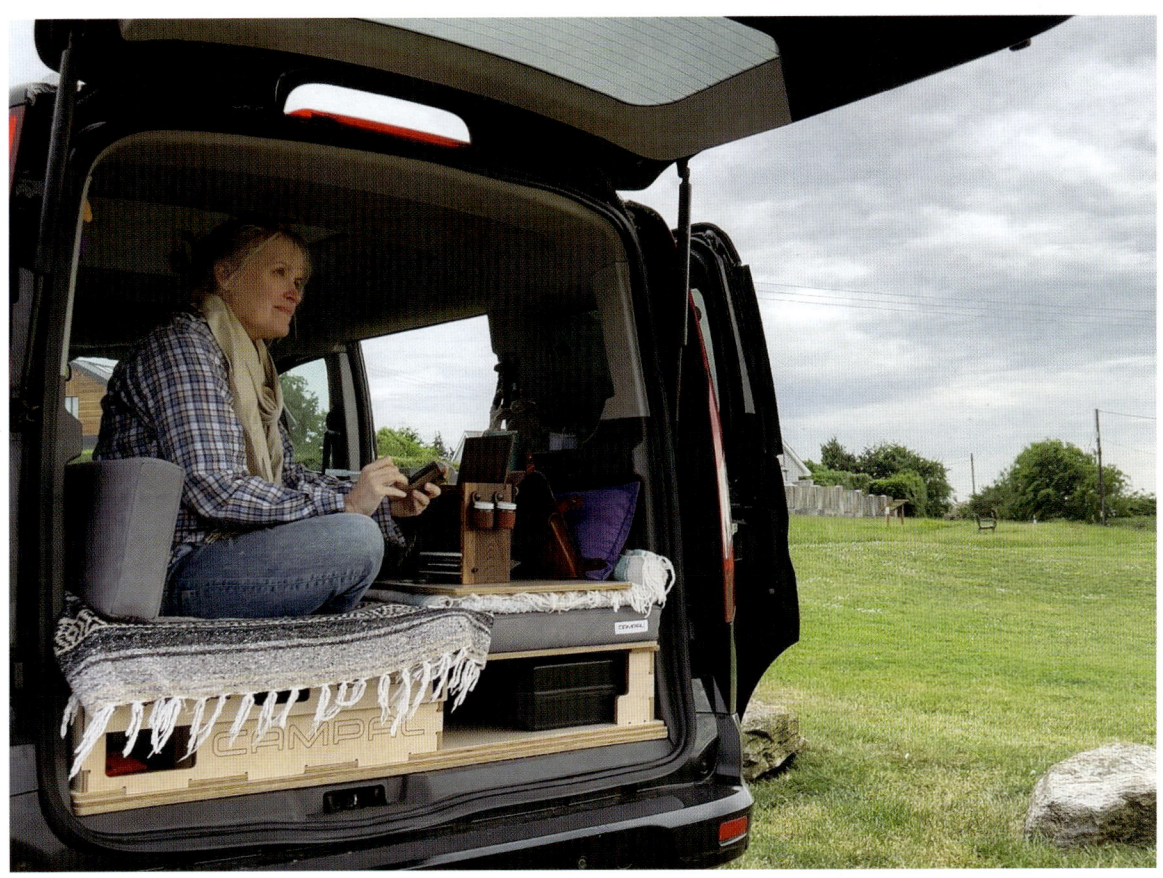

Overcoming Social Anxiety

If you want to try painting outside but are too afraid to try, here are a few tips that can help calm your anxiety.

- **Start Close to Home** – Find a place in your garden or outside your home – you'll have the benefit of being outside within the privacy of your own space. This will also give you the opportunity to see how efficient your art set-up is and to make any necessary changes. Painting from your vehicle can offer the same security of being in a familiar place.

- **Blend In** – Most people feel self-conscious about strangers when they first paint in public, but if your back is facing a wall or a bush, you'll be secluded enough. If you stand against trees or foliage, you'll feel more private – you can even stand beside your car. One benefit of tiny painting is that most people won't even realise you're creating art!

- **Choose Off-Peak Times** – Eventually, you'll feel ready to venture further afield. Pick quiet areas on days when the weather is overcast and fewer people will be out.

- **Venture Off the Beaten Track** – Choose benches or areas that are away from the crowds and less travelled. Even in popular areas, you can find little nooks that blend in. People are less likely to notice you or ask to see your painting if you're off the main path. Honestly, people are unlikely to notice you wherever you are. Remind yourself that most people are preoccupied with their own thoughts and companions and won't be interested in you.

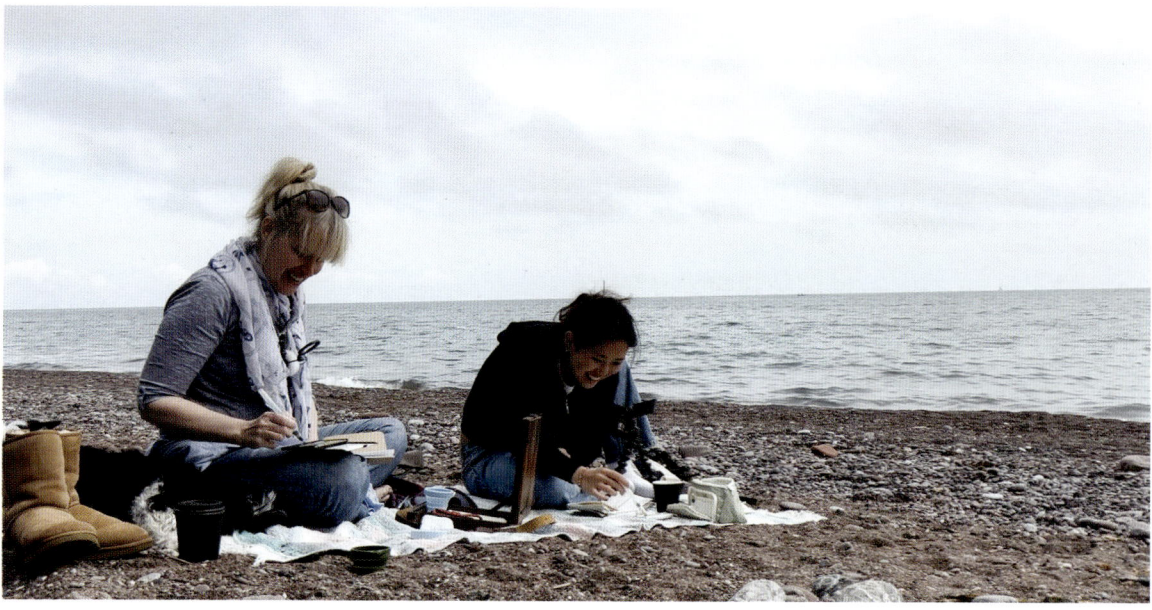

• **Bring a Friend** – Having someone else to paint beside makes the painting experience more fun and will help to keep you distracted from any worries you have about being noticed.

The important thing is to just begin, in whatever capacity you feel comfortable. I remember how self-conscious I felt the first few times I painted outside, but I promise, it soon becomes second nature.

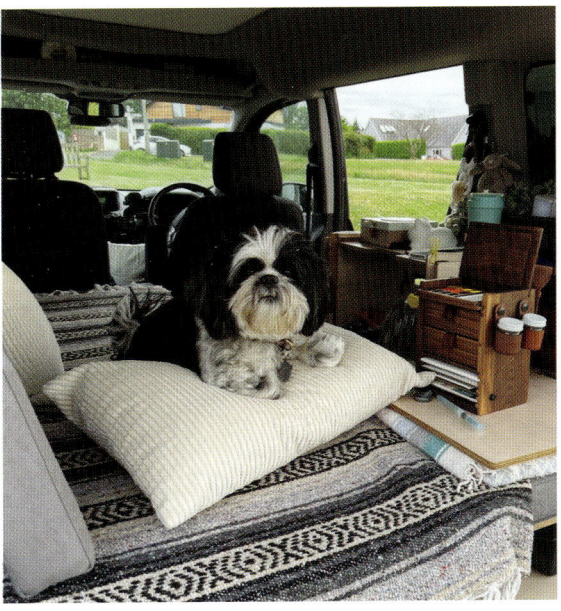

One of the biggest differences between professional and amateur artists is confidence in their ability to create art. So, if you don't have it, fake it. It won't replace learning or practice, but it will go a long way towards making your art better.

Pablo Picasso said, "Every child is an artist. The problem is how to remain an artist once we grow up." John Lennon said it a bit more cleverly: "Everyone is an artist until he's told he's not an artist."

Young children create art with confidence. They aren't worried about what others will think. They'll show you what they made with all the bravado of an art A-lister. But between the ages of 8 and 12, when social awareness and peer pressure creep in, the inner critic emerges. Maybe someone in class has a better drawing, or they look at art on the walls and decide theirs isn't as good. Or maybe somebody has said something mean. So most kids at this age kill their inner artist and deliberately dumb down their art, saying things like, "I can't even draw a stick figure."

But if you can write your name, you can draw. So continue to learn skills and practise, but when you do, silence your inner critic and put on a cloak of confidence. Put your soul into it. Fake confidence if you don't have it. Your lines will be more expressive, and your work will be better.

You can do it. I believe in you.

Choosing a Location

Sometimes you'll have the perfect idea of what you want to paint – a beautiful monument or building, or maybe even a botanical garden. But unless you travel frequently, you'll soon run out of unique locations. The truth is that most of the time you will find interesting things to paint within a few miles of your own doorstep. If you're serious about wanting to paint outside, and it's a practice that you want to do regularly, then you're not always going to have the luxury of an exotic location.

So what do you paint when you have the desire to paint, but you can't seem to find anything that's worthy of painting? One thing I recommend is looking closely at your own world.

ZOOM IN

Here's a scene of an alley with bins lined up (1). At first glance, I might dismiss it. But if I zoom beyond the bins, I can see an interesting arrangement of houses that make an exciting composition (2). The stone walls on both sides lead the viewer's eyes towards the houses, and they are nestled together like best friends sharing a secret. Even the pine trees are leaning in for a listen. Look for scenes that catch your eye, and tell their story with your paintbrush.

LOOK AROUND YOUR TOWN

A few places that have an ever-changing array of scenes to paint are cafes, parks, zoos, and museums. Be a tourist in your own town and visit places you've never been to before. When you're going about your normal day, make a mental note each time something catches your eye. It could be the way a single lamp illuminates a car park at night, or the long shadows created at the edge of a wood at sunrise.

KEEP A RECORD

Make a note of places that make you pause and look more closely, and when you have time return to those places (or paint them immediately). Make a list of houses and shop fronts and barns that have interesting architectural qualities, or that just appeal to you. Keeping a list of locations will make it easier on days when you have the desire to paint but lack the inspiration.

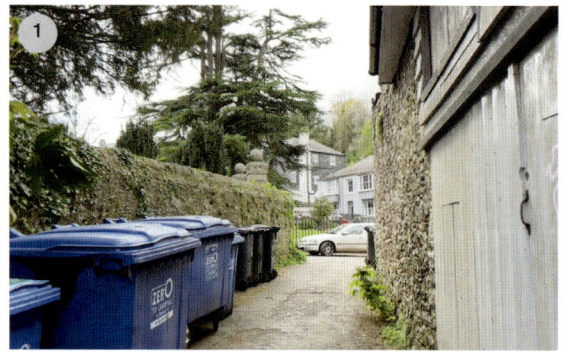

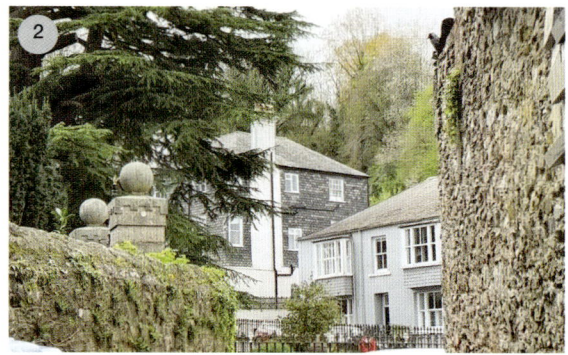

SPECIAL CONSIDERATIONS

If you're planning to paint in a tourist spot or a crowded location where you will be further away from your home or vehicle, there are a few things to consider.

1. I'd recommend arriving early or staying late so that you can avoid the worst of the crowds. Research the area in advance to find recommendations of particularly pretty spots or features. I often phone ahead to ask when their least busy days are.

2. Before you leave, check and double check your bag and art kit to make sure you have everything you need to paint comfortably, including water and a snack. I usually pack the night before to avoid any last-minute forgetfulness.

3. Make sure your phone is fully charged and take a portable power bank because you will likely be taking extra photos or videos, and you don't want to lose battery power.

4. Wear comfortable shoes and take an umbrella. It's helpful to keep a checklist of important items that you always want to bring.

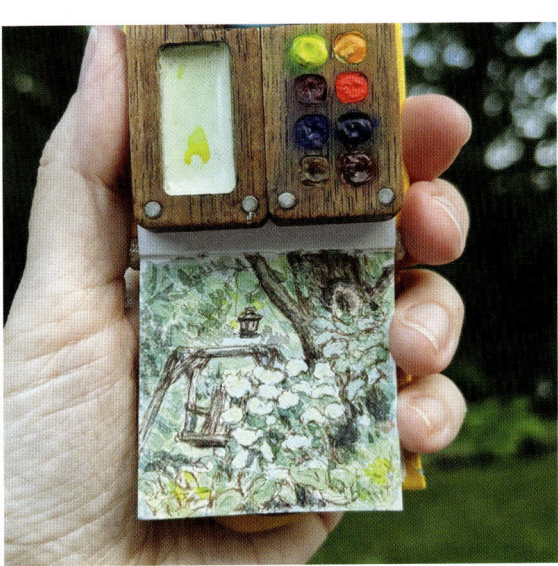

25 IDEAS OF THINGS TO PAINT

- Rooftops
- Flowers or Trees in bloom
- Treetops in all seasons
- Interesting Shadows
- Fences and Gates
- View from a Window
- Weeds (in pavements, walls, etc.)
- Fields (details of bushes, trees, and furrows)
- Corners of Houses as they intersect
- Flower Patches (especially wildflowers)
- Beaches, Rivers, Lakes, or the Sea
- Sheds and Greenhouses
- Laundry hanging out to dry
- House or Building in your neighbourhood
- Bicycles
- Reflections (puddle, window, lake, wet pavement)
- Bird Feeders or Bird Baths
- Doors and Doorways
- Archways
- Shop Fronts
- Abandoned Vehicles
- Clouds
- Your Garden
- Wildlife (swans, ducks, cows)
- Religious or Historic Buildings

When to Paint

Experiment with painting at different times of the day or year. You could even follow in the footsteps of the masters like Claude Monet and paint the same scene again and again at different times of the day, during different weather situations, and throughout different seasons.

Here are a few things to consider:

THE SEASONS

Spring

As the earth emerges from its deep slumber and the days grow longer, you'll have opportunities to paint a more blended landscape. You can find budding trees, snowdrops, daffodils, and busy birds building their nests, contrasted with the stark branches of late blooming trees, puddles, and muddy ground. You'll have more cloudy and rainy days, so it's an ideal time to paint from your vehicle and study the contrasting colours.

Summer

During the summer months, the colours are brighter, the earth is abloom, and the sun rises earlier and sets later, leaving you many uninterrupted hours to paint outside. Sunrises and sunsets create longer, glorious displays of colour and light. Places that were closed during the winter open again, making the choices for painting trips endless.

Autumn

The symphony of colours in autumn is an artist's paradise. You'll still find the greens of summer but they will be layered with pale and golden yellows, rusty oranges, and brilliant reds as the leaves give one last performance before they fall. This is a wonderful time to explore the capabilities of your palette.

Winter

The sun doesn't reach the same heights in the sky during winter, so you may notice that scenes you loved during summer might lack brightness and can sometimes even appear gloomy. The shorter days mean that your window of time to paint is more limited, but it's a great season to study the structure of deciduous trees without the cloak of their leaves. Any bright pops of colour will be more pronounced against the muted and darker landscape. If you live in an area where it snows, you'll have opportunities for observing how shadows play on snow.

TIME OF DAY

Morning Light

As the sun rises low in the sky and the landscape wakes up, you'll find longer shadows. Because the earth hasn't yet warmed up, you can often find misty and dramatic scenes. Although the sun creates warmth as it crests the horizon, it is cooler and bluer than evening light because of the shorter wavelengths. This contrast provides unique opportunities for observing the interplay between light and dark values and warm and cool colours. You'll need to move quickly, however, since the shadows will change your scene if you take too long. Focus on the larger shadow shapes and highlighted areas.

Midday

The sun rises higher in the sky during the middle of the day, making shadows less dramatic. Focus on a composition that relies more on the arrangement of the objects than on the effects of light and shadow. If it's sunny, find a place in the shade.

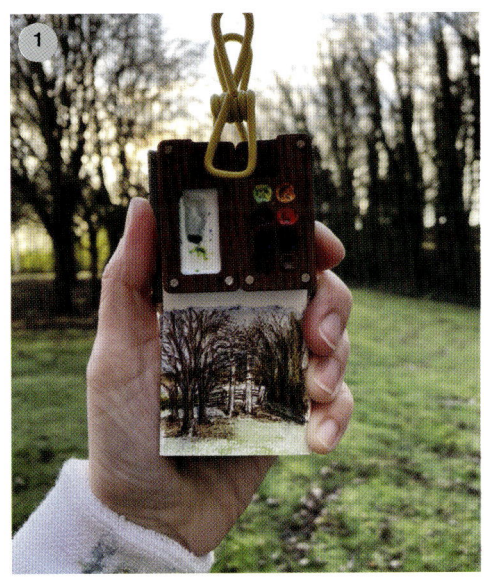

The Golden Hour

Filmmakers often shoot iconic scenes in the late afternoon and early evening because the sun casts long shadows and a golden glow across the landscape as it sets. The light is warmer and redder than morning light. As with the morning light, you'll need to move quickly to capture your scene before the shadows change.

OVERCAST DAYS

Painting on a day where the sun doesn't make an appearance can be a gift. The colours on cloudy days are softer and you can count on the scene remaining the same for longer durations.

Painted on a winter morning at sunrise. The contrast between the glowing light and cooler shadows in the woods provided an interesting challenge.

FINDING BEAUTY IN THE MUNDANE

Many people think that to paint outside they need to brave the crowds to paint fancy landmarks like castles or other places of significance. But the truth is that there are interesting scenes to be found everywhere if you just stop to look for them. Whether it's a rainy view of distant hills from your car window, or a pretty strip of land beside a busy road with the sunrise shining through the trees, you can find beauty in the mundane. You just need to look for it.

When I first started painting plein air, sometimes I'd drive for hours in search of the perfect scene (and usually not find it). But you can paint your own garden. Or someone else's. You can paint at parks or cafes or local neighbourhoods. You can paint anything, anywhere, and in any weather. One thing I know is that I'm always glad I did – and I hope you try it too!

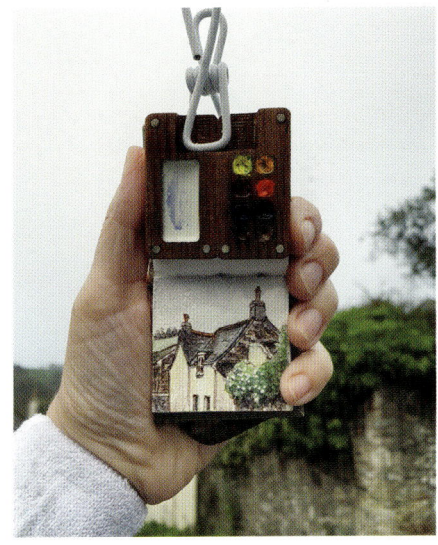

Painted from my car on a rainy, winter's day in an alley while I waited to collect artwork from my printer. Stolen moments like these can provide unexpected instances of zen.

Chapter Five

PLEIN AIR PAINTING
(The Process)

After you've arrived at your location, art kit in tow and excitement brimming, it can be overwhelming to know where to begin. The idea of painting that feels inspiring in its conception can too easily be derailed by crowds of people, a shift in the light, or by somebody sitting right where you had planned to paint.

Be flexible. Remind yourself that this is all part of the painting adventure. If the "perfect" scene you'd envisioned painting isn't available, maybe there is a better one waiting for you to discover.

In this chapter, I'll explain the process of painting on location, from the moment you arrive, to setting up your workspace, choosing and painting your scene, all the way to packing things up and heading home, a tiny painting safely tucked away in your art bag.

You're here. Now what?

When you arrive at a location, make a note of where the nearest public toilets or cafes are. If you're painting in a remote area, this may not be an issue, but in public places it's useful to know where the amenities are.

Even if you think you know where you want to paint, take a little walk to get a feel for the place and find scenes that appeal before choosing your favourite; remind yourself that you're there to explore and discover exciting new vistas and that it's important to be open to new ideas. Don't spend too long on this or you'll run out of time to paint!

Taking a walk will bathe you in the environment. You'll see the colours and textures up close, serenaded by birdsong, rustling leaves, and the soft hum of the world around you. Feel the wind caress your face. Breathe in the scents unique to your location.

If it sounds romantic, that's because it is. When you paint outside, you are joining a centuries-old tradition that thousands of other artists have participated in before you. Listen for their whispers to guide you. Imagining that you are the main character of your life will open you up to a world of creative possibilities.

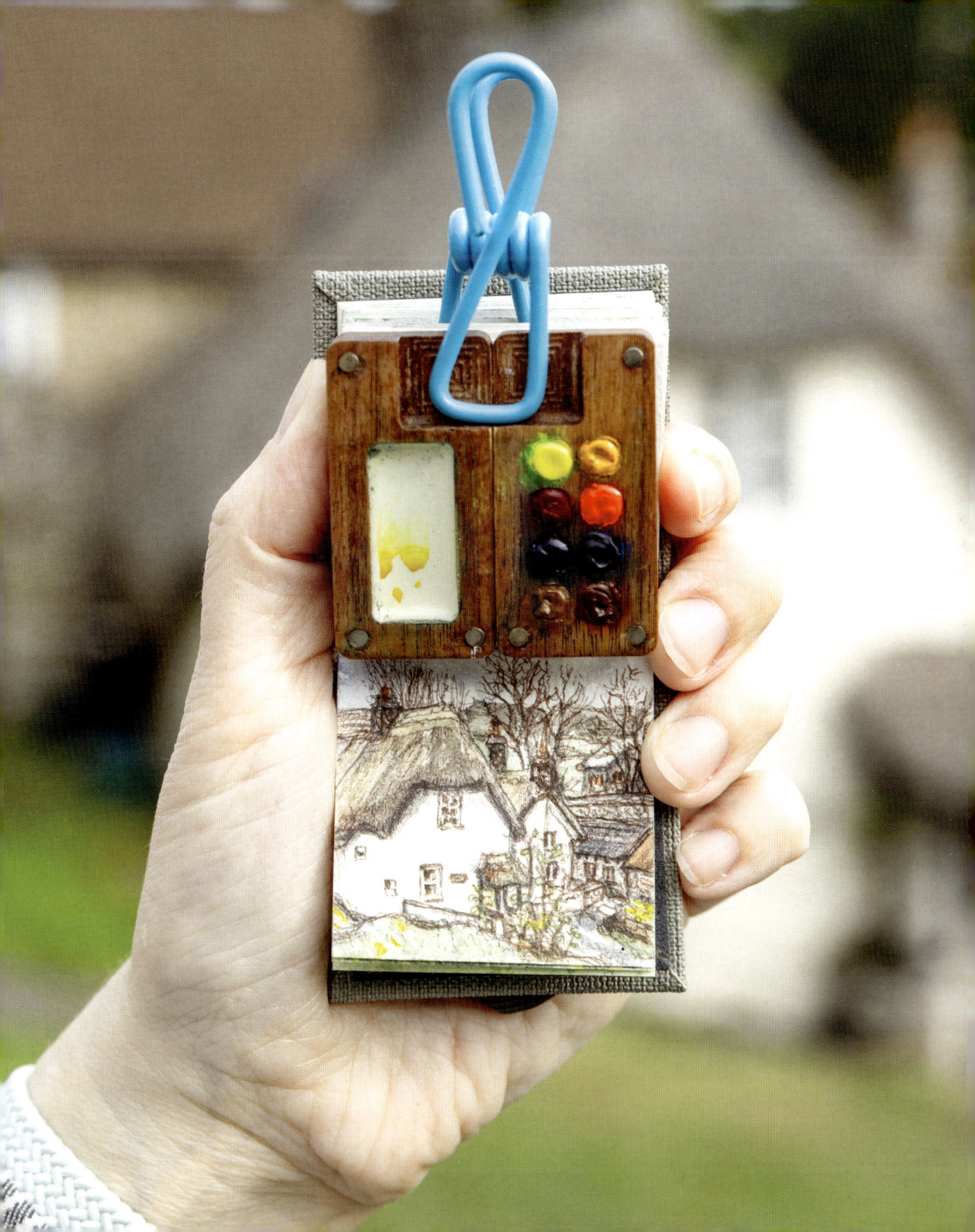

Choosing the Perfect Scene

In cooking we can find a perfect recipe that, if carefully followed, will produce delicious results every time. With painting it's very easy to get the composition "wrong", but with a little bit of planning and some basic knowledge about space (see Composition in Chapter Three), you can find winning compositions.

Here are some things you can do to achieve success every time:

1. Choose something that catches your eye – If you are drawn to a scene, chances are there's something about it that will hold universal appeal.

2. Home in on that subject and use your viewfinder – See how your subject looks with a frame around it. Many times, a scene that looks jaw-dropping in the real world fails to impress once you crop only a section of it. Play around with different configurations until you find one that fills the space in a pleasing way. Sometimes this means scrapping your original idea and finding a new scene to focus on.

3. Make sure to think about your foreground, middle ground, and background; try to include interesting elements in each. Which one of those zones will contain the main focus?

4. Determine what your FOCAL POINT will be – What drew you to the scene in the first place? Was it the way the light and shadows flickered together, or something more fundamental, like a characterful building? Decide what the "main character" of your painting is and make sure that the other "supporting roles" complement it in some way.

USE YOUR COMPASS

While choosing your subject matter, it's helpful to track the sun and select areas that you know aren't going to be swallowed up by undesirable shadows before you're done. Using your compass to determine where west is will help you.

Here are a few things to remember:

• If you're painting in the afternoon or evening and you're facing north, your shadows will fall towards the right of any objects in front of you.

• If you're facing south, they will fall to the left.

• If you're facing west, you will likely be squinting against the sun and everything you paint will be backlit – this can be dramatic, but challenging.

• If you're facing east, you will see your own shadow in front of you, but everything you want to paint will be in full sunlight.

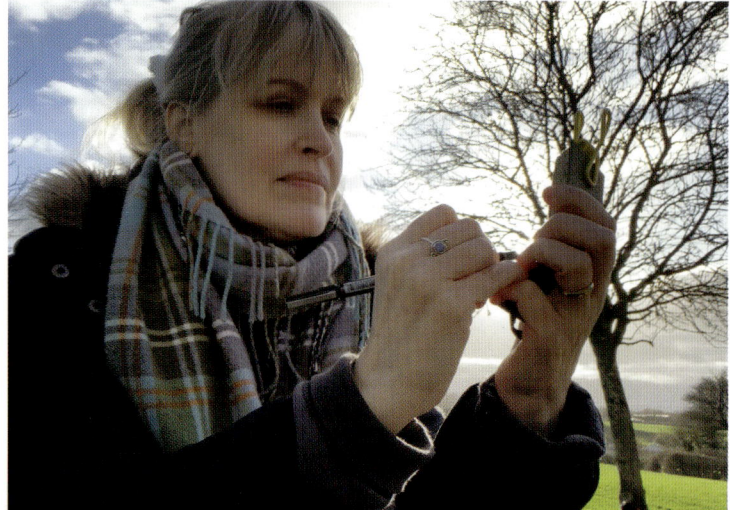

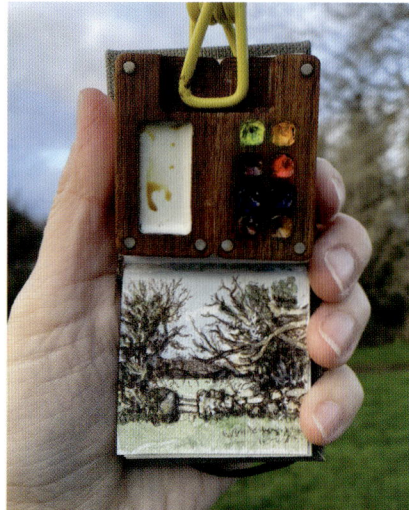

THE STAR OF THE SHOW

In this scene, I wanted the folly, the tiny building on the other side of the lake, to be the main star of the show. Every other element needed to draw attention towards that building, while keeping the eyes moving across the paper.

Selecting the View

Here, the folly is clearly the focal point (1), but there are some issues. For one thing, the lake divides the composition in half, drawing the viewer's eyes off the page in both directions. The little bush on the right isn't strong enough to bounce the attention back to the folly. Although each of the elements is beautiful in its own right, as a unit they don't provide enough visual interest. This was an almost but not-quite-right composition.

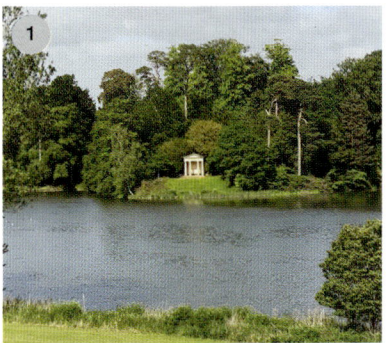

I continued to walk along the lake, keeping my focus on the folly and looking for other objects that might frame it better. This view with the linden tree (2) helps "block" the viewer's eyes from travelling across the lake and off the page on the left, but in doing so accidentally draws the attention straight up and out of the composition.

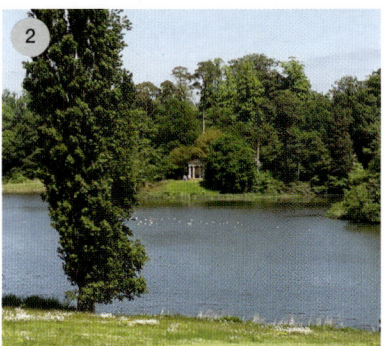

This next view was a contender (3). The dogwood in full bloom was breathtaking, but, unfortunately, too much so. It competed with the folly for the viewer's attention, creating two focal points.

I settled on this view lower to the ground where the grasses are long and the branch of an ancient oak tree reaches towards the folly (4). The trunks of the trees to the right of the folly also lean diagonally, serving as "implied lines" that point towards it. The pale green strip of grass below the folly helps draw the eyes towards it, as do the array of sage and golden bushes that frame it. Even the flowering rushes in front of the lake, dotted with white blooms, point towards it. Each element is individually unique, but they all work as the support cast to draw the viewer's attention towards the folly.

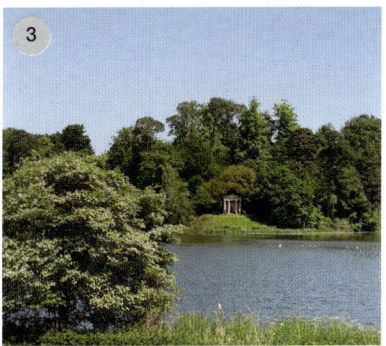

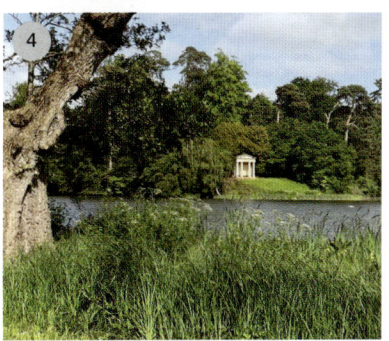

Setting Up

Once you've chosen your scene, find a vantage point where you can clearly see everything. Sometimes, the view you've chosen when you're standing looks completely different once you're sitting. If you plan to sit and paint, it's a good idea to bend or sit down when you're choosing your composition.

SITTING DOWN

If you're in a place that's less crowded, and if the ground is dry, you can put down a picnic blanket. It's cosy and you can spread out (plus, the festive feeling of having a blanket helps relax you!). If you plan to use a chair or a sitting mat, you'll want to have items easily accessible in your bag, so prop it up near you. Often, I'll take my art wrap out and place it on top of my bag.

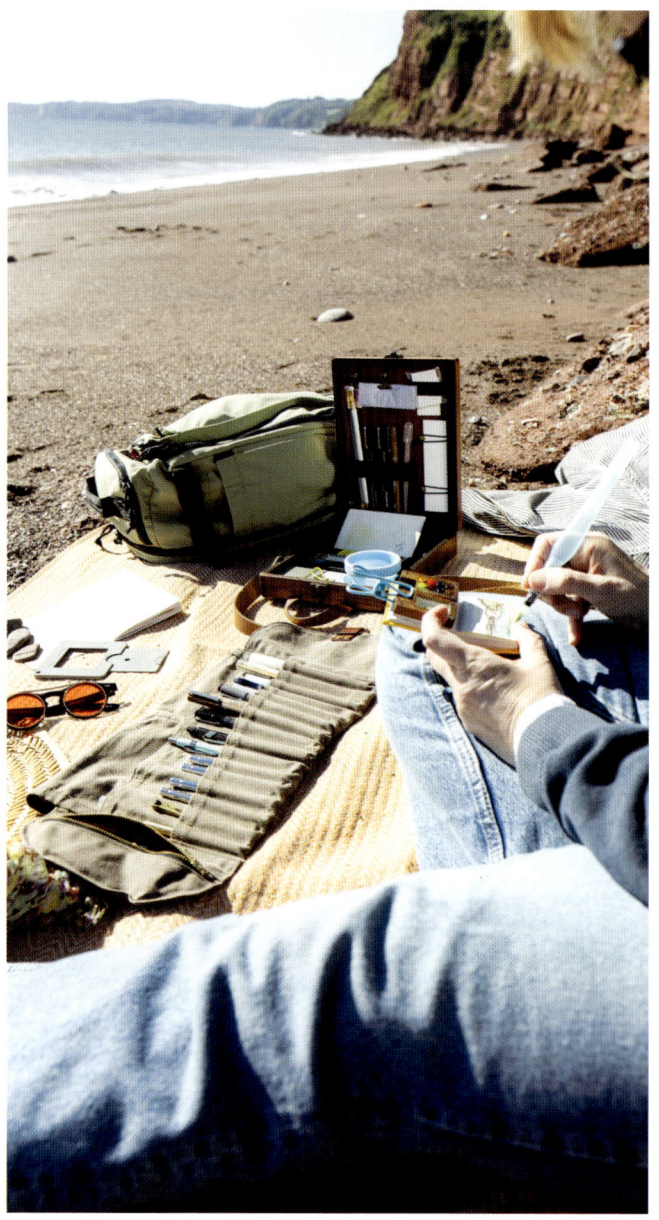

PLEIN AIR PAINTING TIP: KEEP YOUR WORK SHADED

Colours look brighter in the sun. If your painting is flooded with direct sunlight, you will be horrified by how dark and dull it looks when you get home and view it in softer or artificial light. Many plein air artists use white umbrellas or a sun shade above their painting surface to diffuse the light. With tiny painting it's a little bit easier because you'll be holding your painting in your hand and can more easily control how much sunlight falls onto it. Unless it's midday, you can usually just turn your body slightly to put it into shade.

PLEIN AIR PAINTING

STANDING UP

If you're planning to stand and paint, you'll want to consider how to access all your supplies. Even with a tiny painting, you'll want to use pencils, pens, and brushes, so plan a way to easily reach them. I've done several things over the years. In the beginning I put the things I knew I wanted to use in my pockets, but this was awkward, and it was easy to lose things.

One thing I've learned is that having a dedicated space for each item in your kit ensures that you can easily find what you need and that you won't lose anything! You won't want to waste time searching for an item when you're in the creative zone. If you're planning to stand and paint – and this may be your best option if you're in a busy location – you'll want to find a way to access everything.

I've experimented with aprons and even wrapping my Sendak art wrap around the front of my body and strapping it on with a belt (1). All these ideas work, but the thing that I've found to be easiest in all weather is to have a small bag that fits one of my art kits that I can wear diagonally across my body (2). I'll often fold my art kit or art wrap "inside out" and put it into my bag so that it's easier to reach the items on both sides.

Experiment at home with different configurations and see what feels best for you. Having a small bag that you wear also makes you inconspicuous, so if you struggle with social anxiety, this might be your favourite option.

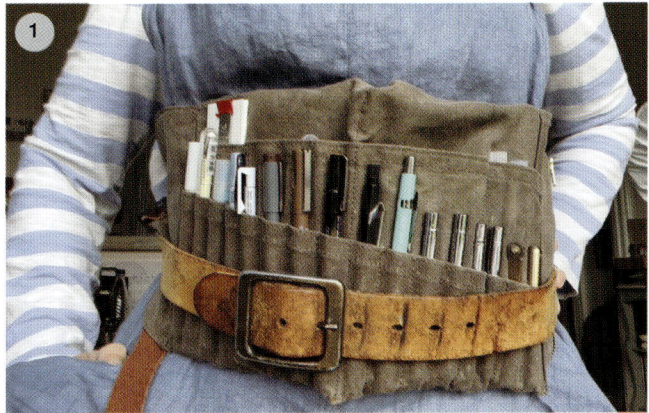

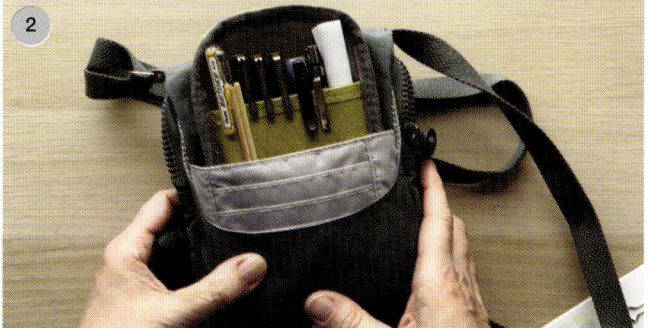

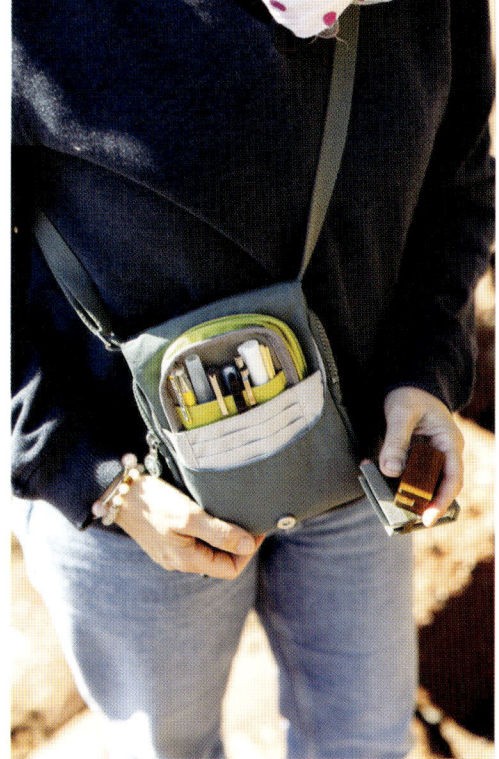

Drawing What You See

Once you've selected where and how you want to paint and chosen the perfect composition, it's time to place those items onto your paper or canvas. This can be tricky in any situation, but is even more so in a tiny painting. Placing items on a small canvas so that they aren't too big or small, and so that they are accurate to what you see, takes a bit of practice. Here are two ways you can study the placement of the objects in your scene so that your compositions are accurate every time.

UNIT OF MEASUREMENT

Getting your proportions correct is essential when you want to paint a realistic scene. Using a measuring guide, such as a knitting needle or bamboo skewer (see Extra Essentials in Chapter One), will help you measure the objects in your scene against one another to determine how large or small they are. You can use a pencil or paintbrush to do the same thing, but paintbrushes have a taper, and the thickness of these items makes it trickier to get accurate measurements – especially when you're working small.

Here's how to do it:

1. Hold one arm out straight in front of you. Don't bend your elbow because you'll want to repeat these measurements several times, and the only way to ensure accuracy is to keep your arm straight.

2. Tilt your head slightly towards your outstretched arm and close one eye. If you're measuring with your right arm, close your left eye, and vice versa.

3. Line up the top of the measuring guide with the top of the object you want to measure. Move your thumb down the guide to mark the bottom of the object. You now have a measurement you can use to compare to everything else in your scene.

In this scene (right), I've used a knitting needle to measure the top half of the clock tower (1) and noted that it's the same length as the bottom half (2). I can also take this same measurement and turn the knitting needle sideways to see how far the distance is to the edge of the trees or the white building behind. I can see, for instance, that the width of the white building is only slightly longer than the top section of the clock tower if I measure from the edge of the building to the far right of the building (3).

This same method can be used to measure any element in the scene and compare it to others. I find that it's most useful to find something that is of small or medium size in your scene and compare that to everything else.

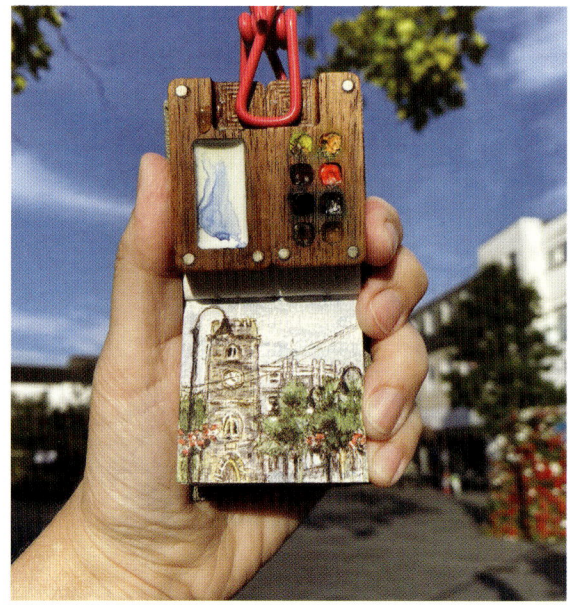

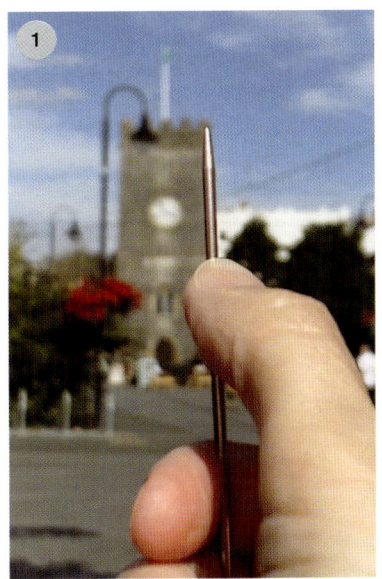
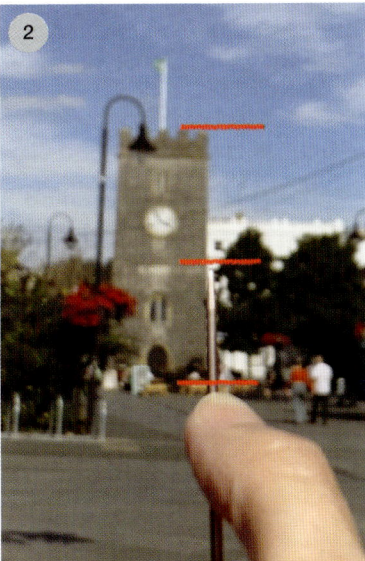
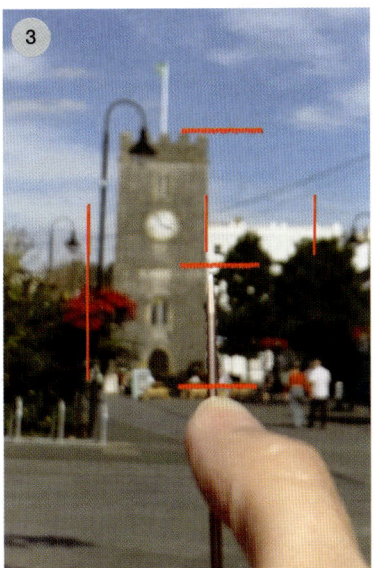

ART TIP: PRETEND YOU'RE AN ALIEN

My best art advice ever (according to one of my students) is to draw like an alien. Too often, artists allow their brains to interfere with what their eyes really see. To fix that, pretend you're an alien who's just landed on the planet and your job is to draw and paint everything that you see (you're from an advanced planet that supports the arts). You've never been on this planet before, so you don't know that trees have thousands of leaves. You only know that you see light parts and dark parts and some areas in between, so that's what you record. You don't know that there are thousands of strands of hair on the average person, but you can see areas of shadows and highlights, and that's what you draw and paint. And the same applies to everything else. If you pretend that you're an alien, you remind your brain to stay out of the way and allow your eyes to do the work.

HORIZONTAL AND VERTICAL SWEEPS

Another way to check proportions with a measuring guide is what I call "horizontal and vertical sweeps".

You can be as intricate as you like with this method; it is a wonderful way to place objects correctly in a scene. Using a unit of measurement to check proportions and further assessing them with horizontal and vertical sweeps will train your eye and improve the accuracy of your drawings.

Here's how to do it:

1. Begin as you did with the unit of measurement by holding one arm out directly in front of you.

2. Turn the measuring guide so that it is perfectly horizontal and place it at the top of your scene, then slowly move it down the scene the way a printer scans a print. Stop whenever the measuring guide touches an element in the scene and notice what you see below or above it.

3. Next, turn the measuring guide so that it is perfectly vertical, place it to the left of your scene, and slowly move it across the scene to the right. As above, pause each time the measuring guide touches something new in the scene to see how it is placed among the other elements.

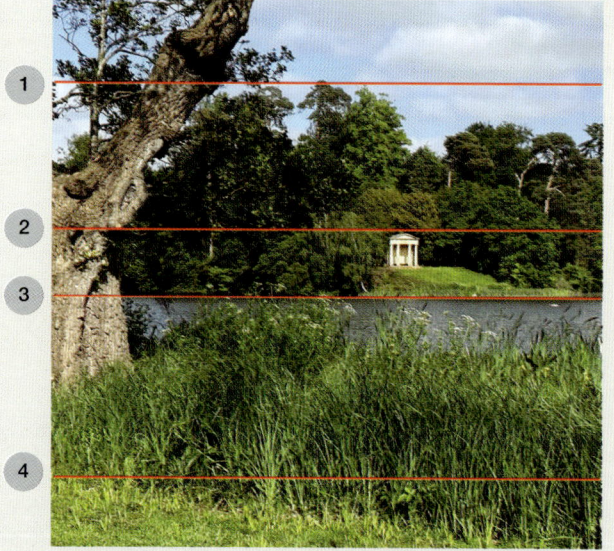

Here, I've marked four horizontal places where I paused to assess the scene:

Moving down, I paused the top line as soon as it touched the top of the tallest tree (1). This shows me how much sky is above it and how much space is below it before it hits the shorter trees.

The next place of note is the top of the folly (2). Looking to the left, I can see that the bend in the tree aligns with the top of the building.

At the third horizontal sweep, I paused at the top of the lake (3) where I can see which of the flowering rushes extends above it.

For the fourth horizontal sweep, I stopped at the top of the lighter grasses below the darker flowering rushes (4). From this I could see that the flowering rushes were at an angle to the base of the page.

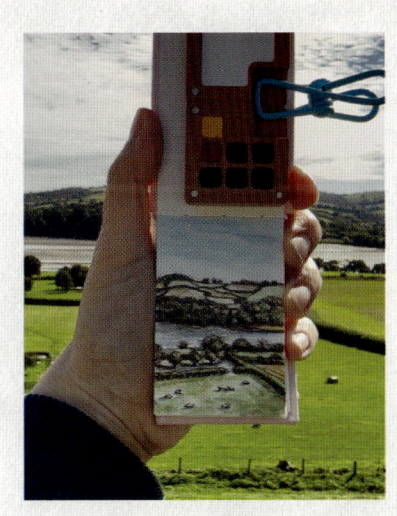

TINY PAINTING TIP

Unless you have a lot of time to allow your painting to dry between stages, the wet-on-wet technique (adding washes to wet paper) isn't as effective for tiny paintings. Instead, use the wet-on-dry technique, where you add wet paint to the dry surface of the paper.

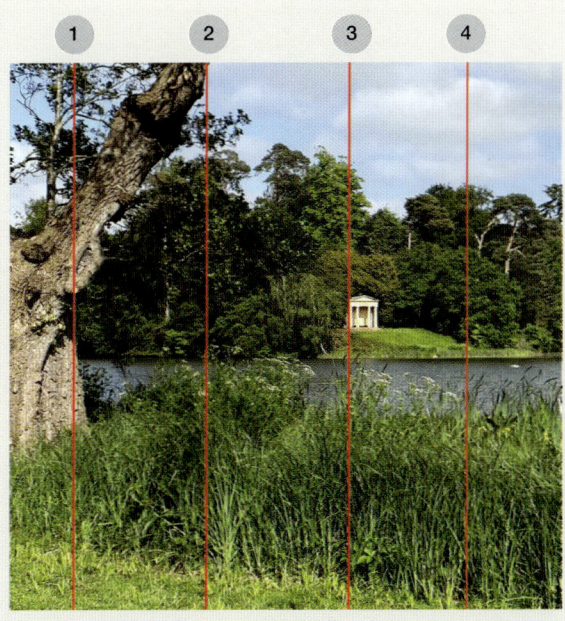

Here, I've marked four places of note in the vertical sweep:

Starting from the left, the first place is the bend in the tree (1). This line shows that the base of the tree angles slightly to the right of this line. It further shows me a shape in the negative space between the tree branch and the line that I can use to draw it correctly.

The second vertical sweep stops at the right edge of the tree branch (2) and shows me that it ends about a third of the distance across the top of the page. It also shows me the relation of the trees behind it.

The third vertical sweep stops at the left edge of the folly (3). I can see that it is to the right of centre and that the tallest trees fall mostly to the left of this line and ever so slightly to the right of it.

The fourth vertical sweep stops at the edge of the folly's grassy patch (4). I can see that the trees with the white trunks fall to the right of this line and that the light grassy patch ends at the middle point of the tree above it.

THE LINE-AND-WASH PROCESS

When I create a tiny painting, I almost always use a technique known as line-and-wash. This is where you combine an ink drawing and a watercolour painting. There are various ways one can approach this, but I like to use a three-stage method as follows: the Sketch, the Ink, and the Colour.

When you paint outside, the light is constantly changing and your time is limited, so it's important to get your whole composition down as quickly as you can. With watercolour, it's a little trickier because darks take longer to build. When you add the drawing element of a line-and-wash painting, it further delays your application of colour.

The Sketch

The first stage is the sketch. If you're new to art, this part can take a while. That's okay. Never compare yourself to other artists because you don't know how much practice they've had or what level they're at. Even some people who haven't painted for decades might have devoted hours to creating art as a child. Art isn't a contest, so try not to allow your internal critic to make it one.

Give yourself permission to play – and to fail. My first plein air paintings were awful, but that didn't mean I wasn't having a wonderful time. Remind yourself that it's all a learning process and have fun with it.

After you've used your viewfinder to choose a strong composition and taken a few moments to check your proportions, it's time to place your first marks with a mechanical pencil. It's helpful to start with your horizon line, because from here you can anchor the drawing and decide which items belong below or above it.

Next, put in some basic shapes. Look for the largest simple shape you can find. Use the tips above to help you place another object besides, above, and below it. Slowly break things down into smaller shapes. If you're painting a building, for instance, start with the general shape of the building and then add windows, doors, or architectural details.

Pay attention to your light source. Where is the sun and where are the shadows? Lightly sketch these in. I recommend drawing just enough so that you know where the key features are placed. You can add details during the next stage.

TINY PAINTING TIP

If possible, do not use black ink on your tiny paintings! It will dominate the tiny scrap of paper and make your work look more cartoonish. Use a dark brown, sepia, or grey fineliner or ink with a fountain or dip pen instead. I prefer to use the smallest nib possible for tiny paintings because the thinner lines blend in more seamlessly with the rest of the painting. If you're using fountain pens, there are a variety of waterproof inks available in different brown and grey hues that are fun to explore. I'd recommend using an extra-fine nib, but make sure to clean it regularly because the waterproof ink can get clogged.

The Ink

Beginning artists are often tempted to draw or paint everything with the same amount of detail, but that's not how the human eyes perceive things. When you look at one object, everything around it blurs slightly. Even many realist artists will choose to keep one object slightly sharper and more detailed than the rest. This more closely mimics the way people see the world. Consider this as you draw and paint. Allow your focal point to receive the most love and detail.

HOW MUCH TO PUT IN?

With line-and-wash you are the one who decides how much detail you want to add. Study different artists from the past and present who have used this technique to see how they have approached it. Try adding more or less to see which you prefer. I like for my ink drawings to look complete irrespective of whether or not I add colour. In fact, sometimes I love the drawings so much that I don't want to paint them! The more you explore this method of painting, the more your own style will develop.

THE INKING PROCESS

This is my favourite stage of the tiny painting because it's where everything starts to come together.

Begin with lighter lines first, using a combination of hatching, stippling, and scribbling to create different values and patterns (see Understanding Value in Chapter Two). Slowly build your darker values, but make sure to leave plenty of white and mid-tones as well. It can be easy to go overboard on a tiny painting, so try not to push things too far at this stage. Remember that your drawings will look better if you have a range of values.

Look at the subject as much as you do the painting. Study the way the trees move in the wind and create lines that mimic their movements. Do the same for other organic objects, like bushes, grasses, and foliage. Vary the marks for different areas. This can be harder with tiny paintings because your real estate is limited, but it's possible. Squint at the scene to find the darkest shadows, and build textures in those areas.

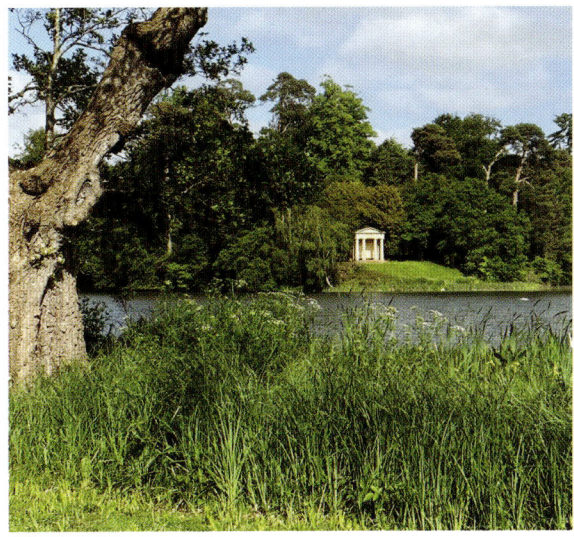
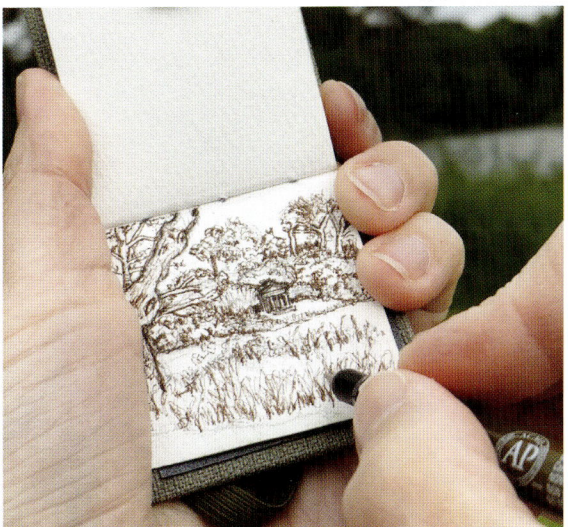

APPLYING MASKING FLUID

Once the inking is complete, look for the areas that you want to remain light or that will be the lightest values, and determine whether you can avoid those sections when you're painting, or if you'd like to mask the paper with masking fluid. This is the best stage to add it to those areas. Apply the masking fluid thickly or it will be more likely to tear the paper when you later remove it.

For plein air painting, a masking fluid liquid pump marker works great. These come in a variety of nib sizes, but I recommend the smallest ones you can find (0.1 or 0.2). You shake them, pump the nib on a piece of scrap paper to get it started, and then dab or draw the areas that you want to be protected. The colour of the masking fluid in my marker is blue, which makes it easy to see when it's time to remove it.

You can use any making fluid for this; I merely use the markers for convenience. When they work, they are miraculous. But when they die off or stop working, they can be frustrating. If yours stops performing, check to see if any of the masking fluid has dried on the nib and peel it off. Sometimes, when you pump the nib, it will spit a blob of masking fluid onto your scrap paper. If this happens, treat it the way you would a dip pen. Dip the nib into it and then paint it on the paper. Even with all of these flaws in the design, I still prefer to use them. They dry in about a third of the time as the masking fluid sold in bottles, and for the convenience and portability, they're worth it.

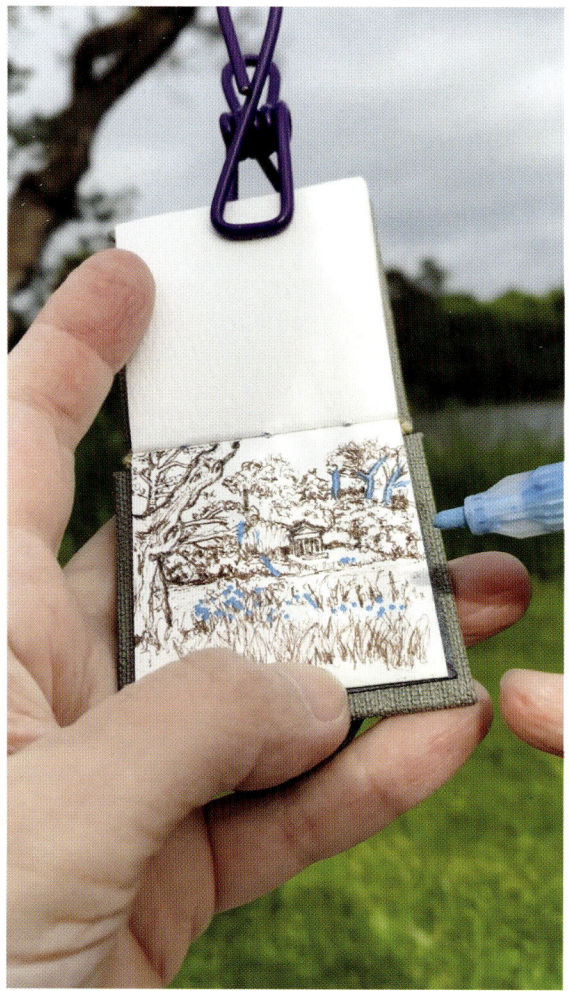

SKETCHING TIP

If you're using hot-pressed (smooth) paper, you will have a more difficult time creating a variety of marks in ink. With cold-pressed (textured) paper, the nibs will glide and sometimes even skip across the surface, creating interesting effects.

The Colour

Your drawing is like the frame of a house – it shapes the space where everything else will live. Once it's completed and all of the elements of the scene are in place, the pressure is off, and you can sprinkle in the colour that will give it life. Working with a limited palette will ensure that your tiny painting has colour harmony. It will also make it easier to achieve the results you want. Refer to Colour in Chapter Two for more about using your limited palette.

USING A WATER BRUSH

If you've never tried a water brush, you're in for a treat. Their clever design makes travel painting much easier, especially for tiny paintings. The handle holds water, eliminating the need for a separate water source.

There are several different designs on the market, but my favourites are the Pentel Aquash brushes. You can refill them by unscrewing the top and filling the reservoir with water (some other brands require you to turn the tops anticlockwise). The bristles are synthetic, so they do stain, but they also keep their point, which is important. The cap snaps onto the bottom for convenience while painting.

Another bonus of water brushes is that they are self-cleaning. Gently squeeze the handle to release a drop or two of water through the bristles and wipe it on a clean cloth. You may need to do this a few times for cleaning darker colours.

Some brands have a button on the barrel that you can depress to release the water, but others, like the Pentel Aquash brushes, maintain a steady flow, which means the bristles stay wet. This is important for washes or wetter applications of the paint, but other times you might require the bristles to be merely damp.

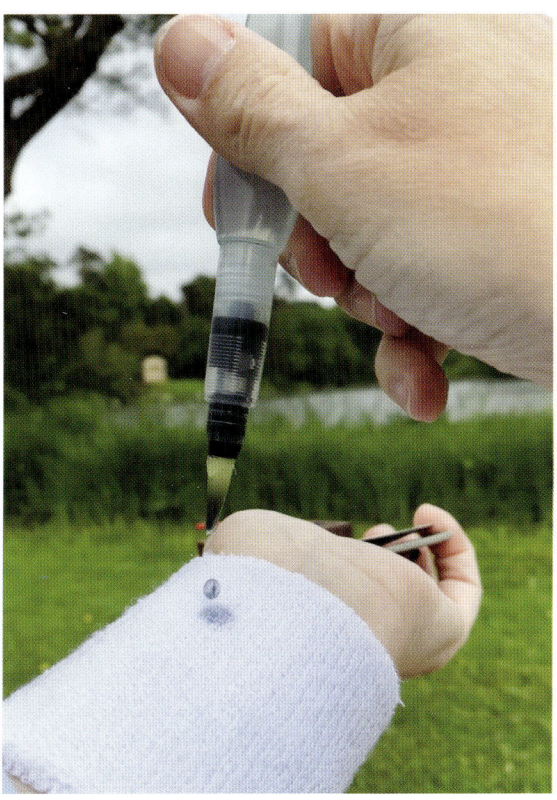

Tips for controlling the water:

• If the bristles are facing downward, more water will flow through them, maintaining an even flow. This is ideal for first layers and washes (1).

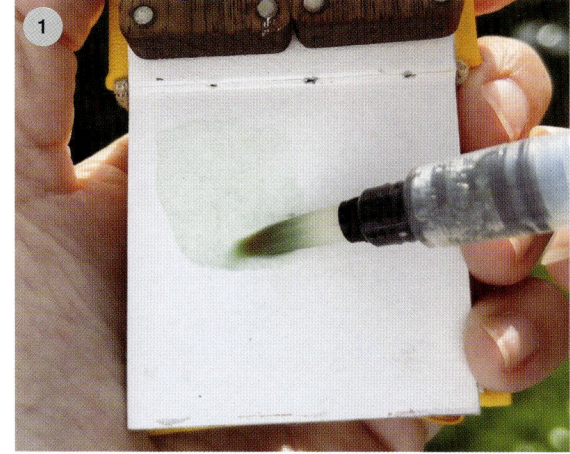

• If you want the bristles to be damp instead of wet for thicker applications of paint, hold the sketchbook upright and paint with the bristles pointing upwards. This will stop the water flow while keeping your bristles damp (2).

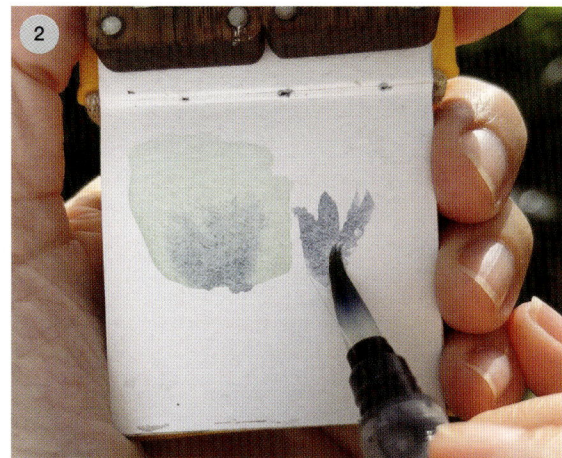

• For a dry-brush effect, blot the bristles on a cloth before adding and applying the paint (3).

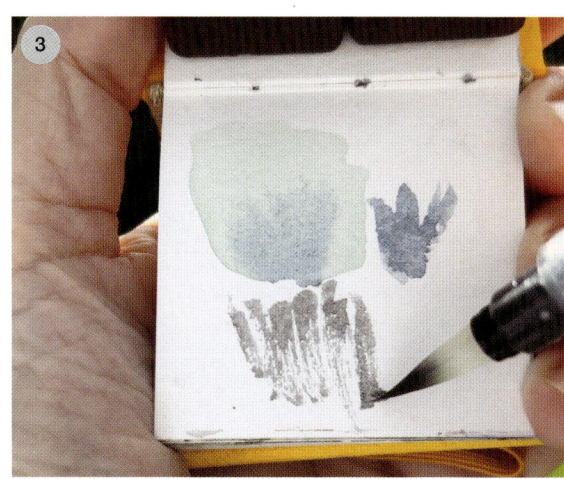

PLEIN AIR PAINTING

WORKING FAST

Remember that the goal when plein air painting is to work quickly. Working in layers is the best way to do this. Watercolour is a less forgiving medium, so it's important to leave plenty of light areas. You can always make passages darker by adding subsequent layers, but you can't easily lift paint once you've committed.

Look for your light source, squinting to see values. Remember the rules of atmospheric perspective (see Space in Chapter Two), and search for them in action. With a tiny painting, I will often exaggerate some of the characteristics of atmospheric perspective, remembering that the furthest objects are bluer and have less variation in value, and the closer items are darker, brighter, and have more contrast.

CHASING THE LIGHT

Consider where the shadows might be deepening in certain areas and put in any light colours you want to include during the first layer. Commit at this stage and don't be tempted to add extra shadows later, even if the light changes.

Remember that you're capturing the moment that first attracted you to the scene. You want to be careful not to "chase the light", a term plein air artists use to refer to changing your painting multiple times throughout the painting process. Doing this will not only change your original plan, but it will also run the risk of making your painting less compelling. You already "caught" the light when you decided on the scene, so the chase is over and it's time to commit.

SEARCHING FOR SHADOWS

I've already emphasised the importance of including a range of values in Chapters Two and Three, but I can't stress this point enough – if you're having trouble making the three-dimensional world look three-dimensional, search for the shadows. You'll want to search for the highlights too, of course, but mostly the shadows! They are everywhere and will make your painting look more realistic.

Here are a few tips:

- In trees, there will be shadows deep within, but also along and on the ground beside the trunks and below the canopy of leaves.

- Buildings normally have shadows in key areas, like where they meet the ground, under the eaves, and above and below windows and doors.

- Search for your light source. Even on overcast days, the sun is travelling across the sky and illuminating your scene – it might even peek out from behind a cloud. Knowing its position will help you discover where the softer shadows are likely to be.

- There are curved objects everywhere! Objects that are rounded or curved will have a highlighted area and will move into shadow as it turns away from the light source. They will also cast a shadow on the surface below them.

- Look for the interplay of different elements in your scene and the unique shadows they cast on one another. This will help add dimension to them.

- Squinting will help, and so will snapping a photo and converting it to black and white.

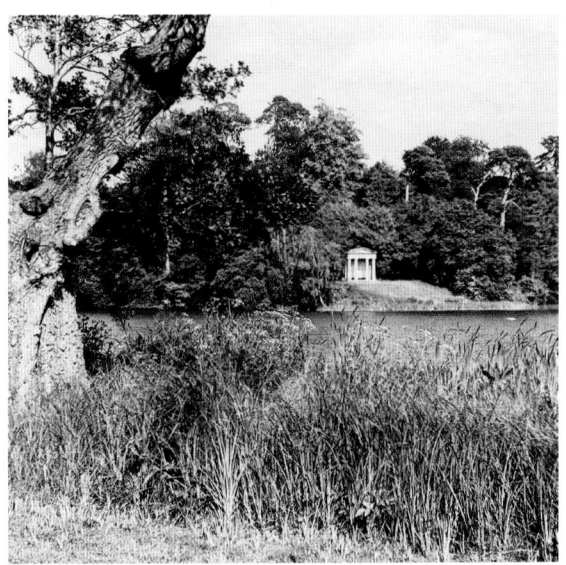

HOW TO SEE THE TONAL VALUE IN COLOUR

Learning to tell how dark or how light a colour is takes practice, so don't worry if at first it seems elusive.

Here are a few things that can help you in this process:

1. Use a Value Scale – Keep a value scale tucked in your art kit (see Understanding Value in Chapter Two). If you have a hole punched into each value, you can hold the strip in front of the objects in your scene to see their relative value. Look at each object through the holes until it most closely resembles one of the values to determine its relative lightness or darkness. Squinting will help you see the various nuances.

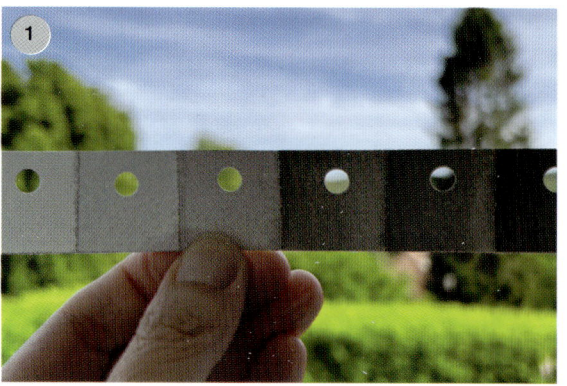

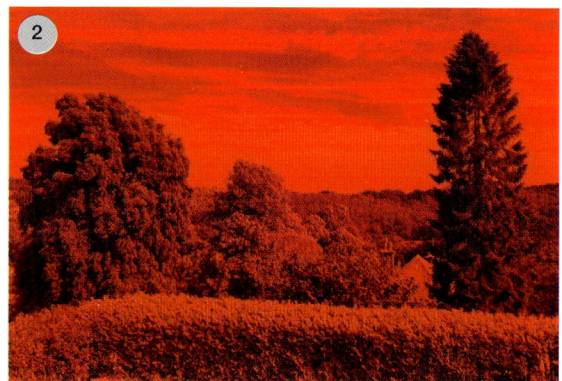

2. Use a Red Filter – Do you know that cliché about looking at life through rose-coloured glasses? It turns out that it's helpful advice for artists as well. Since there are an abundance of greens and blues in landscapes, looking at them through a red lens highlights the various values. A red filter absorbs blue and green light, allowing red and a little yellow light to pass through it. This is useful for seeing the variety of values in a scene, although it's not perfect. Blues and yellows will appear a little darker, and reds will look slightly lighter than they actually are. Even so, they are a helpful teaching tool to reveal the variety of values in a landscape. It will show you subtleties that you might not have noticed without it. I carry an inexpensive pair of red-tinted sunglasses with me that I can pop on at any time. You can also purchase pieces of red plastic and cut your own to bring with you.

PLEIN AIR PAINTING

The Three-layer Painting Method

For tiny plein air paintings, I use a three-layer method to get pleasing results each time. This is helpful for gradually building layers and keeping a freshness to your colours.

FIRST LAYER

The goal for the first layer is to cover the entire painting with the lightest values you see. Unless you have a lot of time to allow your painting to dry between stages, the wet-on-wet technique (adding washes to wet paper) isn't effective for tiny paintings. Instead, use the wet-on-dry technique, where you add wet paint to the dry surface of the paper.

Tips for the first layer:

• You can "drop" additional colours into the layers before they have dried. Because the surface is so tiny, they will often blend together with the colour below into one uniform colour. You can create beautiful effects this way. If you want to add more distinct patches of other colours on top, however, it's easiest to do this in the next stage.

• Don't use an overly wet brush to add paint to an area that hasn't completely dried. Doing this is likely to create streaks and blooms in undesirable ways.

• Blend your colours in your mixing well to the consistency that you want them to be BEFORE applying them to the surface. If you put down a colour that is too dry or dark and try to blend it out with water, you will create streaks.

• Make sure that your brush isn't too wet because a little goes a long way with a tiny painting. A modest amount of water in a larger painting would be an ocean on a tiny painting.

• If your colour is too dry or pigmented, you can add a drop of water to the mixing well to thin it. Strive for thinner, lighter washes of colour in the first layer.

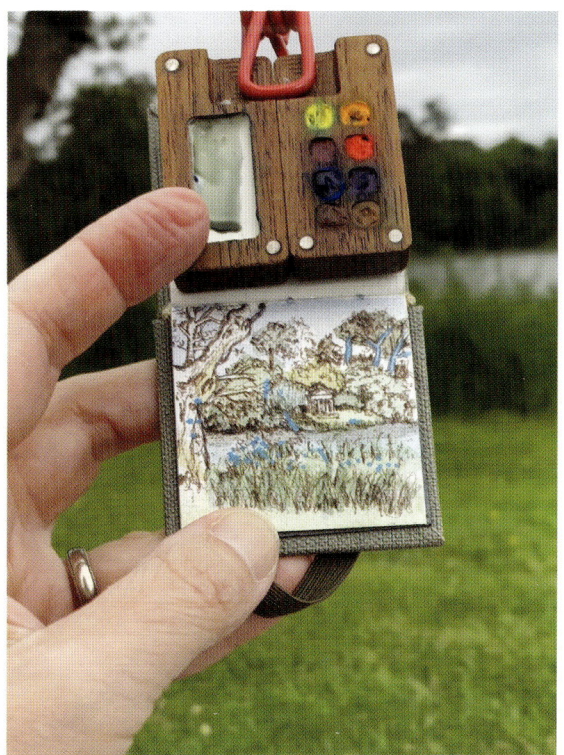

• Avoid having too much water on your brush. Use the edge of your palette or blot it on a cloth before picking up the paint in the well.

SECOND LAYER

If you've applied your first layers lightly enough and without too much water, the paper should dry quickly. It's a good time to take a little break, have one of those beverages you packed, and study the scene thoughtfully. The drying time is a gift because it forces you to slow down and really look at the colours in your scene.

If it's raining or there is excessive moisture in the air, the drying process will be slower. Conversely, if it's hot and arid, the layers will dry quickly. Use the weather as your guide to help you determine how much water you need for each layer. During the second layer, you will add mid-tone colours.

Tips for the second layer:

• Make sure to leave lighter values where you see them! This is where a pointed round brush really shines. You can use the tip of the brush for adding drops of colour strategically.

• Find the colours that have mid-values and apply them to the areas where you see the mid AND dark tones. This will add dimension to the shadows and darker passages during the final painting stage.

• If you have a larger patch of a lighter value (a patch of lighter grass, for instance), look for the COLOURS in that area. Dot them in sparingly to create a textured, realistic look (but be careful not to overdo things and lose the light value altogether). The ground isn't smooth, and grass isn't flat. Learn to spot the variations in tone and colour to achieve a more realistic effect.

• Spread the love! I learned this phrase from artist Kathie Odom, and it's a catchy way to remember that every scene you paint is loaded with colour. Search for it. After you apply a colour in one area, look carefully for other parts of the scene where you see that same colour and dot it in.

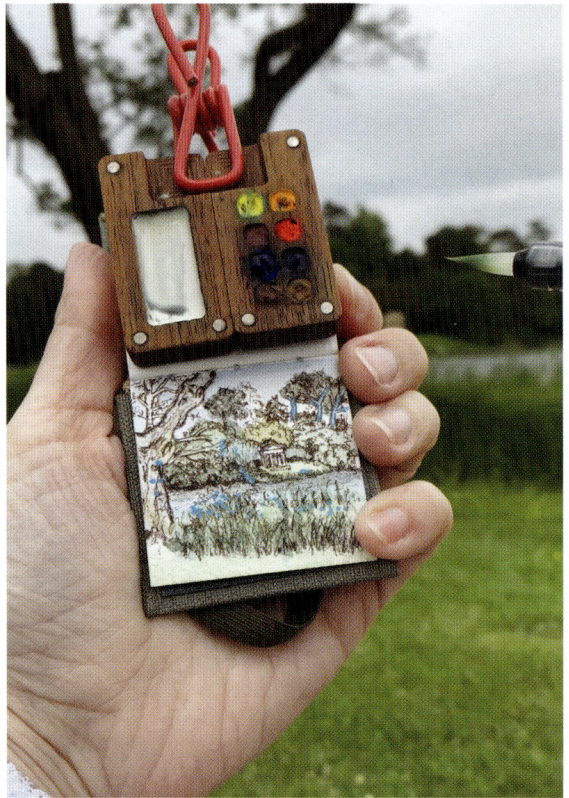

• Look for complementary colours. It may not seem apparent at first, but greenery has a lot of reds and oranges sprinkled in. You can spot them among the branches, the leaves, and patches of earth. Dot them in where you see them to enliven your colours. This works well for lighter values as well. If you have a pale-yellow wall of a house, for instance, look for the violets in the shadows around it and dot them in. Remember that mixing complementary colours together will lessen the intensity, but placing them side by side will cause them to enhance one another. You can use this knowledge to great effect.

THE FINESSING

The first few stages of the painting process are straightforward, but what do you do after the scene has been filled with colour and still doesn't look complete? Welcome to the finessing stage. This is the most mysterious stage because it requires small steps to bring your painting to completion. Many artists stop after the first two layers, partly because they fear they will ruin their painting if they continue, and partly because they simply don't know what to do next.

Tips for finessing:

• Remind yourself that it's normal for your painting to go through what is commonly referred to as the "ugly stage". It can be disconcerting to have gone from a lovely, confident drawing, to a delicate wash of colour, to a mix of indistinct values. If your painting lacks excitement, that's because it probably lacks a range of values. This is when you want to add your darkest values.

• Keep your brushstrokes tiny. Remember that you are finessing and tweaking areas that need a bit of extra refinement. The time for longer brushstrokes is over. Be cautious and strategic.

• After you've added your darkest values, give your paper a few minutes to dry. Take a little break. If you're sitting, stand up. Move your body, whether by taking a little walk or doing some shoulder rotations, neck stretches, or spinal twists. Take a few deep breaths in and exhale. You're painting a landscape that is alive and constantly moving in little ways, so moving your body will help you capture that energy. It's important to put a little distance between yourself and your painting while it dries because it will better enable you to view it objectively.

• Remove the masking fluid. This is equally exciting and horrifying. Liberating the whites that have been protected throughout the painting process will bring new dimension to your painting, but it will also leave many undefined edges. You can use a vinyl eraser or your clean fingertip to do this, but it doesn't always do a clean job. I recommend using a natural rubber pick-up. These are made from a natural crepe rubber and are terrific at removing masking fluid, which contains latex made from the sap of rubber trees.

• Clean up any rough edges created from the removal of the masking fluid, but be careful NOT to randomly outline things. Study the edges of the objects in the landscape. Sometimes, they will be hard and require a touch up of paint along one edge. Other times, they will have a softer, blended edge. To create a soft edge, take a barely damp brush with stiffer bristles and gently feather out the edge. This can take a bit of practice, but it will produce a lovely, natural effect.

• Squint or hold up your value scale to find the darkest values. These will usually be found in the deepest recesses of trees, or where any vertical object in the landscape meets the earth. You'll also find darker shadows under the eaves of roofs or above windows. Study the scene carefully and be judicious with where you add them. One window might have a deep shadow above it, while another might not.

TINY PAINTING TIP
Use tiny brushstrokes. It may seem obvious in a tiny painting, but smaller strokes in the second and third layers will help your painting look more textured and three-dimensional.

- If you feel that a few edges would benefit from being sharper, you can do this with a fineliner or fountain pen, but don't outline everything arbitrarily.

- Add any bright pops of colour. If you've preserved the white of the paper because there are bright, yellow flowers in a bush, for example, this is the time to add those flowers. Remember to "spread the love" with any new colour to other areas of the composition because this will create a more pleasing rhythm to the painting.

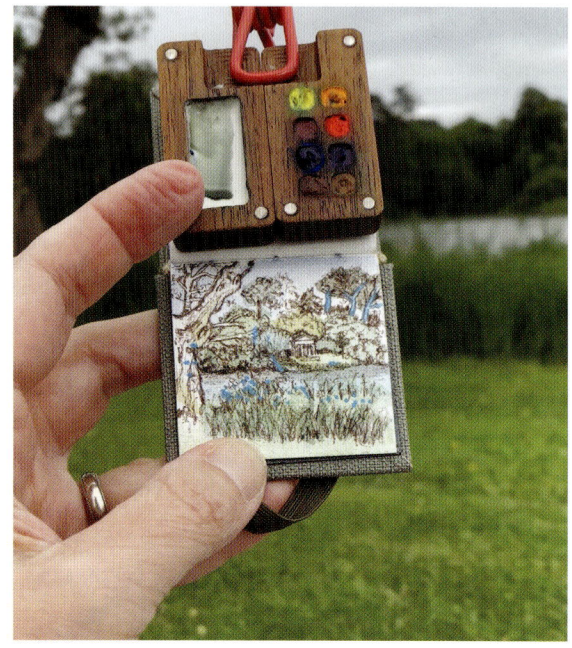

HOW TO KNOW WHEN YOU'RE DONE

Recognising when your painting is finished can be a delicate dance. You've devoted hours of your life swaying to a rhythm of line and colour, and you might become afraid that you'll ruin things if you keep painting. To be honest, many artists are a bit afraid that they'll push things too far, especially if they're new to painting. Sometimes, it's instinctual – you just know that it's perfect and that you're finished, but more than likely you'll have a little doubt. Does your painting need anything else? Does it even look good? No matter how many years you've been painting, these doubts never completely go away.

Tips to help you decide:

- Step back several paces and observe your painting. This will give you a fresh perspective. Even a tiny painting should look balanced and recognisable at a distance.

- Look at your scene through a red filter and then look at your painting through the same filter. Do the values look similar? Have you even added enough value? Your completed painting should have a range of values.

- Take a photograph of your painting. Somehow, this process alone will reveal areas of weakness. Change the photo to black and white. This can feel like a bucket of cold water thrown over you in the middle of a deep sleep. If your painting looks complete in monochrome, it's probably finished. If not… well, you'll see which areas still need attention.

- Take a break. Go for a walk and come back at least 10 minutes later. Look at your painting with fresh eyes. When you're painting, you become so immersed in the process that it's easy to lose objectivity. Taking a break will provide that.

- Be fearless. If you think your painting needs a little more, it probably does. You will learn more from overdoing things than you will if you never try. Remind yourself that if you were able to create a painting once, then that means you have the skills to create it again.

- Film yourself painting. This might not be as helpful in the moment, but it will provide an air of neutrality to your painting process, as well as being educational. I have learned more about when to stop painting from watching myself push paintings too far than I have from anything else.

- Ask a trusted artist-friend or teacher if you have one. Choose someone who you know will be honest with you. If they can suggest things you might still need to do, it's a bonus.

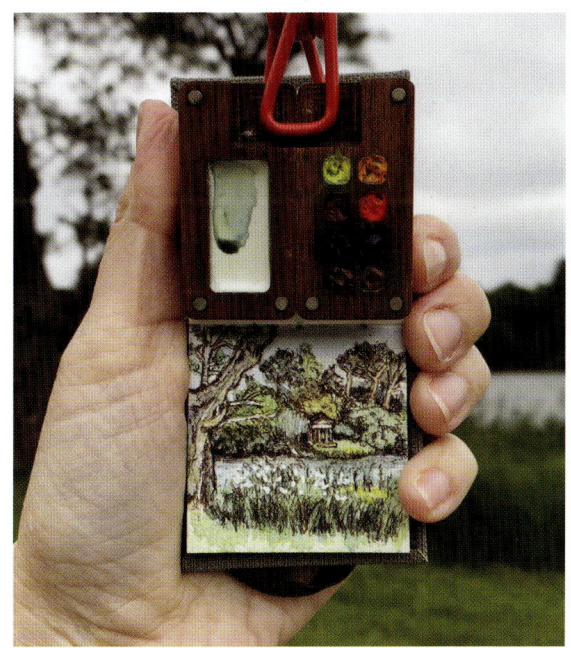

PLEIN AIR TIP: PACKING UP

The beauty of painting in watercolour and ink is that it's relatively simple to pack up at the end of a painting session. I usually give my mixing palette a wipe with a tissue, close it, and put it away, along with the rest of my supplies. Because tiny paintings are so small, they are often dry enough by the time you put everything else away to simply close your sketchbook or pochade box. If your painting is on a loose sheet, you might want to place it beneath a clean one to make sure it doesn't get marred during transport.

If my painting is still too wet by the time I've packed up the rest of my supplies, I'll usually just carry it with me in one hand for a few minutes until it's dry enough to put away. Many of my tiny painting adventures end with my tiny painting riding beside me on the passenger seat of my car.

Chapter Six

PAINT OUTSIDE WITH ME

(Step-by-Step)

There's something uniquely satisfying about watching a painting come together, from the conception to the first sketch, to mixing the colours and painting each brushstroke. Step-by-step demonstrations offer a window into that process – they allow us to slow down, observe closely, and learn by doing. In this chapter, I'll walk you through five small paintings, sharing how I approached each scene from start to finish.

But here's what I'd like you to remember: these demos are just one part of the journey. The real growth happens when you step beyond the page – when you take the concepts we've explored so far and begin to make them your own. Try these lessons, yes – but then, go outside. Wander. Discover the little corners of the world that catch YOUR eye. That's where the magic really begins.

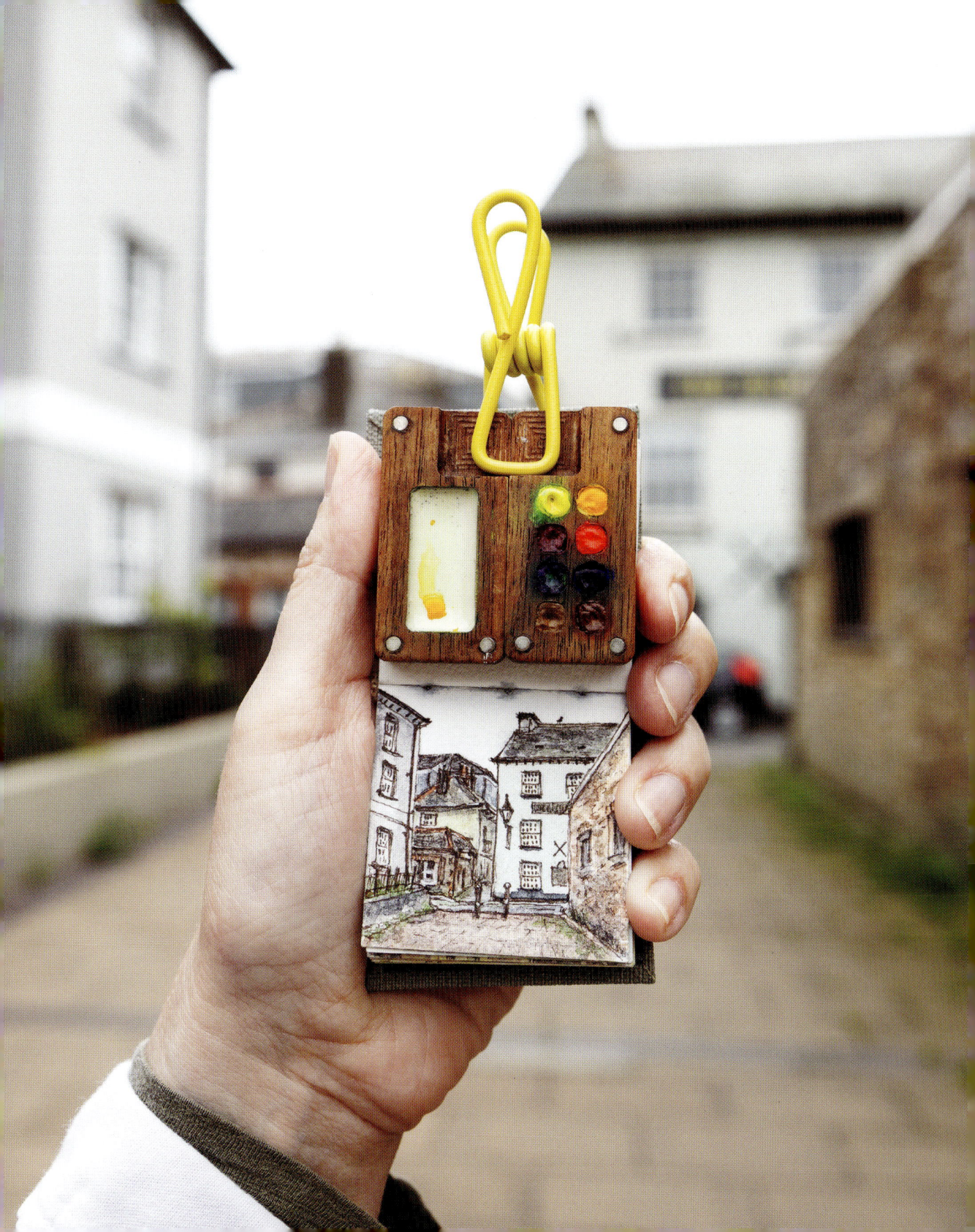

Charming Townhouse

I stumbled upon this quaint townhouse while driving around in the rain, looking for something to inspire me. The Chinese hawthorn and magnolia trees framed the roofline like something out of a storybook. I couldn't resist. I parked my car on the side of the road, rolled down the window, and enjoyed a front-row seat of this charming scene – sheltered from the weather, sketchbook in hand, and ready to capture its beauty.

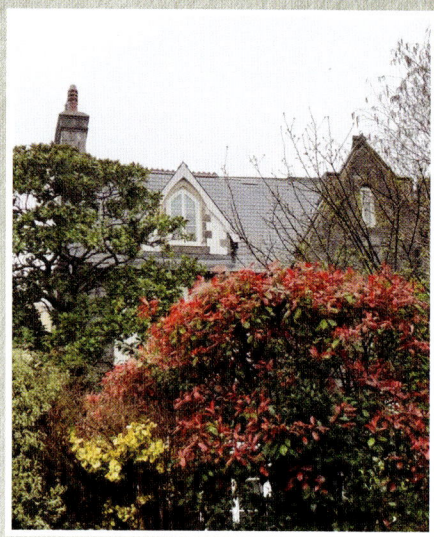

THE SKETCH

Using my viewfinder, I played with the composition until it felt just right. I began by sketching the peak of the dormer on the left – this would be my focal point. Everything else in the painting would serve not only to frame it, but also to gently lead the viewer's eyes towards it, so placing it in a strong position was vital. Once I was happy with its placement, I sketched in the second dormer, followed by the surrounding trees and bushes.

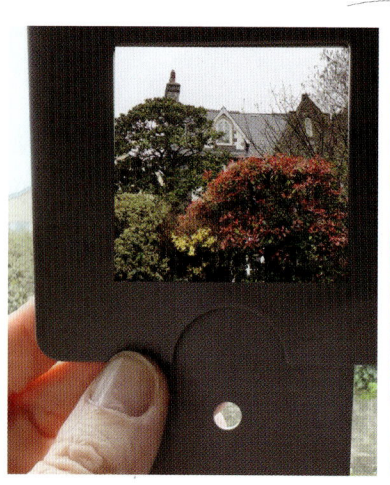
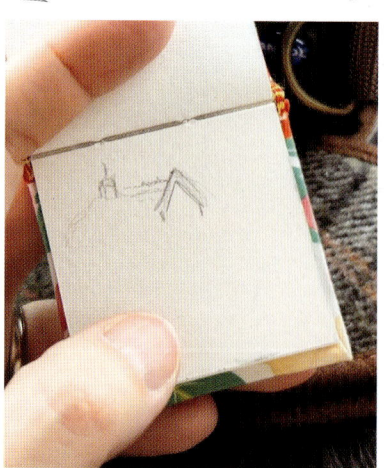
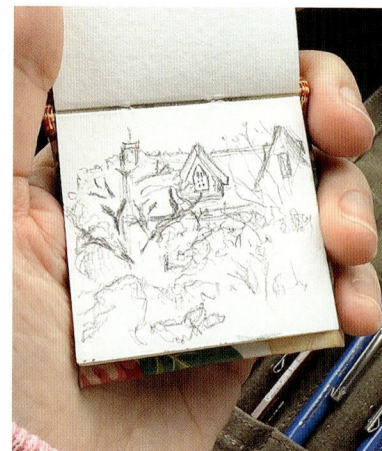

When it comes to foliage, I tend to be quite loose and scribbly with my lines at the drawing stage. I will define those forms later with ink and watercolour. My goal here was simply to suggest their placement, rather than to get caught up in the details.

To preserve the brightest whites in this scene, I used a masking fluid pen to cover the eaves of the first dormer, the window frame of the second, and a few lighter accents on the windows of the house peeking through the trees. This enabled me to paint freely without worrying about losing those crisp, white areas by accident (1).

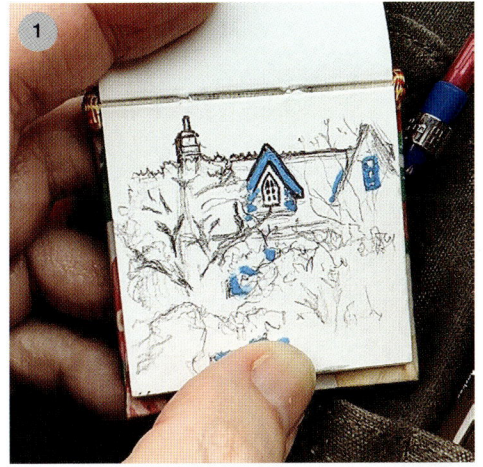

THE INK

Now for my favourite part – adding the ink! Using a brown fineliner, I began by sketching in some of the elaborate woodwork at the top of the roof, as well as the chimney. Next, I drew the first dormer and the window within it. I outlined the dormer's woodwork around the masking fluid to ensure that it would remain crisp and focused. Notice how the panes of glass in the curved window are represented with just a few dots of ink. With a tiny painting, it's not always possible – or even desirable – to include every detail. Sometimes, a suggestion is enough to add realism and charm.

After inking the second dormer, window, and the rest of the rooftop, I carefully drew each tree and bush. I was mindful not to outline each form, but, rather to find a distinctive "pattern" in each one and to use expressive lines to echo that pattern. There is a natural rhythm to objects in nature, and one of the joys of being an artist is finding creative ways to capture them. I made sure to vary the spacing of each mark: darker areas had lines closer together, while lighter areas were spaced further apart (2).

SKETCHING TIP: KEEP IT LOOSE!

When you're sketching or inking, resist the urge to clench the pencil or pen. A tight grip can stiffen your lines. Instead, try holding your tool further back with a relaxed hand. The looser your grip, the looser – and more expressive – your marks will be.

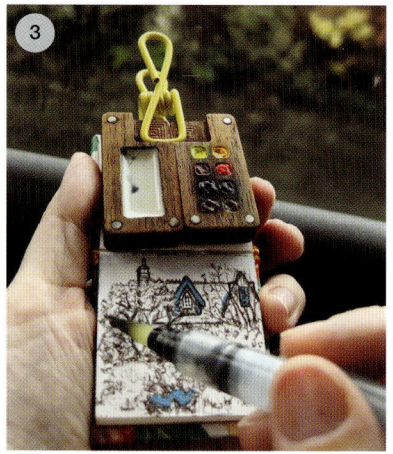

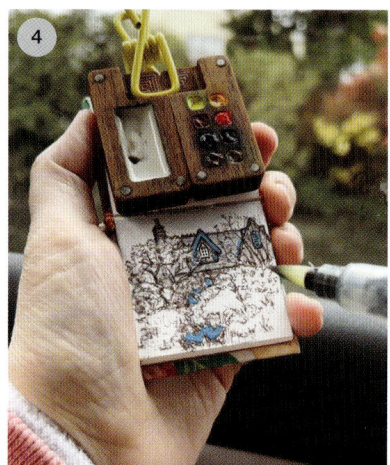

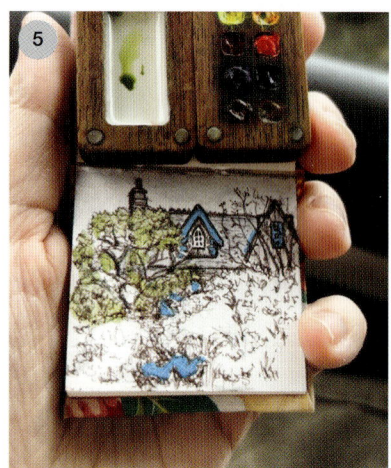

THE COLOUR

First Layer

Sky – The sky was overcast – a pale, whitish grey – but even stormy skies have colour. Look for it. Using a soft, watery mixture of French Ultramarine and Transparent Red Oxide, I dropped it into the sky above the house and behind the magnolia tree on the left. Then I added a bit more Transparent Red Oxide to the mix and dotted it along the top of the page to create a subtle illusion of depth (3).

House – Both the rooftop and the house were shades of grey, but with slightly different undertones. For the roof, I mixed French Ultramarine with Transparent Red Oxide, leaning the mix towards blue. I then added a bit more of the Transparent Red Oxide to the mix to shift the colour to a softer, brownish grey for the house. The difference between the two hues is subtle, but it's these small variations that help a painting look more natural and realistic (4).

Magnolia Tree – The photo doesn't quite capture how brilliant the foliage looked against the greyness of the day – and this is one of the many reasons I encourage artists to go outside and paint from life rather than relying solely on photographs. The vibrant spring leaves of the magnolia tree stood in stark contrast to the muted grey of the house. Starting with a clean palette, I mixed New Gamboge and Phthalo Blue, with just a tiny dash of Transparent Red Oxide to gently tone it down. I dotted this mixture into the clumps of leaves, making sure to leave small gaps where the sky and distant yellow house peeked through (5).

Hawthorn – One of the things that caught my eye about this house was the wonderfully overgrown hawthorn shrub in front of it. I love the challenge of trying to emulate the intensity of brilliant colours in nature, and the leaves of this bush were an intriguing blend of rusty pinks and newer, spring greens. To recreate that glow, I mixed a watery blend of Pyrrol Scarlet and Quinacridone Rose to create a pinkish-red. I dotted this mixture along the edges and into the centre of the shrub, making sure to leave space for the clusters of green leaves. The pale pink not only provides a striking contrast against the grey of the house, but also complements the vibrant green of the magnolia tree beside it (6).

Cheesewood Bush – The cool, pale green of the cheesewood bush on the left is one of those colours that can be tricky to capture in watercolour. Because it's among the lightest values in the scene, I needed to mix a very diluted hue to match both its brightness and tone. Starting with the existing mix of reds from the hawthorn, I added Phthalo Blue and Transparent Red Oxide to create a cool, bluish-green (7).

PAINT OUTSIDE WITH ME

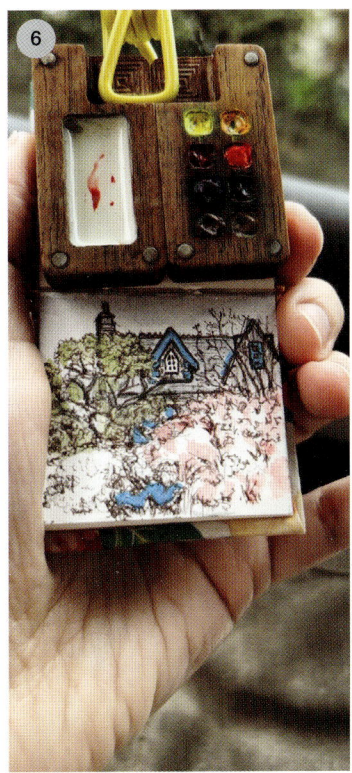

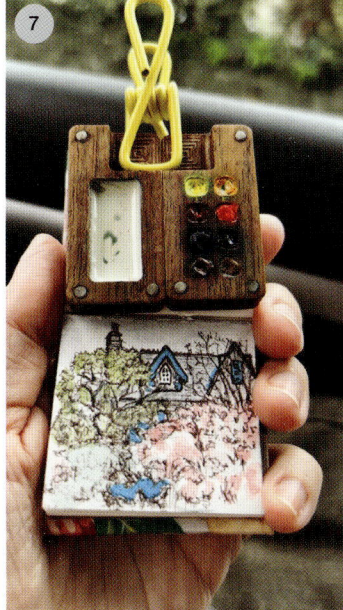

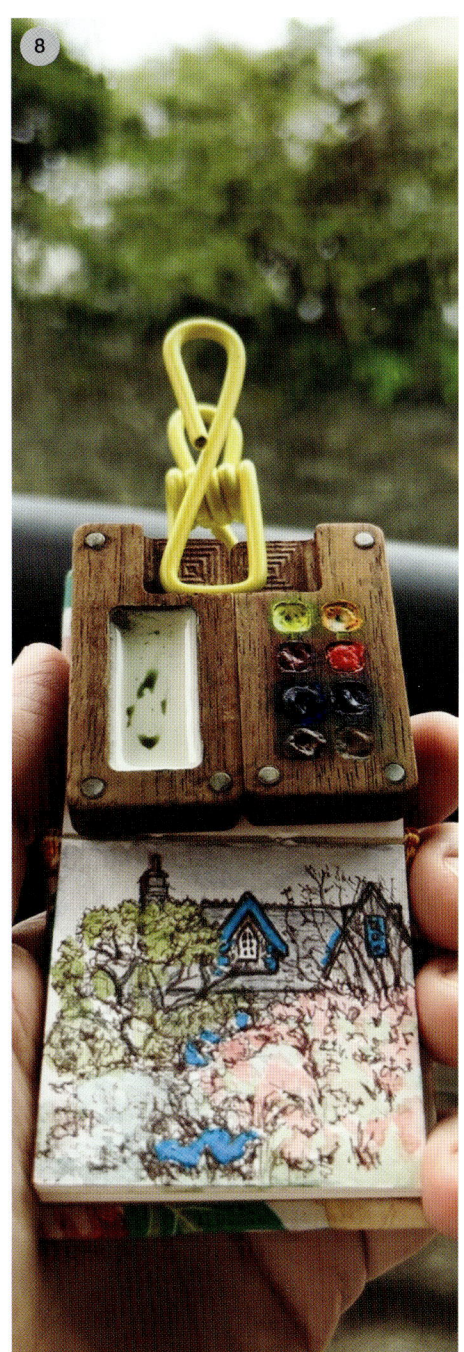

Second Layer

Hawthorn – Once the pinkish colour on the hawthorn had fully dried, I added the surrounding green leaves. For this, I mixed a mid-toned green from French Ultramarine and Hansa Yellow Light and gently dotted it into the foliage.

Evergreen – To create a cooler, darker green for the base of the evergreen spindle tree in the centre, I added a touch of Phthalo Blue and Transparent Red Oxide to the previous green mixture. I also used this colour to deepen the shadows beside the cheesewood and within parts of the hawthorn (8).

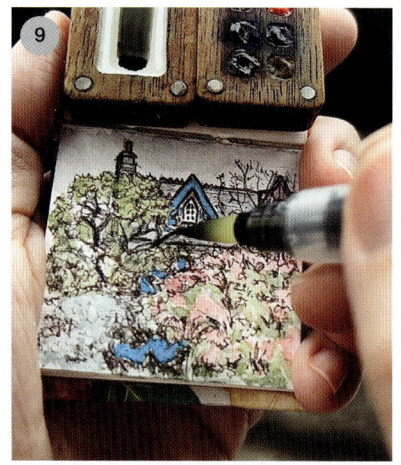

THE FINESSING

Adding Darks – After the first layers of colour had been painted, it was time for one of the most satisfying parts of the process – making everything pop. One of the best ways to do this is to squint at your scene and observe where the darkest values fall. In this composition, the branches of the magnolia tree were quite dark, so I deepened them with a mix of French Ultramarine and Transparent Red Oxide added to the previous mixture. I also used this darker colour to enhance the shadows beneath the roof and around the dormers (9).

Hawthorn – To add more dimension to the hawthorn, I mixed a slightly more pigmented version of Pyrrol Scarlet and Quinacridone Rose. I dotted this richer colour at the base of each cluster of pink, making sure to leave plenty of the paler, first layer visible. This contrast helps maintain the intensity while adding depth to the bush (10).

Pops of Yellow – To suggest the pale, yellow house behind the magnolia tree, I mixed New Gamboge with Hansa Yellow Light. After adding a drop of water to lighten the mixture as much as possible, I gently dotted the colour into the spaces between the leaves, letting it peek through as a soft, glowing hint in the background (11).

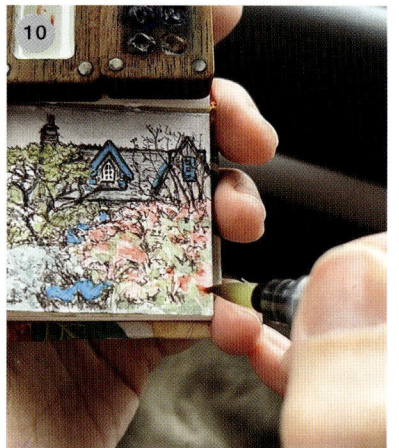

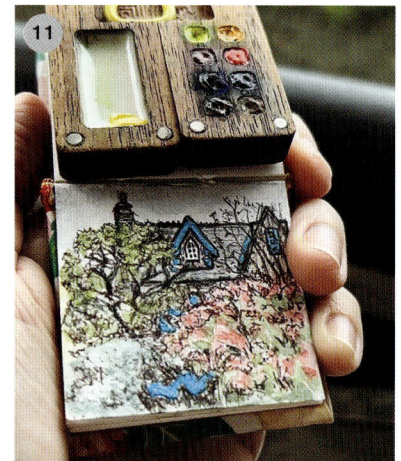

PAINTING TIP: SPREAD THE LOVE!

Every time you use a new colour in your painting, take a moment to study the entire scene. Look closely – where else is that colour hiding? Gently dot it into those areas as well. This simple practice helps create colour harmony, rhythm, and a beautifully balanced composition.

PAINT OUTSIDE WITH ME

Removing the Masking Fluid – After I had achieved a satisfying balance of light and dark tones and felt the painting was just about finished, it was time to remove the masking fluid. When I'm painting on location, I usually use a vinyl eraser pen to carefully lift it. Lately, though, I've found that a small piece of natural rubber pick-up is even easier to use and leaves a cleaner result (12).

More Ink – At this stage, I touched up the painting by refining the dormer windows and adding a bit of cross-hatching to some of the shadowed areas in the foliage. There's always a fine line between using ink to enhance a painting and simply outlining everything. The key is to look for the areas with the sharpest edges and only add ink where it will help define those focal points (13).

Evergreen – The dwarf spindle in the centre of the painting added a lovely pop of yellow-green that nicely balanced both the surrounding foliage and the yellow of the distant house behind the magnolia. I mixed a blend of Hansa Yellow Light and Transparent Yellow Oxide and painted it into the white of the paper that had been preserved with masking fluid. I also dotted touches of this colour into other areas of the composition where I saw a similar hue – such as within the magnolia tree – to tie everything together (14).

Step back and admire your work!

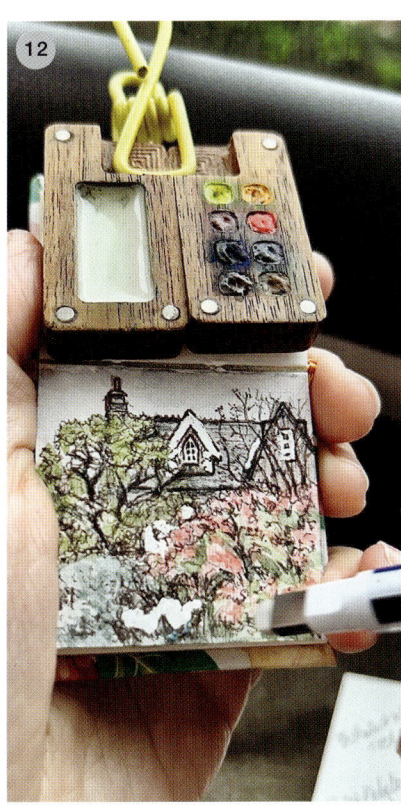

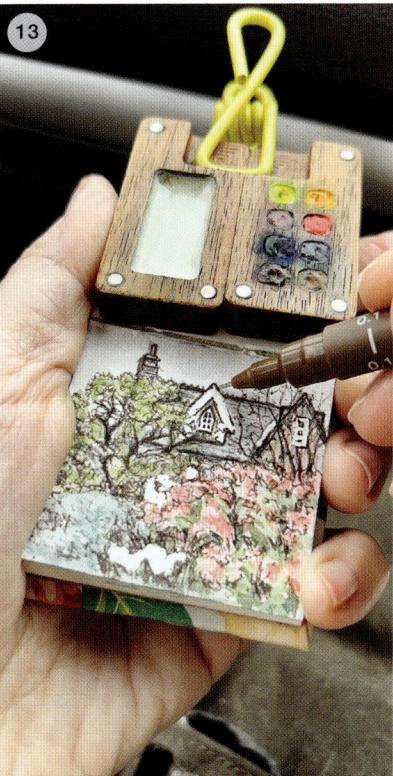

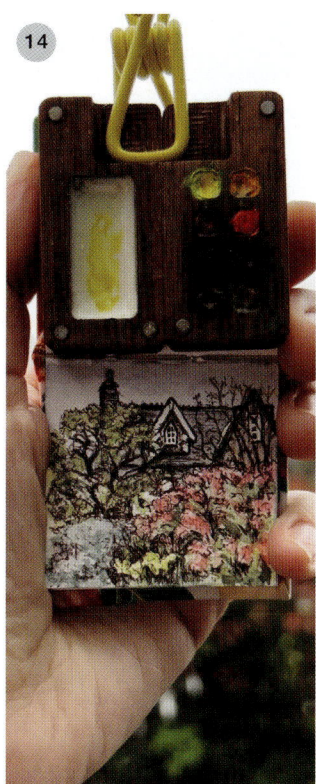

Village Scene

This scene captured my attention because of the wide, pedestrian path flanked by a stone building on the right, a grey, Victorian building on the left, and a Georgian inn painted a warm bluish-green that created a soft contrast against the overcast blue of the sky. The cluster of three overlapping buildings to the left of the inn offers insights into the layered history of this market town, with a low, stone building in the front, a dark grey, shingled building in the back, and a pale-yellow Victorian building sandwiched in between. I loved the way the eaves of the buildings on the sides pointed towards the inn.

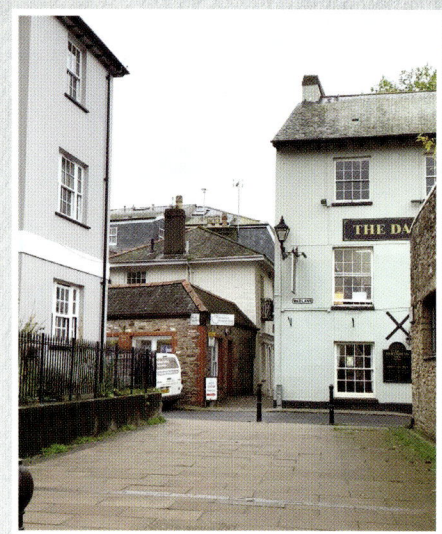

THE SKETCH AND THE INK

I wanted the muted colours to be the focus of this painting, so my sketching process was minimal. After marking the main placement of the structures, I went in with my fineliner and inked each building with clean outlines. I added various textures to the roof of the inn, the stone building on the right, and the pedestrian path. Additionally, I dotted in the windowpanes of the inn and of the grey building on the left (1).

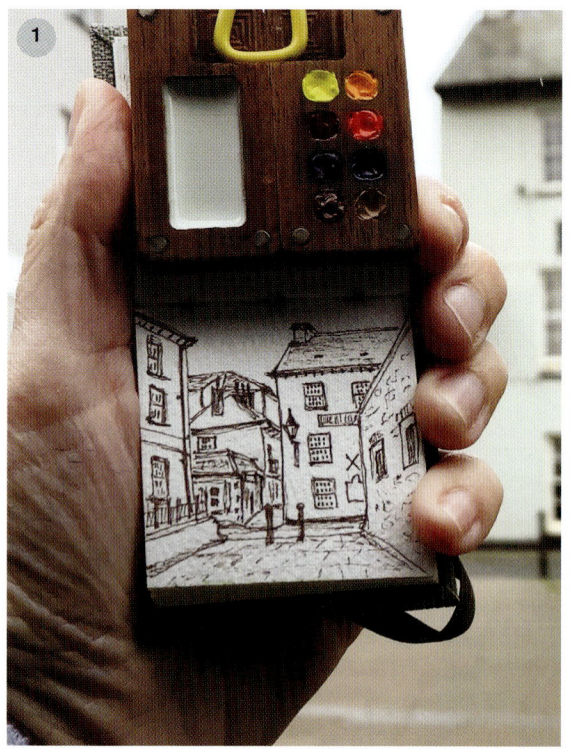

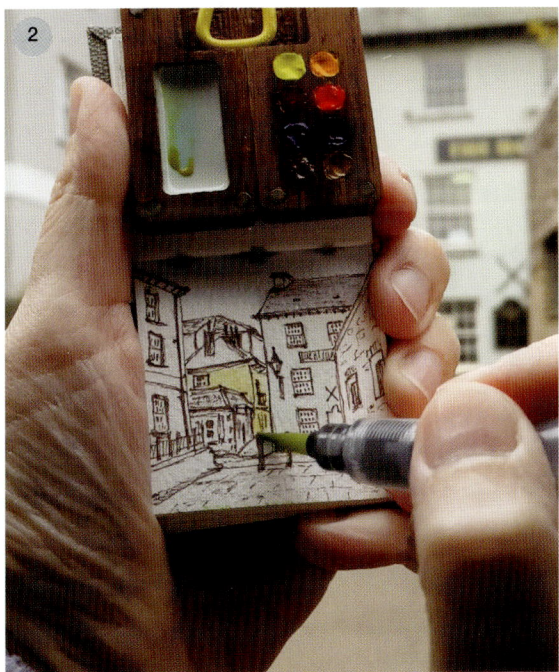

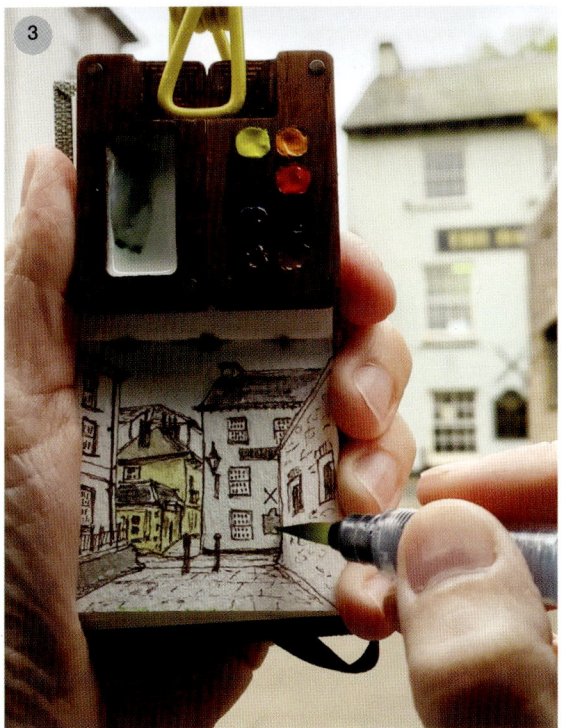

THE COLOUR

First Layer

Sky – The rainy grey of the sky was nearly colourless, so I created a pale grey mix of French Ultramarine and Transparent Red Oxide and dabbed it above the rooftops with a large, pointed round water brush.

Inn – Into that mix, I added some more French Ultramarine to darken the colour for the rooftop of the inn. The tiles looked silvery and wet, so I decided that less was more for this feature. I then added some Phthalo Blue to the mix with a drop of water to keep it pale for the wall, painting around the windows. I applied this mix with a damp brush.

Yellow Building – To enhance the colour of the inn, I mixed Transparent Yellow Oxide and a dash of Hansa Yellow Light for the Victorian building to the left of the inn, and as the base coat for the stone building in front of it. Though slightly more vibrant than the building, I knew it would soften to a lighter hue after it dried. I then adjusted the mix with a touch of French Ultramarine to create a warmer brown for the tiles of the roof, and applied it with a damp brush. I allowed the two colours to bleed together slightly, giving an illusion of a shadow under the eaves (2).

Adding Greys – Into the remaining mixture from the roof of the yellow building, I added some French Ultramarine and Transparent Red Oxide to create a darker grey for the short stone building. I then added a few dashes of this colour to the edges of the roof of the inn, the signs on the inn, the grey concrete wall in front of the grey building, and the windows of the stone building on the right (3).

Adding Reds – I warmed the grey with some Transparent Red Oxide and dotted it onto the stone building on the right. I then added even more of the same colour for the details of the short stone building and the edge of the roof on the yellow building. Using a drier brush, I scumbled this mixture onto the path, leaving flecks of white paper exposed (4).

Second Layer

Stone Building – I watered down some Transparent Red Oxide and dotted it into the stone building to create contrast and depth with the previous layer. The first layer on this structure was still wet, so it was important to use the tip of the brush so that they didn't blend together too much.

Roadway – Into this mixture I added some French Ultramarine for the dark strip of road.

Grey Building – For the cooler grey of the building on the left, I added some more French Ultramarine and Transparent Red Oxide to the mixture of the roadway and painted a watered-down layer of this colour to the grey building, taking care to avoid the windows and the white, horizontal strip in the centre of the building.

Distant Building – Adding some more French Ultramarine to this mixture, I dotted in the areas where the grey shingles framed the building (5).

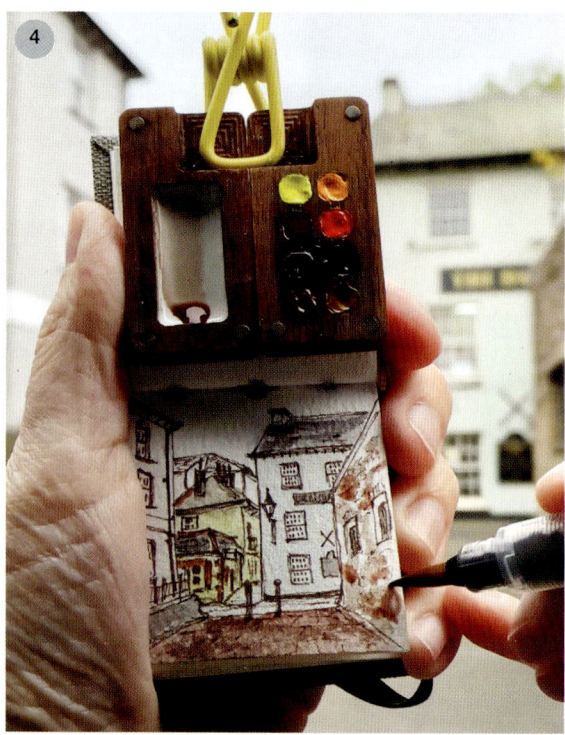

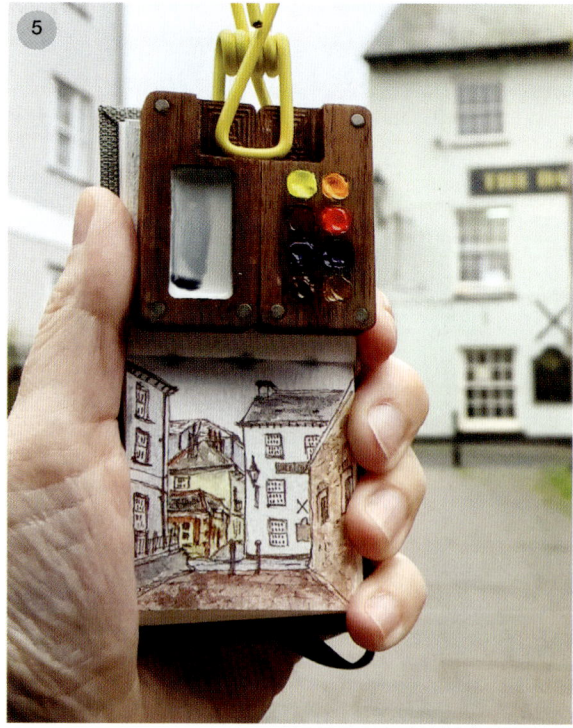

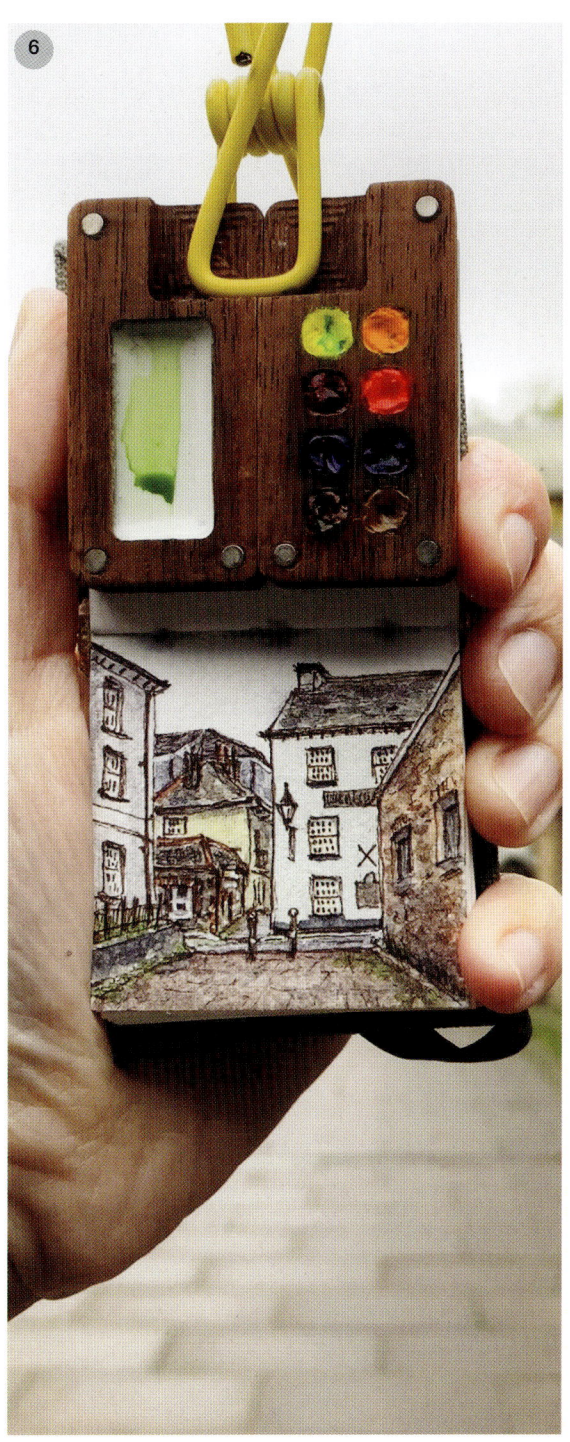

THE FINESSING

Adding Yellows – With a pale blend of New Gamboge and a dash of Hansa Yellow Light, I added pops of yellow to the windows of the inn. I spread a few dots of this colour onto the yellow building.

Adding Greys – Mixing a darker, more pigmented grey with French Ultramarine and Transparent Yellow Oxide, I added touches of this colour along the top of the cement wall in front of the grey building, the black posts at the end of the walkway, the rooftops of the distant grey building and the inn, and the base of the stone buildings. I warmed it up slightly with some Transparent Red Oxide for both stone buildings, dabbing it on with the tip of the brush and leaving space for the previous layers to shine. I also added a dash of this colour to the side of the yellow building to create a shadow from the inn.

Adding Greens – To indicate the pops of green weeds along the edges of the walkway, I mixed a green with Hansa Yellow Light and French Ultramarine and dotted it along the edges of the buildings (6).

Step back and admire your work!

Spring Garden

Sometimes the simplest scene can provide inspiration. These spring daffodils sprouted from my unruly lawn, providing a vibrant contrast to the blue of the pot behind them. Even though the daffodils were heavy with dew and the greens in the pot needed pruning, the combination of yellow and blue stole the show on this otherwise dull April morning. The urge to capture the moment in my sketchbook was too strong to pass up. I welcomed the idea of zooming in on a small section of the garden – creating a still life of sorts.

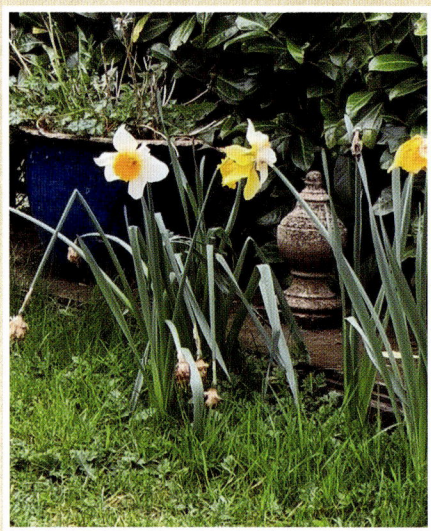

THE SKETCH AND THE INK

I used my viewfinder to place the three daffodils exactly where I wanted them to be in the frame, focusing on the triangular angles of the petals. It's important in scenes where there are many leaves or stems to look for the general movement of the objects and resist getting caught up in counting numbers (1).

I sketched this section, making sure to keep some of the stems bent and curved instead of counting exactly how many there were. Because the plant in the blue pot was similar in colour to the laurel bush behind it, I focused instead on the placement of the pot behind the largest daffodil. Similarly, I sketched in a few prominent leaves of the laurel bush, but didn't mimic exactly where each leaf was.

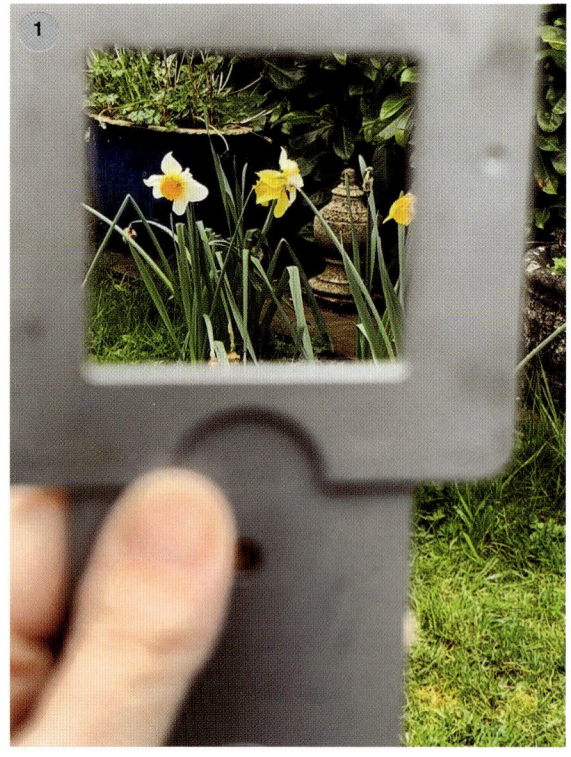

PAINT OUTSIDE WITH ME

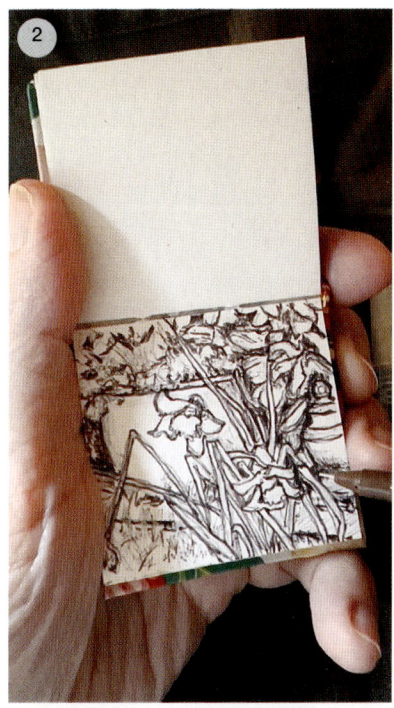

With a brown fineliner, I then traced over my sketch, hatching the areas where the shadows were darkest – deep in the laurel bush and around the blue pot and garden ornament. Notice how I varied the line weight in some areas, barely allowing the nib to touch the paper – this allows for variety in the mark making as well as a wider range of values. The tiny painting has three main textures: the curving lines of the laurel bush with deep shadows, the longer, thinner angled lines of the daffodil stems, and the light hatching of the grass (2).

After the ink, I applied a thick layer of masking fluid to the lightest areas of the daffodils, stems, and rim of the blue pot to preserve them while I painted the other elements. I waited for this to dry completely before adding the colour (3).

THE COLOUR

First Layer

Laurel Bush – I painted a wash of French Ultramarine and New Gamboge across the laurel bushes behind and around the pot and flowers with a large, pointed round water brush. I added a bit more of the French Ultramarine and a dash of the Transparent Red Oxide to darken the colour in the mixing well. Using the tip of my brush, I then dotted it into the darkest areas of the laurel bush, where I had hatched the shadows during the inking stage. The first layer was damp (not wet) and the newer colour was also applied with a damp brush. This allowed the edges to blend softly, but for the colour to generally stay in place.

Grass and Plant – Into a clean mixing well, I combined French Ultramarine and Hansa Yellow Light with the tiniest dash of Transparent Red Oxide to slightly lower the intensity of the green. With a light, sweeping motion, I applied this colour to the grass and the patch of greenery in the blue pot. The bristles on the brush were only slightly wet, and I angled the brush upwards to control the flow of water from the brush.

Blue Pot – To create the brilliant, deep blue of the pot, I mixed French Ultramarine and Phthalo Blue and applied it to the pot. While it was still wet, I added some more French Ultramarine to the mix and dabbed it into the shadowy areas with a damp brush: under the rim and to the left of the pot. This subtle variation helps to create dimension.

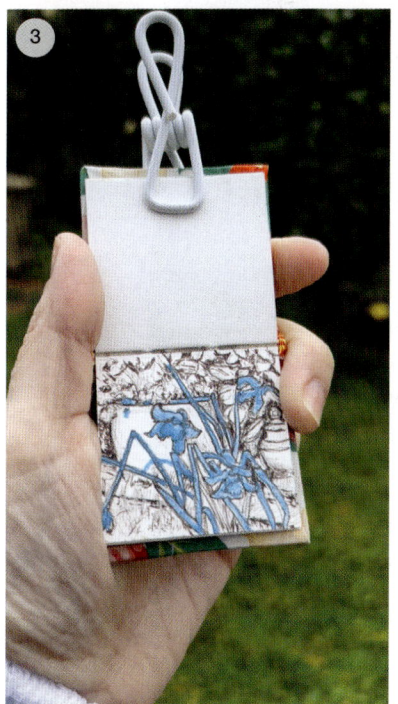

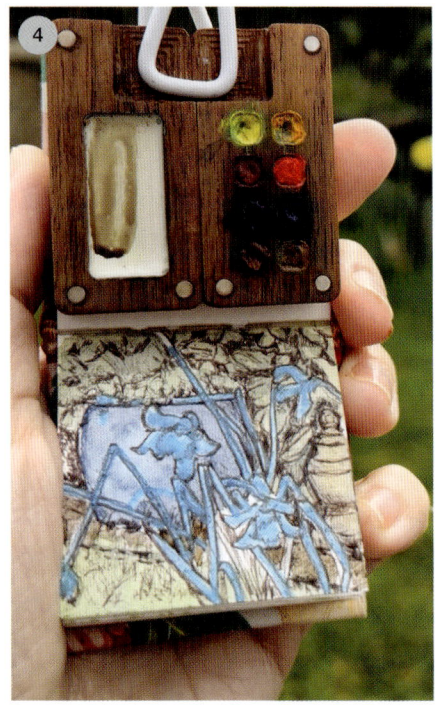

Garden Ornament – I warmed the blue left over in the mixing well with Transparent Red Oxide and applied this to the base of the garden ornament. Watering it down slightly, I applied this same mixture to the rest of the ornament. While it was still wet, I added a touch of New Gamboge and Hansa Yellow Light to the mixture and dabbed it onto the ornament in the non-shadowed areas. I then added a little more Transparent Red Oxide to the mix for the base of the ornament.

Wooden Deck – To create the darker brown of the wooden deck below the pot and ornament, I added some French Ultramarine and Transparent Red Oxide to the colour in the mixing well and applied it, careful to add it between the stems of the daffodils. The darkness of this value will later provide contrast for the lighter value of the leaves (4).

Second Layer

Laurel Bush – After the first layer was completely dry, I mixed a warmer green with New Gamboge, Phthalo Blue, and a dash of Transparent Red Oxide to desaturate it, and then dotted this across the laurel bush. I avoided the shadowed areas and left some of the lighter colour below to help create depth. To this mix, I added some French Ultramarine and a dash of the Transparent Red Oxide and dotted this into the shadowed areas. To spread the love, I added some of this mixture to the left of the garden ornament.

Blue Pot – I mixed French Ultramarine and Phthalo Blue to a thin consistency and glazed this over the first, dry layer. Into this mix, I added some more French Ultramarine and Quinacridone Rose to create a slightly violet hue. I dotted this into the shadowed areas beneath the rim and at the base of the pot.

Grass and Plant – With a clean mixing well, I mixed a brighter green with Hansa Yellow Light and French Ultramarine. I dotted this colour into the grass and the green of the plant in the blue pot, using the tip of the brush to create short, small strokes that left some areas of the previous layer untouched.

Adding More Shadows – I cooled down the brighter green mixture with French Ultramarine and Transparent Red Oxide. Using the tip of my brush, I applied this darker colour to the shadowed areas behind the daffodils, in the deepest parts of the garden ornament, and into the darkest shadows of the laurel bush. The differences are subtle but noteworthy (5).

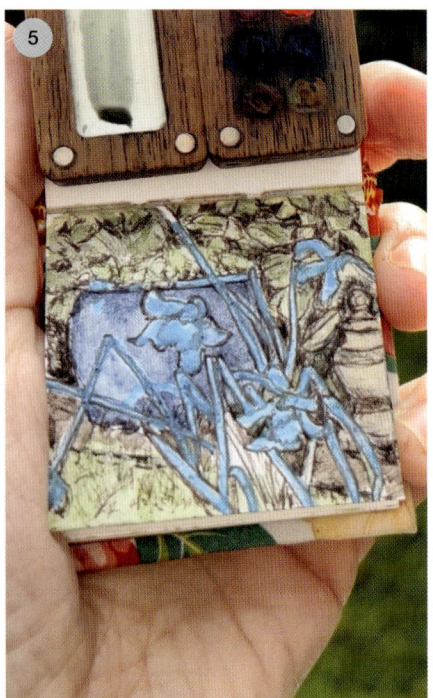

THE FINESSING

After allowing everything to dry, I removed the masking fluid. This exposed the daffodils and stems and the rim of the blue pot, which all needed colour.

Daffodils – I created a pale, watery mix of yellow by combining Hansa Yellow Light with a dash of New Gamboge and applied this to all three flowers with a damp brush (6).

Garden Pot and Ornament – Into a clean mixing well, I mixed a watery blend of Transparent Red Oxide with a tiny dash of French Ultramarine. I applied this with a damp brush to the rim of the blue pot and the curved areas of the garden ornament.

Leaves and Daffodil Stems – To capture the pale, cool brightness of these leaves, I mixed Phthalo Blue with a touch of Transparent Red Oxide. I watered this mix down and then carefully brushed this over all the leaves with the tip of my damp brush, being careful to avoid the flowers.

Finishing Touches – For the centres of the daffodils, I mixed a more saturated golden yellow colour using New Gamboge and a touch of Pyrrol Scarlet.

After everything had dried, I added a second layer of the Phthalo Blue and Transparent Red Oxide mix to the edges of a few of the daffodil leaves (7).

Step back and admire your work!

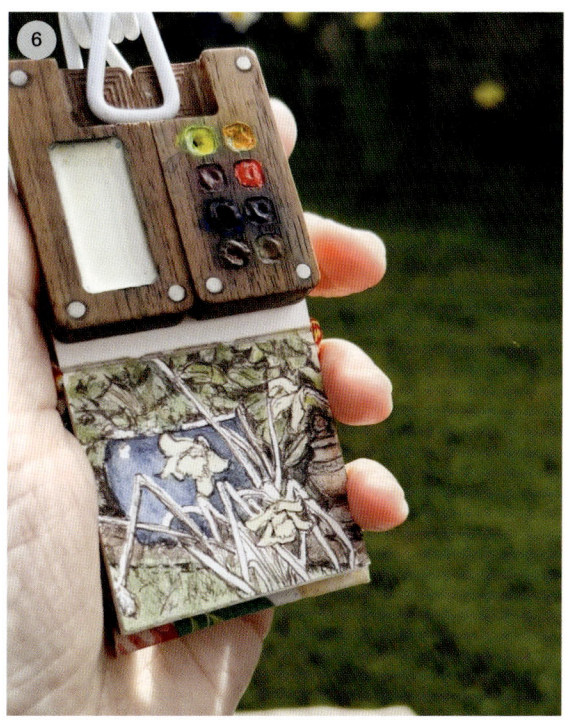

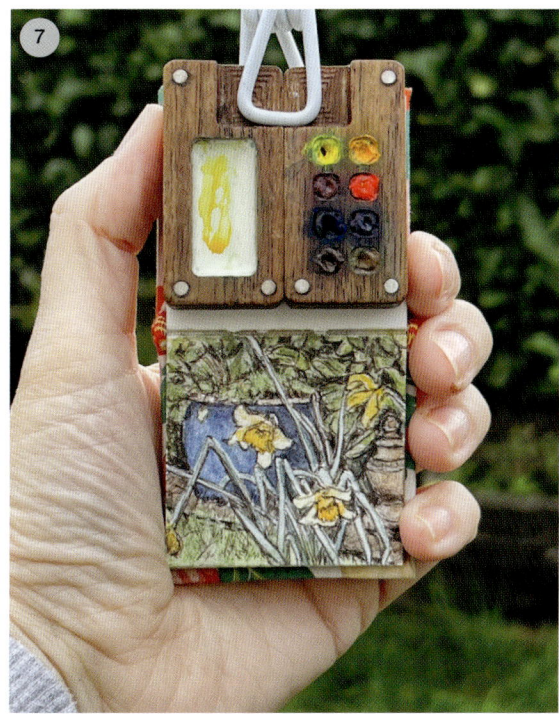

Seascape

I think seascapes are always a little more powerful if you can find some interesting elements – a few rocks peeking up in the foreground, a distant shoreline, or a peninsula of land reaching out to sea. This estuary scene provided so many charming features that it practically begged to be painted. When I began the sketch, the tide was out, leaving more of the wet shore exposed, but I knew it would return during my painting, covering the area with seawater. A heavy mist enveloped the scene, creating a monochromatic colour scheme that left much opportunity for colour play.

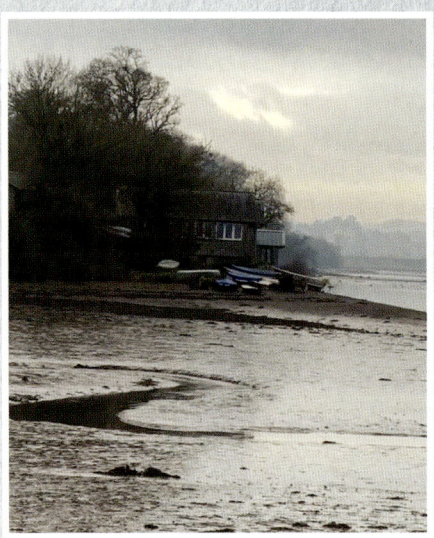

THE SKETCH AND INK

The charming cottage on the edge of the estuary held stories of fishermen past and present with its collection of canoes and kayaks sprinkled around it. The slanted rooflines of the neighbouring sheds and the wisps of branches that reached up to the sky provided a soft, cosy framework that I wanted to capture. I created a light sketch of the buildings and trees, anchoring it to the land and placing the distant shoreline on the horizon.

Once these elements were in place, I added ink with a brown fineliner. I carefully drew in the main cottage and a few of the boats in front of it. In scenes like this, where there are multiple objects, it can sometimes be more effective to select only a few of them to avoid a cluttered look. Because the painting was already so tiny, I chose to include three boats at various angles. I scumbled the tip of my fineliner along the water in the foreground to indicate the shadows of the shallow water, and used a series of wispy lines to provide the

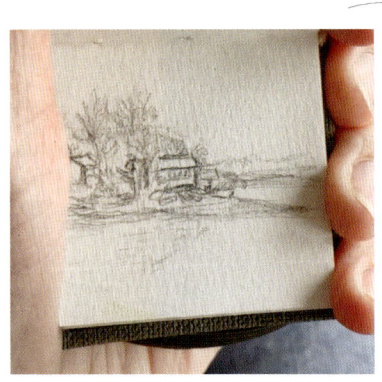
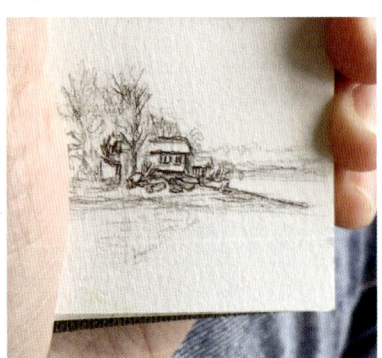
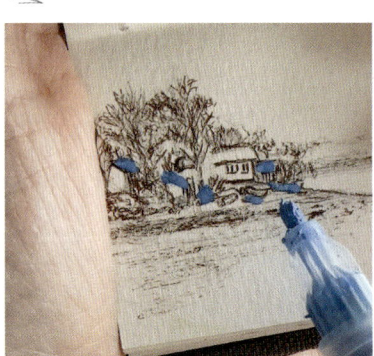

PAINT OUTSIDE WITH ME

framework of the towering trees. I then used my masking fluid marker to cover a few areas where the values were lightest: the tops of the roofs and a few of the boats.

THE COLOUR

First Layer

The first layer was predominantly painted with variations of French Ultramarine and Transparent Red Oxide using my large, pointed round water brush. As I finished one area, I tweaked the colour in the mixing well by adding more or less of each colour as described below.

Horizon Line – I began with a bluish-grey mix of French Ultramarine and Transparent Red Oxide to establish the distant horizon to the right of the cottage. Into this mixture, I added a drop of water to the mixing well and dabbed it above this strip to give the illusion of the misty morning.

Sky – I added a touch of French Ultramarine to the watery mix and painted the sky with horizontal sweeping motions, making sure to leave areas of white to indicate clouds.

Cottage – Adding some more Transparent Red Oxide to redden the mix, I painted the roof of the cottage.

Shoreline – For the darker, reddish earth of the shoreline, I added a touch of Quinacridone Rose and Pyrrol Scarlet to the mix. I applied this to the area below the boats and above the waterline.

Shed and Trees – To further warm the mix, I added a bit more Transparent Red Oxide and dotted it on the shed to the left and the trees in the centre. I then cooled down this mix by adding a touch of the French Ultramarine and dotting that into the trees above the shed and directly above the cottage. I also dotted this colour into the base of the trees to indicate the deeper shadows.

Cottage – I darkened the above mixture with a little more French Ultramarine and applied this at the base of the cottage and the buildings to the left of it.

Sea – Into a clean mixing well, I combined Phthalo Blue, Transparent Red Oxide, and a small amount of French Ultramarine to create a pale greenish blue for the water. I added a drop of water to thin this mix and then applied it to the area below the shoreline with a dry brush. I was careful to scumble the paint, meaning I lightly skimmed the bristles over the surface to allow the texture of the paper to shine through. I deliberately left a few areas of the paper showing to indicate the highlights on the water. Into this mix, I added a little more French Ultramarine to cool it down and applied it with a damp brush to the distant area of sea to the right of the cottage and below the horizon line (1).

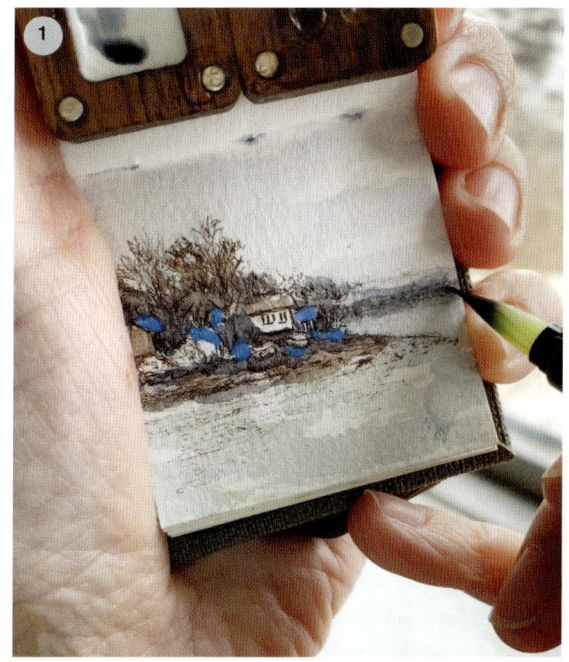

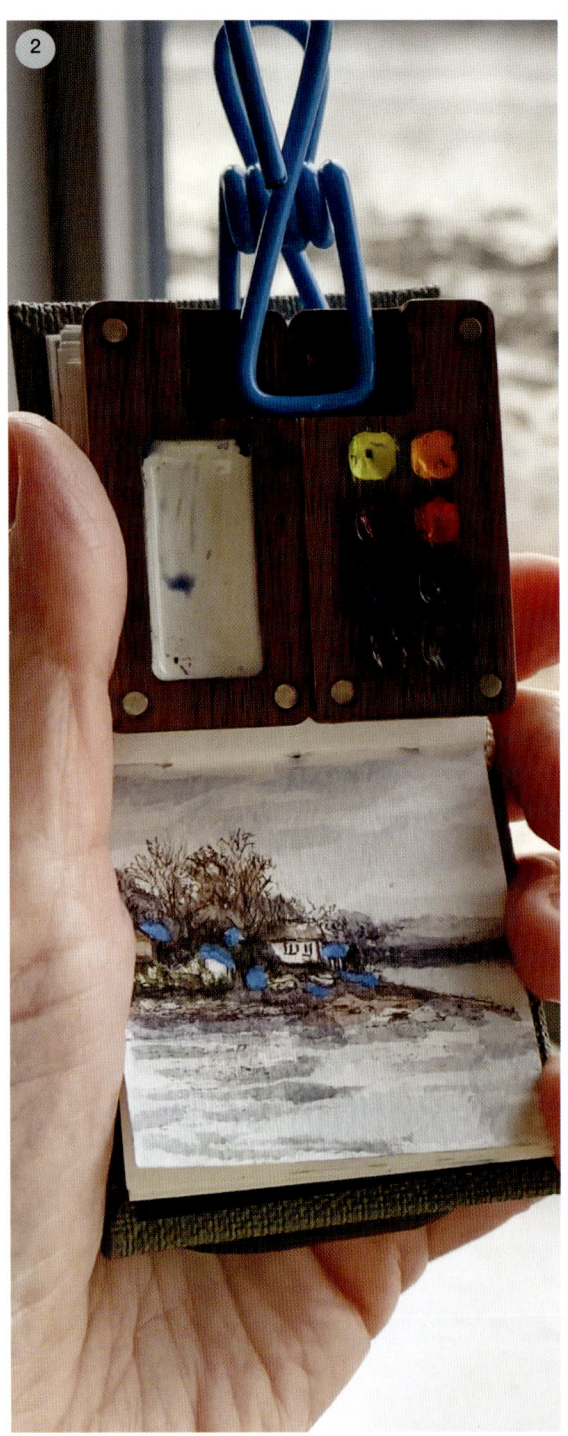

Second Layer

Trees – After the first layer was dry, I mixed a light green with Hansa Yellow Light and French Ultramarine into a clean mixing well. With the tip of a damp brush, I dotted this colour into the areas to the left of the cottage and in front of the sheds on the left to indicate the newly budding trees. I added French Ultramarine and Transparent Red Oxide to darken the green and dotted it into the base of the foliage and shadowed areas beside the main house.

Adding Shadows – I darkened the above mix even further with more French Ultramarine and Transparent Red Oxide, leaning the colour more towards red for a warmer feeling. I dotted this under the eaves of the shed on the left, below the trees, and in a few areas of the shoreline. This not only darkened those areas, but also added more depth.

Sea – To the colour left in the mixing well, I added Phthalo Blue to create a darker greenish-blue mix. I applied this to the water in the foreground on the left with thin, sweeping lines to indicate the darker areas. I was careful to leave areas of the first layer as well as the white of the paper showing.

Horizon – I cooled down the mixture with some French Ultramarine, added a drop of water to lighten it, and applied it to the base of the horizon line with a damp brush to indicate the base of the land.

Sky – To enhance the feeling of the foggy atmosphere, I added more French Ultramarine to the mix and applied it at the top of the sky with sweeping motions. The darker colour at the top of the page, coupled with the darker green at the bottom of the water, helped to create depth to the composition (2).

THE FINESSING

After allowing time for the painting to dry, I removed the masking fluid. This reintroduced highlights, but required some cleaning up of the edges to integrate them with the rest of the painting (3).

Sheds – Into a clean mixing well, I combined French Ultramarine with a dash of Phthalo Blue. With a wet brush, I added this to the rooftops of the sheds, as well as to one of the boats. I made sure to leave a few strips of the white paper to give the illusion of the light hitting the edges.

Cottage – I added some Transparent Red Oxide to the mix to redden it and, with a wet brush, dotted this onto the cottage, the base of the trees to the left of it, and the earth below the sheds.

Sharpening Edges – With a brown fineliner, I touched up a few edges below the sheds and at the edge of the shoreline. I also added a few more wispy branches to the trees above the buildings (4).

Step back and admire your work!

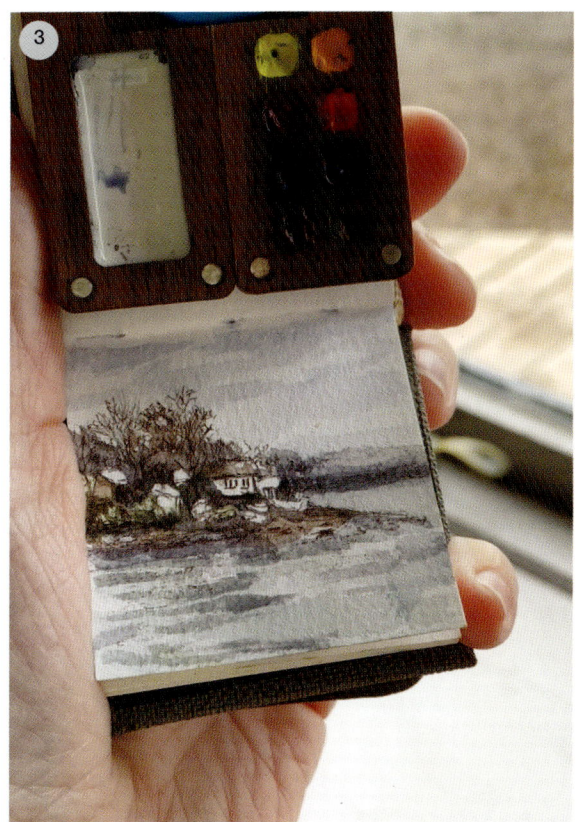

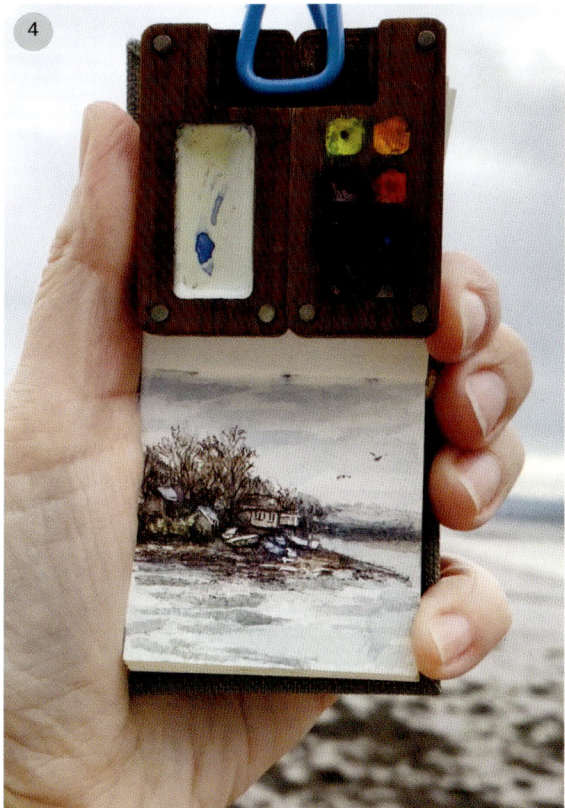

Lost Lamb on the Moors

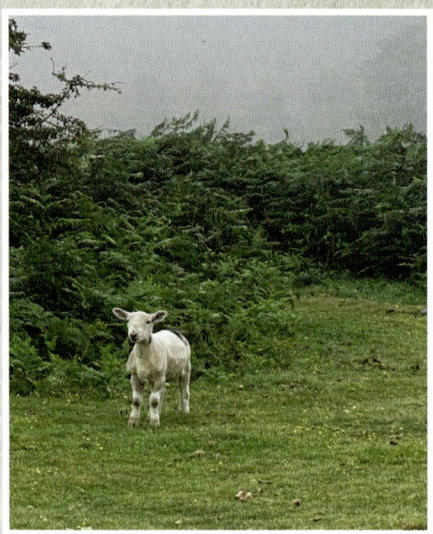

Sometimes, the view you think you want to paint isn't available and you end up with something even better. After a long summer walk in the moors, I returned to my little van just as the rain started to fall diagonally. This prevented me from painting the copse of trees I'd had my eye on, but if I sat in my van with the side door open, I could still paint the scene of the misty heather and gorse, and the distant hills. Just as I settled in, a little lost lamb wandered into the frame and stole the scene (and my heart).

THE SKETCH AND INK

I began with a light pencil sketch, placing the moors and hills where I wanted them and marking a few distinctive areas of heather and gorse. I kept the sketch loose and scribbly to reflect the energy of the blowing wind and rain. As I was sketching, the little lamb appeared and I sketched him quickly, focusing on the contour of the top of his head and the placement of his legs. In a tiny painting, there isn't much room for detail, so I kept the lines minimal.

I used two different fineliners for the inking portion of this painting. I started with dark brown, loosely creating little hatch marks over the sketch in the areas of the hills and foliage. I darkened the area around the lamb, since the bracken was thick and dark behind him. This enabled me to indicate his form without having to add too much detail to his body. Because the mist was quickly rolling in and fading the background, I used a sepia fineliner in the foreground to suggest the warmer, closer colours.

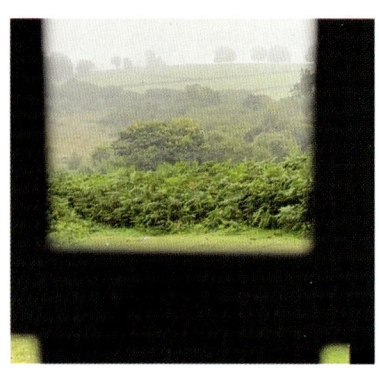

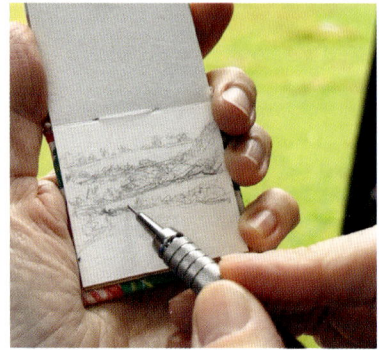

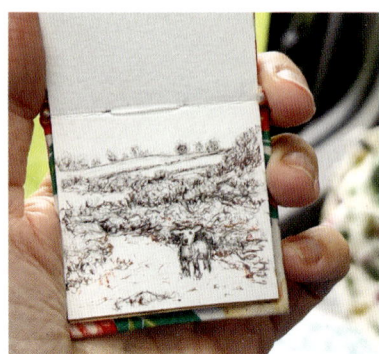

THE COLOUR

First Layer

Sky – Even though the sky was a pale, nearly colourless grey, it was still darker than the lightest value. I mixed a watery, pale grey blend of French Ultramarine and Transparent Red Oxide and applied it across the sky.

Distant Hills – The hills were quite pale and misty. To indicate this fuzziness, I added a touch of French Ultramarine, Hansa Yellow Light, and a dash of Transparent Red Oxide to the mixture left over from the sky, and applied it with a damp brush across the hills and trees closest to the sky area. The wetness of the two sections (coupled with the damp atmosphere) helped them blend together softly. I added a bit more of the French Ultramarine to the mix and dotted this into the trees and shrubs that separated the distant hills from the middle ground.

Middle Ground – For the darker, cooler shrubs in the middle ground, I added more French Ultramarine, Hansa Yellow Light, and Transparent Red Oxide to the mix and applied it with a damp brush. To convey the warmer and redder hills in the middle ground, I added more Transparent Red Oxide and dotted it onto the tips of hills. I also spread a touch of this mixture to the base of the bracken in the foreground.

While the area was still damp, I mixed Hansa Yellow Light, New Gamboge, and Transparent Yellow Oxide into a clean mixing well and dotted it onto the top of the bracken in the middle ground and the edge of the reddish hill to the left of it. The hills to the left contained more Transparent Yellow Oxide and the hills to the right contained more Hansa Yellow Light. It's these subtle variations in colour that help give a lifelike quality to simple scenes.

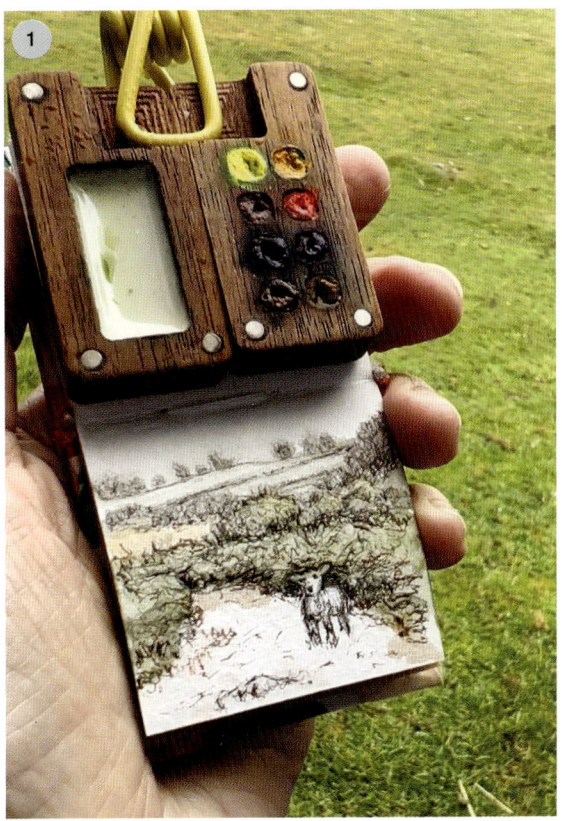

I added some French Ultramarine to the mixture and dabbed it into the base of the bushes with the damp tip of my brush. Next, I added Transparent Red Oxide to the mix and dotted it into the areas that were more yellow or orange.

Bracken in Foreground – I mixed Phthalo Blue, Transparent Red Oxide, and a dash of French Ultramarine and dotted it into the base of the bracken in the foreground and around the lamb. I then added a drop of water to this mixture and spread it evenly across the top of the bracken with a damp brush. This created a pale, cooler base. I immediately added a dash of Hansa Yellow Light and New Gamboge to the mix and dotted it into the bracken in some areas to create warmth (1).

Second Layer

Grass – For the pale grass in the foreground, I mixed more Phthalo Blue and Hansa Yellow Light into the mixing well and desaturated it with a tiny dash of Pyrrol Scarlet. I dotted this into the grassy area, allowing some areas of the page to remain white. I added some French Ultramarine and Transparent Red Oxide to this mixture to create a darker, cooler green and dabbed it at the base of the paler greens.

Bracken in Foreground – I added some Phthalo Blue, French Ultramarine, Hansa Yellow Light, and Transparent Red Oxide into the grass mix to create a darker green that I dabbed into the base of the bracken in the foreground and around the lamb. I was careful to leave areas of the previous layers showing. I added a few dots of this colour to the grass (2).

THE FINESSING

Middle Ground – I created a deep green by mixing French Ultramarine, New Gamboge, and Transparent Red Oxide. I added this to the base of the bushes in the middle ground to create depth and help the paler greens in the foreground stand out.

Bracken in Foreground – I darkened this mixture with a little more French Ultramarine and Transparent Red Oxide for a cooler, dark green and dotted this into the base of the bracken in the foreground. This created more depth and allowed the lamb to stand out and become more of a focal point.

Lamb – I used a white Pentel Milky Brush to enhance a few of the lighter values in the lamb's head, rump, and bottom of his feet. After this had dried, I added a few touches of brown ink to help define his legs, dirty knees, and eyes.

Adding Golden Colours – There is always more colour than you notice at first. I saw several pops of reds and golds throughout the composition and wanted to include them. I added some Transparent Yellow Oxide to a clean mixing well with a bit of water and then brushed this over the body of the lamb. I added a little more Transparent Yellow Oxide and Transparent Red Oxide to darken the colour and dotted it into the bracken and grassy areas and around the rock in the foreground. This helped the painting come to life. Sometimes, it's the final touches that make all the difference (3).

Step back and admire your work!

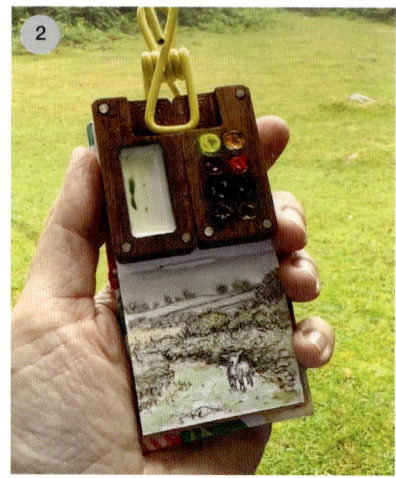

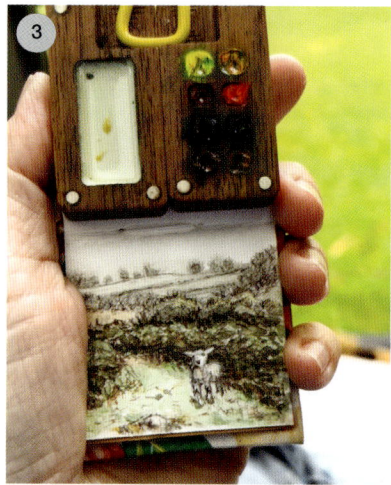

TINY PAINTING TIP

It's important to be cautious when adding any colour to a layer that hasn't completely dried. In tiny painting, the risk of the colours blending on the paper into one new, solid colour is greater.

What Are You Waiting For?

You've collected your supplies, lovingly arranged them in your own custom toolkit, and maybe even completed the lessons and step-by-step paintings in this book. You're now officially ready for some painting adventures of your own! Yay, you!

Go to a beautiful location where you've always wanted to paint, or simply be an explorer in your own garden or town, searching for the perfect scene.

You can do this! I believe in you.

Now go make some magic!

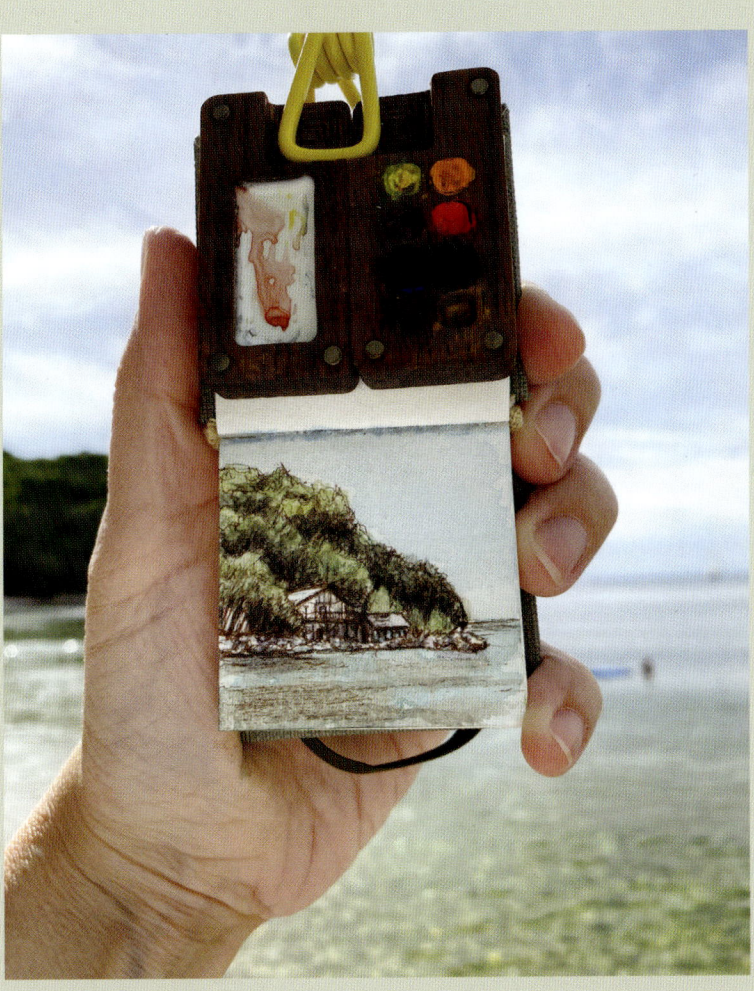

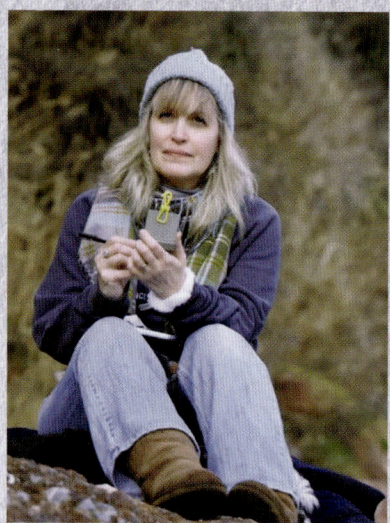

Photo by Aydin Kapancik

About The Author

Leslie Stroz is an artist, illustrator, and former art professor. She shares her tiny painting adventures online so that others can experience a few moments of respite from their busy lives, and is delighted and amazed to have acquired a social media following of over 1.6 million. She lives in Devon, England, with her husband, daughter, and their little black-and-white dog, Poppy, who is her frequent plein air companion.

To see more of Leslie's work or learn about her art retreats, visit: www.LeslieStroz.com

Acknowledgements

To my lovely love, David, who has made all my dreams possible, including a few I'd never even considered. I owe you the greatest thanks. This book, and the ability to pursue my quest of being a full-time artist, would not have been possible without your constant support and companionship. You have shown me by your example what it is to be an artist. Your honour and goodness lights my path. Thank you for being my Hero.

To my clever, irrepressibly talented daughter, Ella Dean, my dedicated scholar, without whom I would never have realised this dream. You are the one who told me to post on social media, which led to an accidental stumble into this art movement of Tiny Painting. Your creativity humbles and inspires me, and your humour brightens my horizons. You sprinkle magic into every realm you create, and I aspire to be like you. Thank you for being my touchstone.

To my darling boy, my soulful son, William James. I can't remember a world when you weren't in it. You are the logic that calms my storms, the keeper of knowledge, my fellow grammarian. Your belief in me eclipses all others, and for you I would paint the world. Thank you for always being up for pursuing a research project with me.

To my mother, Joanne, for nurturing an artistic leaning in me that I didn't see myself, and for taking me to private art lessons when I was child. Thank you for instilling in me your love of poetry, classical music and art. And for praising every scribble I ever created and listening to every story I ever wrote. You watered the seeds of creativity that sprouted this artistic life I live. And thank you to my father, William, gone from us too soon, for giving me the perfect childhood and your unconditional love. I have spent a lifetime striving to make you proud, and I know that you'd be the first to brag about this book.

To my brother, Steve, for decades of pep talks, wisdom and laughter. Your keen business sense has helped me throughout this process, and your reminders to carve my own path instead of following the flock have been a mantra. Thank you for being everything a big brother ought to be. I'll even give you a free book.

To all my family, past and present, who have encouraged and supported me, especially Donna (my constant champion and fellow creative), Jillsy (the talented dark horse), Hilary (my former muse), Sally (my first idol), Chloe (my sister-niece), Zeri (my second daughter), and my Aunt Mary (my first and fiercest fan). Thank you all for helping in your own, unique ways, to keep my fires stoked and my creative flame alight.

To my dearest friends. All of you. You know who you are. And especially to Katey (my soul-sister), Gudi (my soul-saviour), Kitch (my rebel-twin), Eric (my defender), Katrina (my tween), Sally (my pen-pal), and Jo (my creative confidante). You have all played a role in helping me realise my artistic aspirations.

To Poppy, my constant companion and plein air painting pup, who is always excited about going on painting adventures with me, and who is probably responsible for at least half of my social media followers. Thank you for being my sidekick and muse.

To my fellow artists who have inspired me or been my friends along my artistic journeys, especially Katey Monaghan, Sunny Wu, Dr. Amaka Maduanusi (Sketches.n.Scrubs), Cynthia Hawkins, Elizabeth Garber, Joanne Green, Ashley Bravin, Scott Christian Sava, Margaux Kent, Martina Anagnostou, Katerina Kestemont, Charlie Hunter, Eric Jacobsen, and Kathie Odom. Thank you all for galvanising me with your creative energy.

To the team at David & Charles for supporting me throughout this process, especially Nigel Browning, Sarah Rowntree, Jason Jenkins, Sam Staddon, Katie Hardwicke, Katie Crous, and Jessica Cropper. Your belief in me and your cumulative creative contributions have helped make this book a better, sparklier version of itself.

To all my students, past and present, who have inspired me to be a better teacher and artist. It is because of you that I have insights to share. Thank you.

To my Patrons, who supported me financially so that I could take some time off to formulate my art knowledge into this missive. You are my unsung champions! Thank you, lovely artists!

And finally, to YOU, for picking up this book, or following my art journeys on social media, or supporting my art. Without you, there would be no book. Thank you for being here.

Recommended Brands & Supplies

(These are my favourites. You can do an internet search to see where they are available to purchase near you.)

PAINTS
- Daniel Smith
- M.Graham
- Winsor & Newton

PALETTES
- GoDraw
- Blue Star Crafts
- ArtToolkit
- Peg and Awl
- Natsume Handmade

BRUSHES
- Rosemary and Co.
- Pentel Aquash

PENCILS
- Pentel Graphgear

PENS
- Prismacolor Premier
- Staedtler Pigment Liners
- Uni-Pin Fineliners
- Pentel Point Liners

FOUNTAIN PENS
- Kaweco Sport and Liliput
- Scriveiner

WATERPROOF INKS
- DeAtrementis Document Ink (Brown, Sepia and Urban Sienna)
- Rohrer & Klinger Sketch Ink (Lily, Lotte, Thea)

PAPER
- Arches
- Daler Rowney Langton Prestige
- Saunders Waterford

ERASERS
- Tombow Mono Zero
- Pentel Clic Stick Eraser
- Faber-Castell Kneaded

MASKING FLUID MARKERS
- Molotow Grafx Art Masking Liquid Pump Marker
- Kreul Solo Goya fine, Masking Marker

SKETCHBOOKS
- Inkberry (sold by Go Draw)
- Natsume Handmade

ART WRAPS & PENCIL CASE
- Peg and Awl Sendak and Mini-Sendak
- Lihit Lab

POCHADE BOXES, CLIPBOARD & ART BOXES
- Blue Star Crafts
- Peg and Awl

VAN CONVERSIONS
- Campal Camper Van Conversions Ltd.

Index

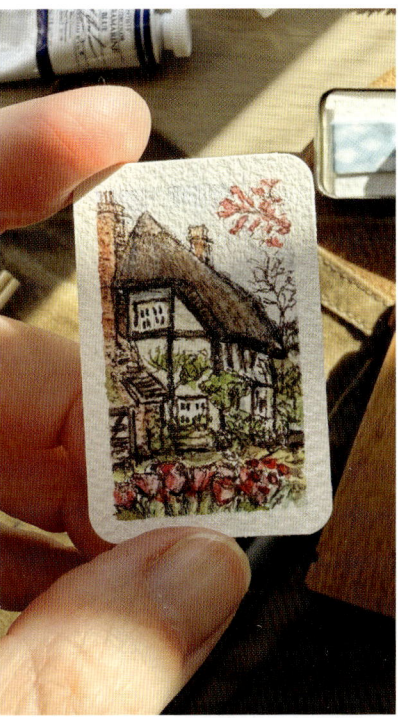

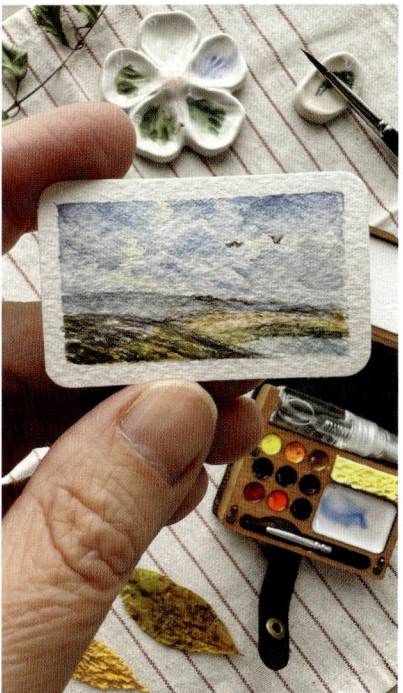

A DAVID AND CHARLES BOOK
© David and Charles, Ltd 2026

David and Charles is an imprint of David and Charles, Ltd , Suite A, Tourism House, Pynes Hill, Exeter, EX2 5WS

EU GPSR Authorised Representative: Logos Europe, 9 rue Nicolas Poussin, 17000, La Rochelle, France
Email: Contact@logoseurope.eu

Text and Artwork © Leslie Stroz 2026
Layout and Photography © David and Charles, Ltd 2026

First published in the UK and USA in 2026

Leslie Stroz has asserted her right to be identified as author of this work in accordance with the Copyright, Designs and Patents Act, 1988.

Names of manufacturers and product ranges are provided for the information of readers, with no intention to infringe copyright or trademarks.

A catalogue record for this book is available from the British Library.

ISBN-13: 9781446316665 paperback
ISBN-13: 9781446316672 EPUB

This book has been printed on paper from approved suppliers and made from pulp from sustainable sources.

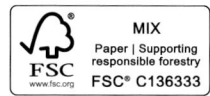

MIX
Paper | Supporting responsible forestry
FSC® C136333

Printed in China by Asia Pacific Offset for: David and Charles, Ltd, Suite A, Tourism House, Pynes Hill, Exeter, EX2 5WS

10 9 8 7 6 5 4 3 2 1

Publishing Director: Ame Verso
Senior Commissioning Editor: Nigel Browning
Publishing Manager: Jeni Chown
Editor: Jessica Cropper
Copy Editors: Katie Hardwicke and Katie Crous
Design: Sam Staddon
Pre-press Designer: Susan Reansbury
Art Direction: Sarah Rowntree
Photography: Jason Jenkins and Leslie Stroz
Production Manager: Beverley Richardson

David and Charles publishes high-quality books on a wide range of subjects. For more information visit www.davidandcharles.com.

Share your makes with us on social media using #dandcbooks and follow us on Facebook and Instagram by searching for @dandcbooks.

Layout of the digital edition of this book may vary depending on reader hardware and display settings.